Through the Paper Curtain

CHATHAM HOUSE PAPERS

The Royal Institute of International Affairs, at Chatham House in London, has provided an independent forum for discussion and debate on current international issues for over eighty years. Its resident research fellows, specialized information resources and range of publications, conferences and meetings span the fields of international politics, economics and security. The Institute is independent of government and other vested interests.

Chatham House Papers address contemporary issues of intellectual importance in a scholarly yet accessible way. In preparing the papers, authors are advised by a study group of experts convened by the RIIA, and publication of a paper indicates that the Institute regards it as an authoritative contribution to the public debate. The RIIA is, however, precluded by its Charter from having an institutional view. Opinions expressed in this publication are the responsibility of the authors.

Through the Paper Curtain

Insiders and Outsiders in the New Europe

Edited by

Julie Smith *and*
Charles Jenkins

The Royal Institute of International Affairs
Chatham House
10 St James's Square
London SW1Y 4LE
http: //www.riia.org
(Charity Registration No: 208223)

Blackwell Publishing Ltd
350 Main Street, Malden, MA 02148-5018, USA
108 Cowley Road, Oxford OX4 1JF, UK
550 Swanston Street, Carlton South, Melbourne, Victoria 3053, Australia
Kurfürstendamm 57, 10707 Berlin, Germany

First published 2003 by Blackwell Publishing Ltd

Library of Congress Cataloging-in-Publication Data has been applied for

ISBN 1-4051-0293-4 (hardback); ISBN 1-4051-0294-2 (paperback)

A catalogue record for this title is available from the British Library.

Set in 10.5 on 13 pt Caslon with Stone Sans display
By Koinonia, Manchester
Printed and bound in the United Kingdom
by MPG Books Ltd, Bodmin, Cornwall

For further information on
Blackwell Publishing, visit our website:
http://www.blackwellpublishing.com

Contents

Contents

Acknowledgments

The issue of insiders and outsiders in an enlarged Europe is one that is of concern to politicians and other policy-makers as well as to business people and academics. We are grateful to the Le Poer Power Trust and to *newnations.com* for their support for a project on this theme, which culminates in this edited volume. In particular, we should like to thank Clive Lindley for his contribution to the framing of the project and to all the participants in the series of research seminars at which the draft chapters were presented. Our thanks go especially to Geoffrey Edwards for reading the entire manuscript and offering rigorous comments and to Camilla Soar and Kim Mitchell for their editorial assistance, which has enhanced the quality and coherence of the book. Finally, we owe a deep debt of gratitude to Margaret May for her sterling efforts in ensuring that the final manuscript went to press in a presentable form. Needless to say, any outstanding errors remain ours.

London, July 2003   C.J.
                                                                          J.S.

About the authors

Peter Doimi de Frankopan is a historian based at Oxford University, specializing in the political, social and economic history of southeastern Europe and the eastern Mediterranean. A graduate of Cambridge University, he was Senior Scholar at Corpus Christi College, Oxford before taking up Junior and then Senior Research Fellowships at Worcester College, Oxford. In 2002–3 he was a Stanley J. Seeger Fellow in Research at the Program for Hellenic Studies at Princeton.

James Gow is Professor of International Peace and Security at King's College London. His books include *Triumph of the Lack of Will: International Diplomacy and the Yugoslav War* (Hurst, 1997), *Slovenia and the Slovenes* (Hurst, 2000), *The Serbian Project and Its Adversaries: A Strategy of War Crimes* (Hurst, 2003) and *Defending the West* (Polity, forthcoming). He was a member of the expert panel advising the UK Secretary of State on the 1997–8 Strategic Defence Review and the 2000 Strategic Context Paper.

Graeme P. Herd is Professor of Civil-Military Relations at the College of International Security Studies, George C. Marshall European Center for Security Studies, Garmisch-Partenkirchen, Germany. He has published extensively on post-Soviet security politics. Recent books include (co-edited with Anne Aldis) *Russia and the Regions: Strength through Weakness* (Routledge-Curzon, 2003) and (co-edited with Jennifer Moroney) *Security Dynamics in the Former Soviet Bloc* (RoutledgeCurzon, 2003).

Charles Jenkins has been Regional Director, Western Europe at the Economist Intelligence Unit (EIU) since 1999, where he is the editor of the *EU Country Report*. From 1975 to 1997 he edited the EIU's quarterly *Country Reports* and *Country Forecasts* on all countries in eastern and western Europe, and various research reports. From 1975 to 1993 he edited *European Trends*. Other publications include *Italy to 2000: Forging the Second Republic*,

About the authors

co-authored (1995), *The Enlarged European Union – A Wider Role?* (European League for Economic Cooperation 2001), *Paying for an Enlarged European Union* (Federal Trust, 1999), and *The Unification of Europe, the EU's Forthcoming Enlargement* (editor and contributor) (Centre for Reform, 2000).

Gabriel Partos is South-East Europe Analyst of the BBC World Service. He writes and broadcasts extensively on the Balkans and central Europe. Some of his output is available on the *news.bbc.co.uk* website. He is the author of an interview-based history of the Cold War, *The World that Came in from the Cold* (RIIA/BBC, 1993).

Matloob Piracha is a Lecturer in Economics at the University of Kent. He has written several papers on migration and strategic trade policy and is currently conducting research on the relationship between foreign direct investment and migration, with a particular emphasis on central and east European countries.

Christopher Preston is a consultant specializing in advising EU candidate countries in eastern Europe on pre-accession issues and public-sector reform. He has worked with the governments of Poland and Lithuania, as well as those of Romania, Croatia and Macedonia. He has written and published extensively on EU enlargement.

Alan Smith is Professor of Political Economy at the School of Slavonic and East European Studies, University College, London. He is the author of *The Return to Europe: The Reintegration of Eastern Europe into the European Economy* (Macmillan, 2000), *Russia and the World Economy: Problems of Integration* (Routledge, 1993) and *The Planned Economies of Eastern Europe* (Holmes and Meier, 1983), and editor of *Challenges for Russian Economic Reform* (RIIA/Brookings,1995).

Julie Smith is Head of the European Programme at the Royal Institute of International Affairs, Assistant Director of Studies at the Centre of International Studies, Cambridge University, and Fellow in Politics at Robinson College, Cambridge. She has published widely on various aspects of European politics and integration. Her publications include *The New Bilateralism* (with Mariana Tsatsas) (RIIA, 2002), *Europe's Elected Parliament* (Sheffield Academic Press, 1999), *Democracy in the New Europe: The Politics of Post-Communism* (co-edited with Elizabeth Teague, Greycoat Press, 1999).

Roger Vickerman is Jean Monnet Professor of European Economics at the University of Kent. His main research interest is in the economics of integration and he works on issues such as transport, regional development, migration and labour mobility, with a particular interest in the effects of enlargement. He directed the project on migration and labour market dynamics for the ESRC's 'One Europe or Several?' Programme.

Kataryna Wolczuk is Lecturer in Ukrainian Studies, Centre for Russian and East European Studies, European Research Institute, University of Birmingham. She is the author of *The Moulding of Ukraine: The Constitutional Politics of State Formation* (Central European University Press, 2002) and co-author of *Poland and Ukraine: A Strategic Partnership in a Changing Europe?* (RIIA, 2002).

Roman Wolczuk is a researcher on Ukrainian foreign and security policy. He is the author of *Ukraine's Foreign and Security Policy 1991–2000* (Routledge-Curzon, 2002) and co-author of *Poland and Ukraine: A Strategic Partnership in a Changing Europe?* (RIIA, 2002).

1

Introduction

JULIE SMITH

The enlargements of the European Union and of the North Atlantic Treaty Organization (NATO) scheduled to take place in 2004 will have a major impact across the whole continent of Europe. They will affect those states left outside the two organizations as well as new and current members. Indeed, so great are the potential ramifications that in a clear parallel with the Iron Curtain of communist times, the spectre has been raised of a 'paper curtain' being erected between the new 'insiders' and the new 'outsiders'.

For 40 years Europe was divided by the Iron Curtain and citizens on either side lived under contrasting and competing regimes: to the west, liberal democracies practised free-market economics; to the east, one-party states had command economies. Similarly, states in the east and the west formed part of different security communities: most west European states were members of NATO, relying primarily on the United States for their security, while most central and east European (CEE) states were members of the Warsaw Pact, with the Soviet Union serving as their security guarantor.[1]

Upon the collapse of communism that began in 1989 and the subsequent demise of the Soviet Union in 1991, this divided Europe seemed to have ended for good. One former communist state after another announced its intention of applying for membership of a whole range of 'West' European and Atlanticist organizations: the Council of Europe, the Organization for Security and Cooperation in Europe (OSCE), Partnership for Peace (PfP), the European Union and NATO.[2] In western Europe at least there was a

---

1 There were, of course, exceptions to this dichotomy as some west and central European states, notably Austria and Finland, chose to remain apart from the Western institutions where they would have found their natural allies, often because they were reluctant to antagonize their Eastern neighbours. Conversely, Yugoslavia was far less closely tied to the Soviet Union than were the Warsaw Pact countries.

2 For a discussion of the expanding membership of European organizations in the early 1990s, see Sarah Collinson, Hugh Miall and Anna Michalski, *A Wider European Union? Integration and Cooperation in the New Europe*, RIIA Discussion Paper No. 48 (London: RIIA, 1993), pp. vi–ix.

tendency to presume that Europe was 'reuniting' as central and east Europeans talked of 'returning to Europe'. There was a widely held belief in both East and West that relations between previous enemies were destined to improve.[3]

It gradually became clear, however, that the 'new' European order would not be quite so easy to achieve as many had hoped. Membership of the EU and of NATO did not come as swiftly as many candidates would have liked, causing some hostility among would-be members when it was felt that the EU in particular was deliberately stalling on enlargement.[4] In addition, although the removal of the Iron Curtain might have marked the end of the ideological and military division of Europe, it left the way open for new lines of differentiation across the continent, potentially dividing neighbours who had previously enjoyed good relations, at least since the end of the Cold War.

As a dozen or so states began to prepare seriously for membership of NATO and the EU, other states began to raise concerns about the implications for them of remaining outside these enlarged entities. Indeed, some, notably Ukraine's President Leonid Kuchma, argued that a 'paper curtain' was being erected in Europe, one that had been created by officials in the EU (and, to a lesser extent, NATO).[5] The danger, it was argued, would be the emergence of a newly divided Europe, where the divisions would be reinforced by the requirements of EU and NATO membership, creating new sets of 'insiders' and 'outsiders'. Those on the inside would be privileged in economic and security terms, while those on the outside would be in danger of slipping still further behind the insiders economically. The new divisions would be likely to impede trade and the free movement of people across

3 Indeed, as Graeme Herd notes in Chapter 7 of this volume, there were even some liberal Russians who spoke of a 'return to Europe'. However, the idea that relations were destined to improve, which seemed realistic in terms of straight East–West relations, ignored the tensions that had existed among central and east European states over centuries, tensions that were to re-emerge between some of them in the 1990s. See, for example, William Wallace, *The Transformation of Western Europe* (London: Royal Institute of International Affairs/Pinter, 1990).

4 This delay should not have come as a surprise given how long it took the United Kingdom, Spain and Portugal to accede. Moreover, as noted in 1993 by Collinson, Miall and Michalski, *A Wider European Union?*, p. 6, drawing on work by Richard Baldwin and others, 'Different patterns of economic, political and social development in these countries [Poland, Hungary, Slovakia and the Czech Republic] … make the prospect of early membership unlikely.' However, the fact that Western leaders, notably Jacques Chirac while Prime Minister of France and Germany's Chancellor Helmut Kohl, indicated that enlargement could occur rather swiftly – the dates 1996 and 2000 were both mentioned – ensured that candidates' expectations were raised only to be dampened down again. This resulted in a degree of ill-feeling.

5 Leonid Kuchma addressing a regional summit of 22 Black Sea and Baltic states, cited by Radio Free Europe/Radio Liberty, 10 September 1998.

borders, potentially creating economic and social problems for both insiders and outsiders.[6]

To an extent, this insider versus outsider problem is an inevitable part of the expansion of any organization: members have rights and responsibilities; non-members have neither the obligations nor the benefits of membership. Although these corollaries of membership may not create difficulties in interpersonal relations, they do create potent problems in interstate relations even in our evolving globalized society. First, they may directly harm the interests of those inside the organization as well as those outside. Closed borders between states can impede mutually beneficial cross-border trade, and they can damage security if outsiders feel that the insiders are part of a security club, raising the spectre of a Hobbesian relationship in which insiders and outsiders are mutually suspicious. In the case of post-Cold War Europe this threat seemed real enough when Russia voiced concern about NATO's expansion to the Baltic states, which it perceived as a potential security threat.

Secondly, those left outside may feel that they are being treated as second- or third-class states. This is especially true for states that are not scheduled to join either the EU or NATO in 2004. This feeling could in turn affect states' long-term strategic outlook, potentially reinforcing differences between them as some begin to look to the Russian Federation and the Commonwealth of Independent States rather than the West for allies, as has been the case with Moldova and Ukraine to some extent. Even if these outsider states do not reorientate their geostrategic alliances, the sense of being treated as second-class may nevertheless ensure that they become less cooperative associates of the EU and NATO. In addition, there is a danger that, having been kept outside for a long time, those outsiders who are seeking membership of Western institutions could become 'reluctant' Europeans when they are eventually permitted to join.[7]

There are good reasons for creating hard borders between EU states and their neighbours, notably those connected with achieving the economic and security aims of the Union. However, it is important to be aware that these dangers exist and that they may persist despite the EU's efforts to work with

6 On the positive side, such reinforced borders are expected to reduce the problems of people- and drugs-trafficking.

7 Indeed, the danger of creating 'reluctant' Europeans was present even among those candidates scheduled for membership in the first wave of EU enlargement, owing to a belief among some of them that they were not being treated as equal to the current member states. One noteworthy example was that of Poland and agriculture: Polish farmers were aggrieved that direct payments would be introduced on a sliding scale, ensuring that it would be 2013 before they received the same levels of payments as farmers in the 15 current member states.

outsiders through partnership and cooperation agreements. The EU institutions have recognized this potential difficulty, which the European Commission highlighted in a Communication to the Council and the European Parliament in March 2003, in which it advocated closer links with Europe's eastern and southern neighbours.[8] The Commission's suggestions are in line with the argument of some contributors to this volume that closer cooperation short of stability and association agreements, which confer the expectation of future accession negotiations, may be desirable in order to avert such problems.

THE PATH TO ENLARGEMENT

The EU has been enlarging or discussing enlargement almost since its inception in the 1950s, and in each case accession has taken rather longer than prospective members would have liked. The one exception was the first post-Cold War enlargement, in 1990, which brought the former German Democratic Republic (GDR) into the then European Community within a matter of weeks. When the Berlin Wall came down in November 1989, the scene was set for the GDR to unite with the Federal Republic of Germany. The prospect of a united Germany, for which Germans on both sides of the Iron Curtain had long hoped, was greeted with considerable anxiety by many west European leaders, but Helmut Kohl was determined to seize the opportunities for reunification as they became apparent. Reunification paved the way for the first post-Cold War enlargement of NATO as well as the EU.[9] Because these organizations did not define membership by states' territorial boundaries, the former GDR was able to accede with almost none of the formalities that new members are normally required to undertake.[10] Thus the former GDR preceded the other former communist states in central and eastern Europe in achieving a widely shared ambition to join these two western institutions in a 'return to Europe'.[11]

8 Commission of the European Communities, 'Wider Europe – Neighbourhood: A New Framework for Relations with our Eastern and Southern Neighbours', Communication from the Commission to the Council and the European Parliament, COM (2003) 104 Final, Brussels, 11 March 2003.

9 France's President Mitterrand was so anxious about the prospect of German unification that he conducted a whistle-stop tour round central and eastern Europe arguing that it would not or should not happen, while the Dutch prime minister Ruud Lubbers's hostility to unification was sufficiently vocal for Kohl subsequently to veto his nomination as President of the European Commission in 1994.

10 For a full discussion of the preparations that enabled the former GDR to join the EC, see David Spence, *Enlargement Without Accession: The EC's Response to German Unification*, RIIA Discussion Paper No. 36 (London: RIIA, 1991).

11 This enlargement seemed to set a negative precedent for those who believed the massive exodus of east Germans or 'Ossies' to the richer western *Länder* to be indicative of what

Other states were less fortunate in terms of the rapidity of their progress, as none of them could claim to be a 'kin-state' of an existing EU member. To make matters worse, the difficulties that Germany faced upon unification – public hostility in the west to higher taxes and in the east to a perception that citizens there were not being treated on a par with their western counterparts, as well as recession and high unemployment arising from overly generous exchange rates at the time of German economic unification – rendered Germany less willing than in the past to bankroll European integration. And this happened just when the EU was most in need of German funds in order to facilitate enlargement.

Yet if the EU's paymaster has looked a little less keen to foot the bill than in the past, this has not made Germany less enthusiastic about the idea of enlarging the EU further. Nor does it seem to have put off many potential applicants. In the 14 years since the collapse of communism, 11 central and east european (CEE) states have applied for membership with a twelfth – the former Yugoslav Republic of Macedonia (FYROM) – expected to do so in the course of 2003. Of these 12 states, 10 were granted candidate status in 1997. Five of these states, the Czech Republic, Estonia, Hungary, Poland and Slovenia, began accession negotiations in 1998 along with Cyprus.[12] Five more, Bulgaria, Latvia, Lithuania, Romania and Slovakia, began negotiations in 2000, as did Malta.

In October 2002, the European Commission recommended that eight of the 10 CEE countries already negotiating membership should be welcomed into the EU in 2004. At its summit in Prague in November 2002, NATO recommended that in addition to the Czech Republic, Hungary and Poland, which had joined in 1999, seven more states should become members of that organization in 2004.[13] The exceptions for the EU were Bulgaria and Romania, which had only set themselves a deadline of 2007 to be ready to accede, a date that the Commission accepted in its 'road map' outlining the work these two states should undertake in order to meet the Union's membership requirements. Croatia put in an application for membership in February 2003, in the hope of being able to accede alongside Bulgaria and Romania in 2007 – an optimistic but not entirely impossible goal given

would happen if further enlargement took place too quickly, or who were aware of the environmental and other industrial costs which someone would have to pay to raise standards in new member states of Western organizations.

12 Candidate status was agreed at the Luxembourg European Council held in December 1997, at which it was agreed that the first six states (the five CEE states and Cyprus) could begin negotiations, hence the concept of the Luxembourg Six. Similarly, those states which were permitted to open full negotiations at the 1999 Helsinki European Council took the name of that Council as the Helsinki Six.

13 These were Bulgaria, Estonia, Latvia, Lithuania, Romania, Slovakia and Slovenia.

Croatia's relatively strong economic potential. Other applications are to be expected (as indicated above, FYROM has indicated its intention of submitting an application in 2003), although the chances of membership for Serbia and Montenegro (the former Republic of Yugoslavia) suffered a setback in March 2003 when Serbia's prime minister, Zoran Djindjic, was assassinated. Each future enlargement is likely to bring with it the same sort of issue: how to minimize the negative impacts of enlargement for those states left outside and for border regions, whether inside or outside the EU.

OUTLINE OF THE BOOK

In this volume we consider relations between those prospective EU and NATO members that are expected to accede to both organizations in 2004 and those states that seem destined to remain outside in the medium to long term. The focus is exclusively on the EU's enlargement to former communist countries of central and eastern Europe, not because the accession of Malta, Cyprus and Turkey is unimportant but because the issues associated with these cases are essentially *sui generis*, unrelated to the questions that unite the would-be members from central and eastern Europe.[14] Certainly, questions of the free movement of people from Turkey will be a major issue for the current member states when accession talks are opened sometime after December 2004, and the strategic implications of Cyprus's accession to the EU could also be profound. However, these issues will be somewhat different from the challenges raised by eastern enlargement, which will affect outsiders at least as much as insiders.[15] For the same reason, we do not consider case by case the implications of EU enlargement for all potential new members and new neighbours. Bulgaria, for example, is not covered in any detail because although it is a candidate seeking to join the EU in 2007 the next round of enlargement will not directly affect it (it already has a common border with Greece, so the 2004 enlargement will not change its status). This volume focuses instead primarily on issues facing states with external EU borders and their neighbours on the outside.

The first part of the book comprises three thematic chapters, which set the relations between insiders and outsiders in the wider context of enlarge-

14 Turkey is already a NATO member and as NATO's expansion will not include Malta or Cyprus, the issue of its southern enlargement is not relevant.

15 The accession of Turkey would, of course, make Iraq, Iran and Syria neighbours of the EU, which in turn could create both security challenges and potential migratory pressures. However, the tensions would be qualitatively different from those between, say, Poland and Ukraine or Romania and Moldova. In these cases the outsiders are clearly European and thus in some eyes potential EU members. It is hard to argue that Iraq, Iran or Syria fit into this category.

ment and assess the prospects for interstate relations in the 'enlarged' Europe. Chapter 2, by Alan Smith, considers economics and trade relations. Chapter 3, by Matloob Piracha and Roger Vickerman, analyses the politically salient issues of immigration and labour mobility. In the last thematic chapter (Chapter 4) James Gow looks at security issues in Europe. These issues are explored in more detail below in this Introduction.

The remainder of the book explores interstate relations through five case studies. Chapter 5, by Kataryna and Roman Wolczuk, examines Poland's relations with Ukraine. The former is expected to join the EU in 2004; the latter is not yet an applicant despite occasional indications, so far resolutely ignored by the EU, that it would like to become a member. Traditionally somewhat fraught, relations between Poland and Ukraine improved enormously after Ukraine's independence in 1991, and there is now a considerable amount of cross-border trade. There is concern on both sides of the border lest Poland's accession to the EU damage this newly invigorated relationship. Thus Poland has tried hard to 'Europeanize' Ukraine in the hope of securing stability on its borders and, to some extent, it has been an advocate of Ukraine in Europe. Poland has not been able to prevent the EU from insisting on the introduction of visas for all Ukrainians crossing the border, but has reached an agreement to make the visas easy to obtain and free of charge. In addition, Ukraine has refrained from requiring visas from Poles. At a broader political level, however, Poland has not succeeded in persuading Ukraine to introduce the sort of reforms that closer relations with the EU would require.

In Chapter 6, Gabriel Partos considers two contrasting sets of bilateral relations: between Hungary and Romania and between Romania and Moldova. Right from the start of transition, Hungary was the 'star pupil' among CEE states seeking EU membership; reform in neighbouring Romania was much slower. In contrast to Ukraine, successive Romanian governments have sought EU and NATO membership, seeing positive relations with Hungary as a way to help them succeed. Moldova has viewed Romania as its conduit to the West, although the election of a communist government in Moldova and strong links with Russia and Belarus make its hopes of closer relations with the West somewhat fragile. A particularly interesting aspect of these cases, and also that of Poland and Ukraine, is the vast number of resident minorities from neighbouring states: large numbers of ethnic Hungarians reside in Transylvania (Romania), the majority of those resident in Moldova are ethnically Romanian and some 200,000 Poles live in Ukraine. This mixture of ethnic groups, typical of central and eastern Europe where borders changed so often during the twentieth century, is one of the issues that makes the question of EU enlargement so politically sensitive.

In Chapter 7, Graeme Herd considers the relationship between Russia and the EU, noting that there is scope for cooperation between the two but also acknowledging Russia's strategic interest in close links with the United States. The EU–Russia relationship is extremely important in terms of ties between insiders and outsiders, although Russia is highly unlikely to join the EU or NATO in the short to medium term, despite its links with both organizations, especially NATO.

The relationship between the specific issue of the Russian exclave, Kaliningrad, and the enlarged EU is discussed by Christopher Preston in Chapter 8. With the break-up of the Soviet Union and the new-found independence of the three Baltic states, Kaliningrad, bordering on Lithuania and Poland, was cut off from the Russian 'mainland'. Although this situation did not raise many problems in the 1990s, the prospect of EU enlargement has heightened the exclave's significance. Under pressure from the EU, Poland and Lithuania had to agree that the residents of Kaliningrad should henceforth possess travel documents in order to transit either state on the way to or from Russia. This situation had major implications for Kaliningrad residents, Poland and Lithuania, and also for wider EU–Russian relations, as both Preston and Herd discuss.

In Chapter 9, Peter Frankopan considers the relations between three states that were formerly part of the Socialist Federal Republic of Yugoslavia: Bosnia-Herzegovina, Croatia and Serbia. The federation had been one of the most economically successful states in communist times, but the wars that beset its successor states in the 1990s meant that, with the exception of Slovenia, none were ready to accede to the EU or NATO in 2004. All the same, as noted above, in February 2003 Croatia put in a formal bid for EU membership, declaring its intention of trying to accede in 2007 along with Bulgaria and Romania. This is an ambitious but not entirely impossible task, not least because of the EU's preference for taking in new members as groups rather than individually. The prospects for Serbia, the former Yugoslav Republic of Macedonia and Bosnia-Herzegovina acceding were more remote, but they are all states with reasonable medium-term prospects of joining, despite their continuing domestic political and economic difficulties.

The reason for including a discussion of relations between Bosnia-Herzegovina, Croatia and Serbia in this study is to demonstrate that domestic politics frequently damage states' prospects of EU membership but that, nevertheless, states may be able to recover lost time if they are sufficiently committed to the goal of membership and its political requirements, such as good relations with neighbours and respect for minorities. That said, it is unlikely that these former Yugoslav states would envisage aiding each other in their moves towards EU membership. This is in marked contrast to other cases where states likely to join in 2004 typically feel that it is in their interest to support the applications of their neighbours or at least to ameliorate any ill effects of their accession on them. In the case of former Yugoslavia, old wounds have not healed sufficiently to make this a realistic prospect.

CHANGING INTERSTATE RELATIONS: FROM 1989 TO 2004
AND BEYOND

The end of the Cold War fundamentally altered the economic, political and security maps of Europe. There was a proliferation of (small) countries as three states – the Union of Soviet Socialist Republics, Czechoslovakia and the Socialist Federal Republic of Yugoslavia – broke up, the first two fairly peacefully, the last amid bloody conflict. The result in each case was to increase the number of sovereign states with which the West had to deal. All the emerging democracies across central and eastern Europe, with the partial exception of the successor states to the Socialist Federal Republic of Yugoslavia, also needed to create a wholly new set of trade relations, as they had previously conducted most of their trade with other members of the Council for Mutual Economic Cooperation (the CMEA, also known as Comecon), typically on a bilateral basis via Moscow.

As Alan Smith notes in Chapter 2, most of the former communist states produced low-quality goods during the Cold War, which had to be upgraded if they were to be able to trade effectively with western Europe and, *a fortiori*, if they were to meet the rigorous requirements set for EU members.[16] The ability to redirect their trade to the West has been a good indicator of their progress towards EU membership, with the Visegrad Four (Hungary, Poland, the Czech Republic and Slovakia) and Slovenia the most successful in market adaptation, which has improved income and employment levels. Other states, particularly the Baltics, remained vulnerable to changes in the Russian economy. On accession, those CEE states which are scheduled to join the EU on 1 May 2004 – the Czech Republic, Estonia, Hungary, Latvia,

16 At the European Council meeting in Copenhagen in 1993, the EU outlined a set of criteria that each would-be member was required to meet. These included 'stability of institutions guaranteeing democracy, the rule of law, human rights, and respect for and protection of minorities … a functioning market economy as well as the capacity to cope with competitive pressure and market forces once in the Union … the ability to take on the obligations of membership including adherence to the aims of political, economic and monetary union … the conditions for its integration through the adjustment of its administrative structures, so that European Community legislation transposed into national legislation is implemented effectively through appropriate administrative and judicial structures.' Source: *http:// europa.eu.int/comm/enlargement/intro/criteria.htm* cited by Julie Smith, *An Ever Larger Europe?*, RIIA Briefing Paper New Series No. 14, May 2000, p. 2.

Lithuania, Poland, Slovakia, and Slovenia – will enjoy the benefits of increasingly integrated trade with the 15 current EU members.[17] By contrast, those states destined to remain outside, either temporarily or permanently, may see a decline in their ability to compete in Western markets; they will certainly not benefit from intra-EU transfers, which will give the new insiders a considerable advantage (although Romania and Bulgaria should see some increase in pre-accession transfers). Yet, as noted by Alan Smith in Chapter 2 and also by Wolczuk and Wolczuk in Chapter 5, it is not only the outsiders who stand to lose from the reduction of cross-border trading that is expected to result from EU enlargement. New members such as Poland and Hungary may also suffer from a reduction in the volume of cheap goods being brought over the borders on a daily basis as part of the grey economy.

A reduction of cross-border trade may occur, for two reasons. First, the imposition of the EU's common external tariff will render trade with the new outsiders less attractive for the new member states than in the past. Secondly, as James Gow in Chapter 4 and Christopher Preston in Chapter 8 among others point out, new members are required to implement so-called Schengen *acquis* upon accession.[18] Schengen borders are a natural complement to the EU's internal market, which is intended to ensure a level playing field in European business: as internal borders are removed, member states feel that their external borders must be strengthened. *Inter alia*, this entails the imposition of visa restrictions on many third countries, including the majority of the Union's new neighbours. In several cases this has necessitated candidate states imposing new visa regimes on states whose nationals had previously been allowed to enter their territory freely. This was a particular problem with regard to Kaliningrad. To date, Russian citizens have been able to travel freely through these states en route to or from Kaliningrad, a situation that will change once its two neighbours accede to the EU. After difficult negotiations an agreement on travel formalities for Russians travelling to and from Kaliningrad was reached, but it remains to be seen how it will work in practice.

17 The Copenhagen European Council meeting in December 2002 agreed to accept those states along with Cyprus and Malta on 1 May 2004. All 10 accessions will depend on ratification procedures at the EU level and in the current member states as well as the candidate countries.

18 In 1985 five states – Belgium, France, Germany, Luxembourg and the Netherlands – signed the Schengen Agreement, thereby committing themselves to remove border controls and to allow free movement of people between their territories. The Agreement was supplemented by the Schengen Convention, signed in 1990. The Agreement and Convention plus associated declarations and decisions form the so-called Schengen *acquis*. At the time of writing, all EU member states except the United Kingdom and Ireland were signatories of the Schengen Convention, as were Norway and Iceland. See SCADPlus: Glossary, *Schengen (Agreement and Convention),* available at *http://europa.eu.int/scadplus/leg/en/cig/ g4000s.htm.*

As Wolczuk and Wolczuk discuss in Chapter 5, the need to strengthen borders and to impose a visa requirement is an issue that might create a new dividing line between Poland and Ukraine, which have enjoyed significant cross-border trade since 1991. Despite the agreement to provide free and reasonably easy-to-obtain visas, there will inevitably be some impact on trade once the new regime is implemented. There was also concern in Romania and Hungary that visas would be imposed on Romanian nationals once Hungary acceded to the EU. This was because, despite being a candidate hoping to join in 2007, Romania was on an EU blacklist of states whose nationals were required to have visas in order to enter the Union. However, as Gabriel Partos notes in Chapter 6, the prospect of divisions between new members and those states next in line to join was averted in this case when Romania was dropped from the blacklist along with Bulgaria in 2002.

The free movement of people became a key issue for the EU following the 1986 Single European Act and the Treaty on European Union, introduced in 1993, which allowed for free movement. The 1997 Treaty of Amsterdam went further in bringing asylum and immigration policy within the first, European Community, pillar of the Union. In addition, the end of the Cold War freed up the movement of people from former communist states who had previously been allowed to travel solely in eastern Europe, and even then often only with difficulty. With the prospect of EU enlargement, some member states already facing pressures from asylum-seekers and would-be economic migrants, notably Austria and Germany, were concerned that the extension of the free movement of people would lead to large migratory pressures from the new member states. They thus managed to secure a seven-year transitional period during which citizens of the new member states would not enjoy full freedom of movement. Most existing member states indicated that they would permit free movement as soon as the EU enlarged, however; in any case, although the new members will be economically weaker than the existing members, there appears to be little prospect of mass east–west migration.[19]

If large-scale migration by citizens of new member states is unlikely to occur after enlargement, as Piracha and Vickerman point out in Chapter 3, there remains considerable scope for migration from the outsiders because

19 As Piracha and Vickerman argue, there is little evidence that large numbers of citizens from the first wave of new member states are likely to seek to work in other EU states. See also Christina Boswell, *EU Enlargement: What are the Prospects for East–West Migration?*, European Programme Working Paper (London: RIIA, 2000). The experience of previous enlargements also suggests that the level of migration is likely to be fairly low. For example, more Spaniards sought work in the EC *prior* to Spain's accession than after, perhaps because workers felt that once Spain was inside the EC the benefits of membership would accrue to them anyway, despite the persistently high levels of unemployment in Spain.

the economic disparities between the EU insiders and those outside will be greater. Poland, for example, is already a major recipient of Ukrainian migrants, although they frequently use it as a staging post in moves farther west. In some cases, there is also an ethnic or historical reason for would-be migrants to choose particular states: for example, ethnic Romanians from Moldova might be expected to seek to live and work in Romania and ethnic Hungarians living in Romania might wish to move to Hungary.[20] If EU enlargement does damage the economic interests of the outsiders, their citizens will have an even greater incentive to try to move westwards. (This does not mean that such moves would necessarily be a bad thing for the recipient states: the prospect of ageing populations in western Europe, Piracha and Vickerman argue, signifies that increased labour migration might in any case be beneficial for the EU.)

Although it is current member states that have expressed concerns about migration, it is the new members that face the greatest problems in dealing with would-be migrants from the east. In part for this reason, the EU is taking on some of the burden faced by prospective members, which are required to strengthen and improve the policing of their external borders prior to accession. In a Union without internal borders, the eastern and southern borders of the new member states will, in many cases, become the new external borders. In order to prevent abuses of the system, particularly at a time of global terrorist threats, it is in the interests of *all* members of the EU to ensure that its external borders are policed effectively. Yet, even though the merits of such action might be clear to all concerned, it is nevertheless likely to reinforce new divisions between insiders and outsiders in Europe. Thus the reinforcement of the borders needs to be handled sensitively by the EU: it would not be wise to lower the standards of external border controls, but it is necessary to be aware of the potentially detrimental effects those controls might have on new members and their neighbours.

Just as internal security in an enlarged Europe is a matter of concern for new and old members alike, so too are issues of 'hard' security and military capability. Yet, if the requirement in terms of internal security is to strengthen borders, this might not be the case in matters of broader geopolitical security. As Gow argues, it is difficult to define clearly the borders of Europe in terms of security. The geographical limits of the EU are not particularly helpful in this policy area because national interests are frequently affected by

---

20 It was in part the prospect of large-scale influxes of ethnic Hungarians from Romania and Slovakia that led Hungary to produce its reviled Status Law, discussed by Gabriel Partos in Chapter 6, which sought to offer ethnic Hungarians resident abroad preferential treatment in terms of work and education; this was deemed counter to the interests of those states where Hungarian nationals were resident.

the actions of outsiders, which lead states to act beyond the borders of the EU, as the wars of secession in the former Yugoslavia highlighted all too clearly in the mid-1990s. Moreover, creating inflexible security borders with potentially hostile states may be counter-productive, as Russia's initial hostility to the idea of NATO's expansion demonstrated. For Moscow, NATO remained a potential aggressor. It was reluctant to see the Alliance expand to its borders, particularly if expansion entailed membership for the three Baltic states, which had been under Soviet rule until 1991. Moscow's reaction created great anxiety in the Baltics, which felt that it implied they were vulnerable to possible Russian aggression. As Herd makes clear in Chapter 7, however, by 2002 Russia had signed an agreement with NATO creating the so-called 'NATO at Twenty', indicating, perhaps, that Russia was no longer too worried by NATO as a potential aggressor. Herd argues that there seems to be some scope for Russia to work with the EU on certain security matters, such as Kosovo.[21]

A second consideration bearing on both the EU's and NATO's relations with their new neighbours as both plan their expansion is that many of the new neighbours or new outsiders might themselves become new members in due course. As Gow argues, in many cases it is better to think of security in terms of frontiers leading to other countries and entailing the prospect of further expansion than in terms of fixed borders, which create a sense of 'them' and 'us' and are unlikely to enhance the security relations of insiders or outsiders.

The processes of EU and NATO expansion have been broadly parallel, although NATO has expanded to the east sooner than the EU: Poland, Hungary and the Czech Republic were accepted as NATO members at its fiftieth anniversary in 1999. Although it was not inevitable that the processes would run in parallel, it is helpful that they have done so, as greater congruence between the EU and the European members of NATO may help give more coherence to the European contribution to NATO and also to bolster the EU's own emerging Security and Defence Policy. That at least is the theory but, as Gow points out, it will be hard to secure EU-wide legitimacy for any military action given the differing national interests of the soon-to-be 25 members. The disparate reactions of EU member and candidate states to the prospect and reality of war in Iraq in late 2002 and early 2003 suggested that progress is unlikely to be made in the near future. Nevertheless,

---

21 It must be borne in mind that many scenarios surrounding European and transatlantic security will have to be fundamentally rethought in the aftermath of the war on Iraq. In that conflict Russia allied itself very closely with France and Germany, despite an apparent concern to build up good relations with Washington prior to the war. At the time of writing it was not possible to predict the European security constellations that would emerge.

it remains the case that tackling shared security issues effectively is vital to existing members of the EU and NATO, to prospective new members and to their neighbours who remain outside.

CONCLUSIONS

The enlargement of the EU and of NATO offers manifold benefits to Europe. However, these benefits may not be unalloyed. Just as the reunification of Germany in 1990 highlighted very clearly the problems associated with bringing kin-states together, so too the enlargement of the European Union may create new tensions both between old and new member states and between new members and their outsider neighbours. Just as the euphoria that greeted the fall of the Berlin Wall disappeared quickly when the economic realities of unification began to be realized, so there is a very real danger of something similar occurring when the next wave of states accedes in 2004. Certainly, there is scope for economic difficulty as and when the new members join the euro-zone. New member states may find that they are not welcomed quite as warmly as they anticipated – indeed, the salutary process of negotiating membership has already indicated this. At the same time, the present member states may well find that despite their promises, the newcomers are not willing in practice to accept all the EU's rules and regulations, the so-called *acquis communautaire*. Once they are on the inside, states will have some scope to seek to change some of the policies of the EU, and scope too not to implement the full *acquis*. After all, several current members are notably recalcitrant about implementation.

Apart from internal questions, however, the accession of a large number of new states will alter the EU's external relations profoundly, creating a set of 'new neighbours' with whom good relations will be desirable but not automatic. If the EU is to become the superpower that many wish it to become, it will need to ensure that relations with the new neighbours are conducive to stability and prosperity across Europe. If it fails to do so, it is likely to be weakened, which is not in the interests of the Union or of the outsiders. It is thus incumbent on the EU to deal sensitively and effectively with its immediate neighbours and with those states farther afield which might consider applying in the medium to long term.

2

Economic and trade relations between the European former communist states and the states of western Europe

ALAN SMITH

The break-up of the communist economic system in Europe has involved the creation of new trade relations for the 27 independent states that emerged from the collapse of the Soviet economic empire. This chapter outlines the changing nature of the trade relations of the European former communist states with western Europe. It examines the redirection of trade flows away from trade within the communist region towards trade with the 15 states of the EU and attempts to assess the degree to which the individual states are becoming integrated into EU structures of production and trade.

In the period from the end of the Second World War until its demise the Soviet economic empire consisted of an unbroken, land-based trade zone that comprised the Soviet Union and the European members of the Council for Mutual Economic Assistance (CMEA or Comecon).[1] Two other socialist economies in southeastern Europe, the Federal Republic of Yugoslavia and Albania, which were formally associate members of the CMEA, were not fully integrated into either the Soviet trading system or the economic structures of western Europe.

The collapse of communism led to a significant change in state formation, which in turn affected interstate relations. The disintegration of the Soviet Union itself resulted in the creation of 15 independent states, while the collapse of communism in central and southeastern Europe resulted in the reunification of the former German Democratic Republic with the Federal Republic of Germany and the break-up of Czechoslovakia into two separate states. The disintegration of the Federal Republic of Yugoslavia resulted in the creation of five independent states.

The former communist economies were required to formulate new currency regimes and new policies towards foreign investment and to

---

[1] The CMEA was the body that formally coordinated the trade relations of the communist states. Its members were the USSR, Bulgaria, Czechoslovakia, the GDR, Hungary, Poland, Romania and Mongolia plus Vietnam and Cuba.

develop new trade relations. In the case of the new nations that emerged from the break-up of larger economic units, this involved the creation of a 'new foreign trade' – the replacement of what were once internal, domestic trade links by what is now international trade. These economies, together with economies that remained within the same territorial boundaries, have been forced to seek new markets for their products, new sources of capital and new networks, including links with multinational corporations, in order to replace the trade structures and networks that were an integral part of the communist trade system.

PROBLEMS CREATED BY THE SOVIET TRADE SYSTEM

Economic contacts between the communist states and the states of western Europe were limited during the Soviet era. This reflected partly Stalin's concept of two separate world economic systems, socialism and capitalism, and partly the desire of Western states to limit the transfer of technology that could have military applications. As a result the communist states were isolated from international markets and capital flows, and had limited exposure to international technological innovation and new economic ideas.

The trade system was dominated by the Soviet Union, which in turn was dominated by the Russian Socialist Federal Soviet Republic (RSFSR). Trade and capital flows between the Soviet republics were determined by central planners in Moscow. The RSFSR was a net exporter of energy and raw materials, machinery and equipment, and chemical products to the other Soviet republics, and was a net importer of foodstuffs and consumer goods. The predominant pattern of trade flows between the Soviet Union and the central and southeast European members of the CMEA was established after the outbreak of the Korean War and proved relatively impervious to change. The Soviet Union, with a market of 275 million consumers and an abundant supply of energy and raw materials but with a neglected agricultural sector and a limited capacity for innovation outside the defence sector, became the dominant trade partner for all the central and southeast European economies. It exported energy, raw materials and resource-intensive manufactured goods to each of them and imported machinery and equipment, consumer goods and foodstuffs from each on a barter basis. As a result, trade flows between the Soviet Union and the states of central and southeastern Europe were not sufficiently differentiated to reflect, or benefit from, the different resource endowments, levels of development and skill structures of the individual economies.

Critically, the Soviet Union provided these economies with a guaranteed market for exports of products that had largely become obsolete in the world economy. East European exports to the Soviet Union in many industrial sectors were marked by relatively low quality and technological backwardness, which was also reflected in exports to western Europe that sold for substantially lower prices than their west European counterparts. Civil and heavy engineering products, rather than technologically advanced electronic engineering goods, predominated in the exports of machinery and equipment from each of the central and southeast European economies to the Soviet Union. Low-quality clothing and household utensils (which excluded sophisticated electronic goods) predominated in exports of consumer goods and were intended to meet the needs of a mass low-income market. Exports of foodstuffs consisted of agricultural materials and products with a relatively low degree of processing.[2]

The dominance of the undemanding Soviet market and the centralized state monopoly over foreign trade relations protected enterprises from foreign competition and prevented them from responding to the demands of market economies in western Europe. Their separation from western Europe was aggravated by the low level of capital flows and foreign investment between the market economies and eastern Europe. Although each of the CMEA economies (except the German Democratic Republic) permitted Western multinationals to operate joint ventures on their territory, these arrangements provided the multinationals with very limited rights of ownership and control and did not operate as a satisfactory vehicle for technology transfer from multinational corporations to the host country. A different pattern prevailed in trade relations with Yugoslavia, with some domestic firms developing direct contacts and supply relationships with west European partners.

An attempt to import Western machinery and equipment on credit in order to modernize the CMEA economies in the 1970s, coupled with very limited reforms of the domestic economic system, which left central planning intact (the import-led growth strategy), resulted in a failure to generate exports to repay credits and a build-up of unsustainable levels of indebtedness. This necessitated a contraction of imports in the early 1980s. By the late 1980s, exports to the EC from those CMEA states for which data exist were concentrated on labour-intensive consumer goods (clothing, footwear and furniture), organic chemicals and fertilizers (excluding pharmaceuticals and cosmetics) and ferrous and non-ferrous metals and metal products. Some limited successes were recorded in exports of machinery and equipment and transport equipment, but in each of these cases CMEA

---

2 Alan Smith, *The Return to Europe: The Reintegration of Eastern Europe into the European Economy* (London and Basingstoke: Macmillan, 2000), Chapter 4.

exports were largely limited to exports of relatively unsophisticated products aimed at the lower-quality end of the market.

THE IMPERATIVE FOR TRADE REDIRECTION

The collapse of the Soviet market left the former communist states in central and southeastern Europe with a major economic imperative to redirect trade flows to the industrialized market economies and, given its location, to the EC in particular. The collapse of the CMEA and the Soviet trading systems, together with the absence of functioning payments mechanisms between the CMEA states, meant that there was little prospect of resurrecting trade flows among the former communist economies of central and southeastern Europe to replace the Soviet market. This problem was compounded by the low purchasing power of consumers in former communist economies and was further aggravated in the former Yugoslav and former Soviet republics by the collapse of internal markets.

The majority of former communist economies (with the exception of Russia and, to a lesser extent, Ukraine and Poland) have small internal markets which do not provide domestic manufacturers with the opportunity to reach levels of production that allow them to benefit from economies of scale. This weakens their ability to withstand competition in domestic markets from foreign competitors with access to larger markets which enables them to achieve substantial economies of scale. As a result the majority of medium- and large-scale producers in central and southeastern Europe and former Yugoslavia are dependent on export markets to maintain output and production. The problem was further complicated by the fact that the former communist economies had inherited a capital stock from the Soviet era that was designed to produce goods to meet the needs of defence industries and of low-to-medium-income consumers and thus was not suitable for meeting the demands and tastes of relatively high-income consumers in OECD and EU markets. Consequently, the need to redirect exports to the EU required substantial inflows of capital goods in order to modernize the production structures of the former communist economies, in the form of either foreign direct investment (FDI) or imports of capital goods by domestic entrepreneurs. The lack of domestic financial capital and the degree of control over technology and patents exercised by multinational corporations indicated that FDI would be expected to play a major role in industrial restructuring.

The problem can be illustrated by the case of Czechoslovakia, where the industrial capital stock was designed to meet central planners' demands for obsolete heavy engineering products, defence production and consumer goods for an unsophisticated Soviet market. When this market collapsed, a domestic population of only 15 million low-to-medium-income consumers was incapable of sustaining domestic production. Consequently, the major hope for industrial recovery lay in restructuring output to produce goods for the more sophisticated, high-income market in the EU, particularly neighbouring Germany. However, this required major inflows of physical capital that was not available domestically. The need to compete with existing producers in western Europe who possessed technical know-how, who had already built up complex international supply networks and who benefited from high levels of advertising and brand-name products necessitated the creation of links with Western corporations. Low levels of domestic savings and poorly developed domestic capital markets also meant that this would require inflows of financial capital, some of which would take the form of FDI.

For the smaller CMEA economies in central and southeastern Europe, the problems were of a different scale of magnitude from those initially faced by newly industrializing economies in Southeast Asia, although there were some parallels with the problems faced by Latin American economies in the 1980s. The CMEA economies possessed an operating capital stock in the form of industrial enterprises that provided the major source of employment and security for most households. However, the collapse of the communist trading system meant that the market for the products produced by these plants had effectively collapsed, and there was little realistic possibility that it would recover in the medium term. The EU export market, combined with externally financed reconstruction projects, held out the best prospect of economic recovery in the short term as well as the long term. The problems confronting the Yugoslav economy, which had already developed trade links with Western companies, were initially less acute but were subsequently aggravated by war and the break-up of its internal market. The former Soviet republics faced even greater short-term problems resulting from the collapse of the internal Soviet market. Nevertheless, their geographic location, the potential scale of Eurasian markets and, in some cases, more favourable resource endowments imply a lower dependence on trade relations with the EU in the long term.

TRADE REDIRECTION TO THE EU IN THE TRANSITION ERA AND
PROSPECTS FOR ENTRY

Evidence from gravity models, which attempt to estimate 'normal' levels of trade between countries, indicates that trade between the communist economies and the EC in the late 1980s was substantially below the levels that would normally be expected given the size of their respective GDPs and

Table 2.1: Dynamics of trade between the EU-15 and the European former communist economies, 1989–99 (ecu m)

	EU-15 exports			EU-15 imports		
	1989 (% extra-EU trade)	1999 (% extra-EU15 trade)	% growth 1989–99	1989 (% extra-EU trade)	1999 (% extra-EU15 trade)	% growth 1989–99
Extra-EU-15	392,624	759,796	93.5	434,713	776,707	78.5
Intra-EU	735,004	1,207,773	64.3			
Central Europe	11,271 (2.9)	71,476 (9.4)	534.1	11,297 (2.6)	57,769 (7.4)	411.4
Southeastern Europe	2,581 (0.7)	9,724 (1.3)	276.7	3,349 (0.7)	8,248 (1.1)	146.3
Former USSR	16,666 (4.2)	26,636 (3.5)	59.8	18,714 (4.3)	35,823 (4.6)	91.4
Former Yugoslavia	7,962 (2.0)	16,544 (2.2)	107.9	7,628 (1.8)	10,170 (1.3)	33.3
Total	38,480 (9.8)	124,380 (16.4)	223.2	40,988 (9.4)	112,010 (14.4)	173.2

Sources: European Commission, *External and Intra-European Union Trade,* 1999; International Monetary Fund, *Directions of Trade Statistics Yearbook,* Washington DC (2000) and European Commission, Comext database, published in CD format (Luxembourg: Office for Official Publications of the European Communities).

Note: In this table central Europe consists of Poland, Hungary, the Czech Republic and Slovakia; southeastern Europe consists of Romania, Bulgaria and Albania. Recorded EU-15 trade with former Yugoslavia in 1999 may understate trade with Serbia-Montenegro. Export data for Poland exclude 'shuttle trade'.

their geographical proximity. In the 10 years following the collapse of communism in central and southeastern Europe the growth of trade between the former communist economies and the European Union was dynamic, and the EU became the largest market and the largest external supplier of capital goods and equipment for the majority of the former communist economies. The growth of the trade of the 15 states that currently constitute the EU (EU-15) with the former communist economies was faster than EU-15 trade with all countries outside the EU-15 as the former communist economies took a growing share of extra-EU-15 trade.

As Table 2.1 shows, in the decade between the collapse of communism in Europe and the Helsinki summit's decision in December 1999 to open accession negotiations with all the central and east European applicant states, EU-15 exports to the former communist economies grew by 223 per cent, from ecu 38,480m in 1989 to ecu 124,380 in 1999, while their share in extra-EU-15 exports grew from 9.8 per cent in 1989 to 16.4 per cent in 1999. Over the same period EU-15 imports from the former communist countries grew by 173 per cent, from ecu 40,988m to ecu 112,010m.

However, it is also apparent from Table 2.1 that there are clear regional disparities in the growth of trade between the EU-15 and the former communist economies. It has been predominantly with the central European economies (Poland, Hungary, the Czech Republic and Slovakia); the growth of EU-15 trade with the new states of the former Soviet Union, and with former Yugoslavia, has been far less spectacular. The growth of EU-15 imports from southeastern Europe (Albania, Bulgaria and Romania) between 1989 and 1999, although significant at 146.3 per cent, was far less substantial than the growth of EU-15 imports from central Europe over the same period. The central European economies accounted for 70 per cent of the growth of recorded EU-15 exports to the former communist economies over the period, and for 65.4 per cent of the growth of recorded EU-15 imports from former communist economies, even though these countries account for only 16 per cent of the population of the region. EU-15 exports to central Europe grew by 534.1 per cent, from ecu 11,271m in 1989 to ecu 71,476m in 1999, when they constituted 9.4 per cent of extra-EU trade. Similarly EU-15 imports from central Europe grew by 411.4 per cent to ecu 57,769m in 1999. These figures do not include personal imports by EU citizens of goods purchased in specialized markets in Poland's 'shuttle trade', which are estimated at ecu 3.6 bn for 1998.[3]

A significant proportion of the growth of EU-15 trade with the former Soviet Union can be attributed to trade with the Baltic states. EU-15 imports from these states between 1993 and 1999 grew by 185 per cent, from ecu 1,722m to ecu 4,909m, slightly faster than the growth of EU-15 imports from central Europe of 181.2 per cent over the same period.[4] Similarly the growth of EU-15 exports to the Baltic states of 424.7 per cent, from ecu 1,452m in 1993 to ecu 7,619m in 1999, was faster than the growth of EU-15 exports to central Europe of 174 per cent over the same period.

The growth of trade between the EU-15 and the former communist economies since the collapse of communism broadly coincides with the progress of negotiations for EU membership. The four central European countries, the three Baltic states and Slovenia secured association agreements

3 GUS, *Rocznik Statystyczny Handlu Zagranicznego* [Central Statistical Office, *Statistical Yearbook of Foreign Trade*], Warsaw, 1999, p. 147, converted into ecu.
4 It is not possible to analyse EU trade with the Baltic states for earlier years, as it is generally accepted that the data are highly inaccurate.

with the EU early on, and, barring unforeseen problems with their national accession referendums, will join the Union in the first round of enlargement set for May 2004. The two southeast European states with association agreements, Romania and Bulgaria, will not be part of the first round of enlargement, but they hope, probably optimistically, to be admitted to the EU in 2007. The republics of former Yugoslavia (except Slovenia, whose application is well advanced), Albania and the former Soviet republics in the Commonwealth of Independent States have received no formal offer of entry into the EU, although Croatia and the former Yugoslav Republic of Macedonia (FYROM) have agreements in the form of stability and association agreements that give a *de facto* promise of eventual membership. However, it is possible that the problems of absorbing 10 new members (including Cyprus and Malta) will be so great that the second round of enlargement could be delayed, by which time some of the states without a formal offer of entry might catch up or even overtake Romania and Bulgaria and become full members of the EU by the end of the decade.[5]

To some extent the differential performance by the countries listed in Table 2.1 in increasing trade flows with the EU can be explained by geographical factors, with the greater proximity of the central European economies and the Baltic states to existing EU countries making them more attractive prospects for multinational investors seeking low-wage economies for production for exports to the EU.

The remainder of this chapter will analyse the product structure of trade between the former communist economies and the EU-15 with a view to assessing whether the states that have been more successful in increasing trade flows have been more successful in attracting inflows of capital goods for restructuring their economies. It will also examine the impact this has had on the structure of exports to the EU. This will enable us to assess the extent to which these economies have adapted domestic production to the demands of EU markets.[6]

---

5 Of course, if Iceland, Norway or Switzerland were belatedly to decide to apply for membership, their progress is likely to be somewhat more rapid because they all have stable democracies and meet the other Copenhagen criteria.

6 The Comext database, published in CD format by the European Commission, provides the most comprehensive foreign trade data. They are broken down by commodity at several degrees of disaggregation, by country of origin and by destination for each of the member states. EU trade data from the Comext database have been used to ensure comparability of data between different transition economies, which cannot be guaranteed when national data sources are used. A cross-section of trade in 1998 has been taken to give a comprehensive snapshot of trade flows in that year. Estimates for other years have been undertaken so as to ensure the reliability of the data, but are not included here on grounds of space.

Table 2.2 shows trade flows between the EU-15 and the individual former communist economies broken down by three general product groups: food, beverages and tobacco; fuels and energy; and manufactured goods. The residual between the total and the items shown in the table consists of raw materials, animal oils and waxes, and a small number of miscellaneous items. Figures for intra–EU-15 trade and extra–EU-15 imports and exports are also provided for comparative purposes.

Although significant proportions of the populations of the former communist economies are employed in agriculture and the rural economy, trade in food and beverages accounted for only 4.0 per cent of EU-15 imports from the region, while a further 4.0 per cent originated from agriculture and forestry. These last items, which include timber, were more important in imports from the former Soviet republics, including the Baltic states. The low volume of EU-15 imports of agrarian products can be attributed to a combination of import restrictions, subsidies to EU agriculture and relatively low levels of productivity and of processing and packaging by former CMEA producers, which made their products relatively uncompetitive in Western markets.[7] Food and beverages accounted for 7.6 per cent of EU-15 exports to the European former communist economies listed in Table 2.2; in 1998 the EU-15 ran a surplus of ecu 5.5bn in trade in food and beverages with these economies (ecu 3.1bn of which consisted of the surplus in trade with Russia). There were surpluses in food trade with all countries of the European former communist economies listed in Table 2.2 except Hungary and Lithuania.

Manufactured goods predominated in EU trade relations with former communist economies in the late 1990s, reflecting their preponderance in both intra- and extra-EU trade. Manufactured goods accounted for 87.2 per cent of EU-15 exports to the European former communist economies and for 76.2 per cent of imports from them, compared with 87.6 per cent for total extra-EU-15 exports and 74.6 per cent for extra-EU-15 imports, and with 80.6 per cent for intra-EU trade. Trade in manufactured goods accounted for 90.7 per cent of EU-15 exports to and 89.6 per cent of EU-15 imports from former communist economies in central Europe and for 87.8 per cent of exports to and 90 per cent of imports from southeastern Europe. Manufactured goods constituted a smaller proportion of EU imports (42.5 per cent) from the European former Soviet states, largely as a result of energy imports. These accounted for 41.6 per cent of EU imports from Russia in

---

7 However, the low level of investment in this sector reflects the problems of access to EU markets and competition from subsidized EU products.

Table 2.2: Product structure of EU trade with European former communist economies in 1998 (ecu m)

	EU exports				EU imports			
	Total	Food and bevs	Fuels and energy	Manu-factures	Total	Food and bevs	Fuels and energy	Manu-factures
Total	122,644	9,275	1,857	106,962	93,266	3,722	10,486	71,107
Central-eastern Europe	66,664	2,777	927	60,466	50,561	2,247	1,615	44,349
Poland	27,558	1,375	520	24,719	16,056	1,044	932	13,317
Hungary	16,620	393	109	15,327	14,569	900	253	12,907
Czech Rep.	16,850	777	226	15,262	14,580	242	360	13,116
Slovakia	5,636	232	72	5,158	5,356	61	70	5,009
Baltic states	6,787	703	202	5,638	4,569	172	601	2,659
Estonia	2,662	251	88	2,253	1,761	61	261	1,105
Latvia	1,777	194	103	1,412	1,396	28	259	556
Lithuania	2,348	258	11	1,973	1,412	83	81	998
Southeastern Europe	9,151	638	174	8,038	7,575	329	75	6,819
Bulgaria	2,392	196	59	2,029	2,230	195	28	1,848
Romania	6,206	321	98	5,617	5,129	121	44	4,792
Albania	553	121	17	392	216	13	3	179
Former Yugoslavia	14,469	1,096	403	12,393	8,932	329	32	8,081
Slovenia	6,669	353	160	5,859	5,208	70	6	4,978
Croatia	4,345	325	70	3,798	1,820	54	24	1,542
Yugoslavia	1,754	173	67	1,451	1,064	140	2	852
Bosnia-Herzegovina	836	144	7	654	246	5	0	193
FYROM	865	101	99	631	594	52	0	516
European FSU	25,573	4,061	151	20,427	21,629	653	8,163	9,199
Russia	20,659	3,654	86	16,182	18,934	514	8,076	7,370
Ukraine	3,471	292	58	2,991	2,116	81	84	1,390
Belarus	1,152	61	6	1,028	462	24	3	380
Moldova	291	54	1	226	117	34	0	59
Intra-EU	1,050,971	120,449	30,1503	1,022,98				
Extra-EU	733,272	43,452	13,947	642.511	713.708	49,725	65,276	532.379
Percentages								
Total	100.0	7.6	1.5	87.2	100.0	4.0	11.2	76.2
Central-eastern Europe	100.0	4.2	1.3	90.7	100.0	4.4	3.2	87.9
Baltic states	100.0	10.4	3.0	83.1	100.0	3.8	13.2	58.1
Southeastern Europe	100.0	7.0	1.9	87.8	100.0	4.3	0.9	90.0
Former Yugoslavia	100.0	7.6	2.8	85.6	100.0	3.7	0.4	90.5
European FSU	100.0	15.9	0.6	79.9	100.0	3.0	37.7	42.5
Intra-EU	100.0	11.5	2.9	80.6	100.0			
Extra-EU	100.0	5.9	1.9	87.6	100.0	7.0	9.2	74.6

Source: European Commission, Comext database, published in CD format by the Office for Official Publications of the European Communities, Luxembourg.

1998 (despite falls in energy prices that year) and for 58.1 per cent of EU imports from the Baltic states, to which EU imports of wood and lumber products were important. The EU enjoyed a surplus of ecu 35.8bn in trade in manufactured goods with the European former communist economies in 1998 (including a surplus of ecu 11.4bn in trade with Poland and ecu 8.8bn in trade with Russia).

FACTOR INTENSITY IN TRADE IN MANUFACTURED GOODS

It is apparent from Table 2.2 that trade in manufactured goods predominates in both intra-EU trade and EU imports from the outside world. The growth of exports of manufactured goods to the EU from the former communist countries has been a major factor in sustaining incomes and employment in the latter. It was shown in Table 2.1 that the central-east European (CEE) economies have been more successful than the economies of southeastern Europe, former Yugoslavia and the former Soviet Union in increasing the volume of their exports to the EU. This has also enabled the CEE economies to expand their imports from the EU faster than the other former communist economies have been able to do. Trade theorists have observed that economies with broadly similar levels of development and income, such as the 15 economies that currently make up the EU, tend to trade in products that embody similar factors of production. The preponderant pattern of trade within the EU is in manufactured goods produced by processes that are intensive in human capital (i.e. processes that depend on high levels of research and development and on skilled labour, as reflected in relatively high wage levels). Furthermore, both intra-EU and extra-EU imports of manufactured goods produced by processes that are intensive in human capital have grown substantially faster than imports of goods that are labour- and resource-intensive. Trade in goods produced by human-capital-intensive processes accounted for 75.5 per cent of the ecu 188.7bn growth in the value of intra-EU trade in manufactured goods between 1995 and 1998 (labour-intensive goods accounted for 21.3 per cent and resource-intensive goods for only 3.2 per cent). Goods made by human-capital-intensive processes also accounted for 69.8 per cent of the growth of EU-15 imports of manufactures worth ecu 149bn from outside the EU. This suggests that the former communist economies that have been more successful in gearing their production towards commodities that embody human-capital-intensive processes have been, and will continue to be, more successful in penetrating EU markets than economies that remain dependent on exports of labour-intensive and resource-intensive goods. Furthermore, producers of exports of human-capital-intensive goods, for which demand is growing, are less likely to face pressures for protection from existing producers of labour-intensive goods, for which demand is growing more slowly.

The factor-intensity composition of the exports of the individual transition economies to the EU-15 is examined in Table 2.3 on the basis of categories developed by Wolfmayr-Schnitzer[8] and derived from production methods used in Germany. Manufactured goods have initially been divided into three categories: products that predominantly embody human-capital-intensive processes; products that embody resource-intensive processes; and products that embody labour-intensive processes. Labour-intensive goods largely comprise clothing, footwear and furniture. A substantial proportion of exports of labour-intensive goods is produced under outward-processing agreements that involve the re-export of textile materials and other inputs imported from the EU after the addition of domestic labour. These goods involve a relatively low proportion of value-added in the exporting economy. Resource-intensive products are manufactured goods that embody a high proportion of expenditure on material inputs – mainly steel products, non-ferrous metals, paper and wood products. Human-capital-intensive products that involve a high proportion of skilled labour were further subdivided by Wolfmayr-Schnitzer into high-technology goods, medium-technology goods and other goods requiring 'expert judgment'. High-technology products largely comprise items such as aircraft, sophisticated chemical products, and optical and data-processing equipment.

The breakdown of the structure of EU-15 imports from the former communist economies by exporting regions in Table 2.3 confirms that products made by human-capital-intensive processes were greatest in the exports of the central European economies to the EU in 1998. Those products ranged from 65.4 per cent of exports of manufactured goods for Hungary, which was higher than the intra-EU average of 61.8 per cent, to 34.5 per cent for Poland, which still had a relatively high (42.3 per cent) proportion of labour-intensive exports. However, even in the case of Hungary the proportion of high-technology goods (12.0 per cent) was below the intra-EU average of 16.2 per cent. Hungary's exports of human-capital-intensive exports included relatively high proportions of data-processing equipment and accessories and telecommunications equipment in the medium-technology category. Estonia (43.3 per cent) and Slovenia (47.4 per cent) were also relatively important exporters of human-capital-intensive goods. They are outliers within their respective regions, which otherwise still had relatively high dependencies on exports embodying labour-intensive

---

8 Yvonne Wolfmayr-Schnitzer, 'Trade Performance of CEECs According to Technology Classes', in *The Competitiveness of Transition Economics* (Paris: OECD, 1998), pp. 41–69.

Table 2.3: Factor content of EU imports of manufactured goods from European former communist economies in 1998 (% of imports of manufactured goods)

	Human-capital-intensive				Labour-intensive	Resource-intensive
	Total	High	Medium	Other		
Central Europe	49.7	6.9	30.9	11.9	34.2	16.1
Hungary	65.4	12.0	29.0	24.5	26.0	8.6
Slovakia	51.5	2.3	41.2	7.9	28.9	19.6
Czech Republic	49.1	6.1	35.0	8.0	35.9	15.0
Poland	34.5	4.4	24.9	5.2	42.3	23.2
Baltic States	28.0	3.5	18.7	5.7	48.4	23.6
Estonia	43.3	3.3	35.5	4.6	42.3	14.3
Lithuania	20.9	4.5	7.2	9.2	53.7	25.4
Latvia	10.2	2.3	6.4	1.5	50.9	38.9
Southeast Europe						
Bulgaria	17.3	3.3	12.0	2.0	43.1	39.6
Romania	16.6	1.2	10.0	5.4	65.2	18.2
Albania	5.1	0.2	4.6	0.2	84.2	10.7
Former Yugoslavia						
Slovenia	47.4	4.4	37.7	5.3	35.1	17.5
Croatia	30.6	6.1	20.6	3.9	56.8	12.6
Yugoslavia	18.3	2.9	12.2	3.2	38.1	43.7
Bosnia-Herzegovina	10.3	1.2	6.8	2.3	71.3	18.3
FYROM	9.4	3.3	4.1	2.0	51.5	39.1
European FSU						
Ukraine	28.5	5.4	16.7	6.4	26.7	44.8
Russia	19.8	9.8	8.7	1.4	15.7	64.5
Belarus	16.1	1.2	10.5	4.4	47.5	36.3
Moldova	6.3	0.2	6.1	0	83.4	10.2
Intra-EU	61.8	16.2	38.5	7.1	23.3	14.8
Extra-EU	60.8	24.4	30.1	6.2	27.6	11.6

Source: Estimated from Comext database. Factor intensity categories derived from Yvonne Wolfmayr-Schnitzer, 'Trade Performance of CEECs According to Technology Classes', in *The Competitiveness of Transition Economies* (Paris: OECD, 1998). The percentage figures represent the percentage of total exports of manufactured goods from the given country to the EU-15.

processes. Exports of automobiles contributed to the relatively high levels of medium-technology exports and physical-capital-intensive exports in the human-capital-intensive category recorded by the Czech Republic, Slovakia, Poland and Slovenia. Slovenia was also an important exporter of communications equipment. Estonia's exports of human-capital-intensive products were largely concentrated in telecommunications equipment and parts and in accessories for data-processing equipment, which are labour-intensive within that category.

At the other end of the spectrum, the southeast European economies, Albania (84.2 per cent), Romania (65.2 per cent) and Bulgaria (43.1 per cent), remained highly dependent on exports of labour-intensive goods largely consisting of clothing, footwear and furniture. A clearer regional pattern of Balkan dependence on labour-intensive exports emerges when Moldova (83.4 per cent), Bosnia-Herzegovina (71.3 per cent), Croatia (56.8 per cent) and the former Yugoslav Republic of Macedonia (51.5 per cent) are also included. Finally, the European former Soviet republics (including Latvia and Lithuania) had a relatively low dependence on exports embodying human-capital-intensive processes: Russia and Ukraine had a relatively high proportion of resource-intensive goods in total exports of manufactures, including steel products, which partly reflected Soviet investment in steel production.

IMPORTS OF CAPITAL GOODS AND INFLOWS OF FDI TO THE
FORMER COMMUNIST ECONOMIES

It was argued above that the capital stock inherited from the communist era was unsuited to producing goods in demand in Western markets and that integration with the EU would require inflows of physical capital to modernize production structures. This section compares the success of the former communist economies in attracting inflows of physical capital and foreign direct investment. The first three statistical columns in Table 2.4 provide data on EU-15 exports of physical capital goods to individual transition economies in 1998 expressed in ecu per capita, as a percentage of GDP and as a percentage of total imports.[9] Capital goods consist largely of machinery and equipment (excluding household equipment and consumer durables), transport vehicles (excluding passenger cars), items of specialized optical equipment and other related goods that contribute to increasing a country's capital stock. The EU states are the major supplier of physical

---

9 Data for other years indicate that these flows are not subject to significant annual variation and that 1998 can be taken as a representative year.

Table 2.4: Imports of capital goods and foreign direct investment into European former communist economies, 1989–2000 and 1998

	Imports of capital goods from the EU-15 in 1998			Foreign direct investment into transition economies		
	Ecu per capita	% GDP	% of imports	Ecu per capita 1989–2000	Ecu per capita 1998	% GDP, 1998
Central Europe						
Hungary	644	15.3	39.1	1,641	128	3.1
Slovakia	400	11.6	37.6	649	62	1.8
Czech Republic	635	13.0	38.8	1,756	228	4.7
Poland	234	6.4	32.9	627	114	3.2
Baltic states						
Estonia	620	19.4	34.9	1,170	354	11.0
Lithuania	199	7.7	31.4	540	222	8.6
Latvia	220	9.4	30.9	882	111	5.0
Southeastern Europe						
Bulgaria	80	6.0	27.7	338	58	4.4
Romania	95	5.8	34.3	251	82	5.0
Albania	26	3.2	23.1	145	12	1.5
Former Yugoslavia						
Slovenia	940	10.7	28.2	631	112	1.3
Croatia	288	6.7	30.1	783	154	3.6
Bosnia-Herzegovina	63	7.6	31.6	65	21	2.6
FYROM	94	6.0	21.8	183	78	5.0
European FSU						
Ukraine	26	3.5	38.1	57	13	1.8
Russia	46	2.8	32.7	58	12	0.6
Belarus	41	3.3	36.3	103	14	1.0
Moldova	21	6.0	31.4	85	18	5.1

Sources and notes: Imports of capital goods estimated from Comext database. Foreign direct investment and GDPs estimated from *EBRD Transition Reports* for 2000 and 2001. Cumulative data converted into ecu at the average ecu: $US exchange rate for 1989–2000 and for 1998 at the annual average ecu: $US exchange rate for 1998.

capital to the European former communist economies, and the figures include supplies of capital goods by European subsidiaries of multinationals located outside the EU. Nevertheless, the data suffer from the problem that they exclude imports of capital goods from outside the EU, particularly from the United States and Southeast Asia.

The last three columns in Table 2.4 provide data on net inflows of FDI (from all international sources, including intra-regional ones) into transition economies taken from balance-of-payments data. In addition to providing finance for inflows of physical capital, FDI, which involves the restructuring of existing plants or the construction of new plants, contributes directly to the modernization of the capital stock. It is a major conduit of technical know-how that should enhance the host country's capability to penetrate EU markets. Nevertheless, FDI is only one source of financial capital. It is not used solely for economic modernization and is subject to considerable annual variation.[10] Comparisons with the early 1990s indicate that there is no significant correlation between changes in annual inflows of FDI to individual countries and imports of capital goods, which are relatively more consistent.

Five economies – Slovenia (ecu 940), Hungary (ecu 640), the Czech Republic (ecu 635), Estonia (ecu 620) and Slovakia (ecu 400) – imported high per capita levels of capital goods. In all five cases capital goods imports exceeded 10 per cent of GDP. These five economies also had the highest share of human-capital-intensive goods in exports to the EU in 1998 (see Table 2.3). Estonia, Hungary and the Czech Republic were also major recipients of FDI, on a cumulative basis and as a share of GDP, in 1998. Although Slovakia has been substantially less reliant on FDI to finance imports of capital goods, its exports of road vehicles and components, the majority of which were constructed in plants bought and reconstructed by Volkswagen, came to ecu 1.7bn. They accounted for 31.4 per cent of Slovakian exports to the EU and 65.2 per cent of exports of human-capital-intensive goods. Slovenia has also been less reliant on FDI as a source of capital flows, but it has been a major supplier of components to multinationals and this has involved direct technological links with domestic enterprises, partly on the basis of relations that were developed in the socialist era.[11] Exports of road vehicles and components by either foreign-owned firms[12] or domestic companies with subcontracting links with European multinationals came to ecu 1bn in 1998, and accounted for 19.8 per cent of Slovenian exports to the EU and for 43.8 per cent of exports of human-capital-intensive goods.

Four other economies – Croatia (ecu 288), Poland (ecu 234), Latvia (ecu 220) and Lithuania (ecu 199) – imported intermediate levels of capital goods, which accounted for between 6.4 and 9.4 per cent of GDP. Poland (34.5 per

10 For example, large-scale privatization of utilities may not contribute to an inflow of capital goods in the year of recording although it may result in imports of capital goods in subsequent years.
11 David Dyker, Agnes Nagy, Hedvika Spilek, Peter Stanovnik, Jeffrey Turk and Peter Vince, 'East-"West" Networks and their Alignment: Industrial Networks in Hungary and Slovenia', mimeo, 2002.
12 Renault is the major investor in the Slovenian car industry.

cent) and Croatia (30.6 per cent) also had intermediate levels of human-capital-intensive exports to the EU. The remaining economies all received imports of physical capital goods of below ecu 100 per capita, with Bulgaria, Romania and FYROM faring slightly better than the former Soviet republics and Albania, which received imports of less than ecu 50 per capita. These economies also received relatively low inflows of FDI on a per capita basis.[13] With the exception of Ukraine, these economies all recorded shares of human-capital-intensive exports in total exports of manufactures of below 20 per cent.

CONCLUSIONS

Some fairly clear regional patterns emerge in the relationship between the structure of exports of the former communist economies to the EU and imports of physical capital goods from the EU and flows of foreign direct investment. Three CEE states, Hungary, the Czech Republic and Slovakia, together with Slovenia, have exhibited a high level of integration into the production networks of western Europe, especially that of Germany. These states have all recorded relatively high levels of imports of capital goods as well as high inflows of FDI, and have also had the greatest success in penetrating EU markets for human-capital-intensive goods. Although Slovakia, which also had high levels of imports of capital goods and a high share of capital-intensive exports, was less reliant on FDI, it was demonstrated that a high proportion of exports of human-capital-intensive goods was directly linked to FDI by Volkswagen in the Slovakian automobile industry.

Poland is an interesting central European case, with an intermediate share of human-capital-intensive goods in exports of manufactures (34.5 per cent) and lower levels of imports of capital goods per capita (ecu 234) as a proportion of GDP (6.4 per cent) and as a share of total imports (32.9 per cent) than the other central European economies. The explanation lies in part in Poland's greater size and large domestic market and consequently its lower ratio of imports to GDP, as a greater proportion of demand can be met from domestic production. But Poland's location is also important. It has long eastern borders with the low-income economies of Ukraine and

---

13 The estimates for GDP in ecu for these economies are biased downwards by a greater divergence between the actual exchange rate and an exchange rate measured on a purchasing power parity basis. This biases the ratio of imports to GDP and FDI to GDP upwards in comparison with the central European and Baltic states. In the case of the former Soviet republics, estimates of GDP in ecus were further biased downwards by the collapse of the rouble and consequent devaluations of currencies of economies with strong trade links with Russia in the second half of 1998.

Belarus, and its western border with Germany abuts the poorer regions of the former East Germany. Consequently, domestic producers are still driven by the demands of medium-to-low-income consumers. They have less incentive, or need, than producers in Hungary or the Czech Republic to restructure purely to meet the demands of high-income consumers in the EU. This also means that FDI entering Poland has a greater incentive to meet the demands of the domestic market than to serve as a production base for exports to the EU.[14]

Two other economies, Estonia and Slovenia, are, as has been noted, outliers within their respective regions. They have high levels of imports of capital goods, both per capita and as a proportion of GDP, and relatively high shares of human-capital-intensive goods in exports. Estonia has benefited from high inflows of FDI while Slovenian enterprises have developed close links with multinationals, including serving as subcontractors.

As a result there has emerged a 'core' of countries consisting of Hungary, the Czech Republic, Slovakia, Slovenia and, to a lesser extent, Poland. All of them have common borders with EU economies in central Europe and have developed strong trade links with the EU based on imports of capital goods and exports of human-capital-intensive goods. Estonia, with strong trade and investment links with Finland, can be added to this group. These six countries had all made greater progress than their neighbours in transition by 1998;[15] and they had the largest indicators for 'cumulative liberalization' in 2001, according to the indicators of transition developed by the EBRD.[16]

However, with the exception of Estonia they also had the most favourable starting conditions for transition.[17] The Czech Republic, Hungary, Slovakia and Slovenia have also recorded substantially lower levels of poverty as a proportion of GDP than the other transition economies.[18] Poverty in Poland remains high by the standards of central Europe but low compared with the majority of the economies of southeastern Europe and the former Soviet Union. Poverty in Estonia has fallen from the very high levels recorded in the early and mid-1990s. Croatia is an intermediate case,

---

14 Fiat is the major investor in the Polish car industry and has concentrated production on small cars. This is reflected in a relatively high level of automobile exports to Italy and a low level of automobile exports to Germany.

15 EBRD, *Transition Report 1999* (London: European Bank for Reconstruction and Development, 1999), p. 27.

16 EBRD, *Transition Report 2001* (London: European Bank for Reconstruction and Development, 2001), p.19.

17 EBRD, *Transition Report 1999*, p. 31.

18 Branko Milanovic, *Income, Inequality and Poverty during the Transition from Planned to Market Economy* (Washington, DC: The World Bank, 1998), pp. 68–9, and EBRD, *Transition Report 2001*, pp. 106–213.

attracting relatively high flows of FDI since 1998 (reaching 7.2 per cent of GDP in 1999) and imports of capital goods, which may contribute to a reduced dependence on exports of labour-intensive goods over the next decade. Lithuania and Latvia, while attracting relatively high inflows of FDI and intermediate flows of capital goods, have remained heavily dependent on exports of labour- and resource-intensive goods and have relatively high levels of poverty.

At the opposite end of the spectrum, the other economies of south-eastern Europe (Albania, Bulgaria and Romania), the southern republics of former Yugoslavia (FYROM and Bosnia-Herzegovina) and the European former Soviet republics (Belarus, Moldova, Russia and Ukraine) have low levels of imports of capital goods and FDI per capita. They have made little impact on EU markets for human-capital-intensive goods, have made relatively slow progress in implementing reforms, and (with the exception of Belarus) still suffered from high levels of absolute poverty in 2000.[19] It would be simplistic to attempt to find a common explanation for the economic performance of states as diverse as FYROM, Albania and Russia or to encompass economies that have been affected by wars and those that have avoided war but experienced financial crises and falling output in the mid- and late 1990s. Nevertheless, the arguments outlined above suggest that, especially for states with smaller, open economies, substantial increases in imports of capital goods will be required in order for them to restructure and modernize their economies and be able to penetrate the expanding higher-income markets for industrial goods in western Europe. The arguments also indicate that inflows of FDI or, at the very least, strong relationships with multinationals have played an important role in the technological modernization of the CEE economies, which has contributed to the growth of their exports to the EU.

There are indications that some of the states in southeastern Europe and former Yugoslavia (notably Albania, Bosnia-Herzegovina, Bulgaria, FYROM and Romania) are falling behind the states of central Europe. This is reflected in low rates of growth of both total exports and human-capital-intensive exports, resulting from the inability to attract FDI and to finance imports of physical capital goods.

These economies continue to suffer from high levels of poverty, and could experience a form of vicious circle of low investment, slow modernization and growing uncompetitiveness in EU markets. In the absence of major inflows of foreign capital, imports of physical capital goods that are essential for economic restructuring, and also for promoting exports in the

19 EBRD, *Transition Report 2001*, pp. 106–213.

long term, will be limited to those that can be financed from relatively low export earnings. The relative failure to attract major inflows of FDI results from a combination of factors that are hard to disentangle, but they include the slower pace of domestic liberalization, locational factors, including the greater distance from EU markets, and reduced prospects for joining the EU. Those economies that do not enter the EU in the first round of eastward enlargement will also receive lower transfers from EU budgets than the central European and Baltic states, which may also make them relatively less attractive to private investors. In the absence of developmental assistance, this could result in a significant widening of the gap between the more successful economies which are included in the first round of enlargement and those which are excluded.

3

Immigration, labour mobility and EU enlargement

MATLOOB PIRACHA AND ROGER VICKERMAN

Immigration is one of the most contentious political and economic issues in Europe. Rising unemployment and the rise of far-right political groups, coupled with waves of refugees unleashed by ethnic conflicts not just in Europe following the break-up of Yugoslavia and the Soviet Union but across the world, have brought it centre stage since the late 1990s. This poses particular difficulties for the European Union, especially in the context of its enlargement. One problem is the development and enforcement of Community agreements on asylum and refugee status. This had its most acute manifestation in the nightly attempts by would-be refugees to cross the English Channel into the United Kingdom from a refugee centre at Sangatte in northern France, which finally resulted in the closure of the centre in late 2002. More significant in terms of the development of the EU is the issue of free movement for citizens of future member states; mainly at German and Austrian insistence, lengthy transition periods to full mobility of workers were agreed, although some member states have decided to permit free movement on accession. Furthermore, following enlargement the new eastern borders of the EU may pose additional problems arising from the current openness of these borders and the historical national and ethnic ties which transcend their often artificial nature. The question of migration has to be considered against a background of widespread concern about the lack of mobility within the existing EU to provide the necessary labour market flexibility to ensure competitiveness and permit adjustment within the euro zone.

   This chapter places the various different dimensions of the problem in context using a model of migration which recognizes that within Europe

* The research in this chapter was carried out as part of the project 'Borders, Migration and Labour Market Dynamics in a Changing Europe', financed by the UK Economic and Social Research Council, Grant No. L213252042 in the 'One Europe or Several?' Programme. The research assistance of Sule Akkoyunlu and Bill Collier and the collaboration of Harry Papapanagos, Peter Sanfey and Miguel Leon-Ledesma are gratefully acknowledged.

most migration is not permanent but part of a process of mobility in which both return and serial migration are natural responses to a dynamic economy. We aim to show the beneficial effects of migration for both the home (origin) and host (destination) regions. We also provide some evidence to suggest that there is little difference in the characteristics and intentions of migrants and non-migrants or, more importantly, between those moving legally and those moving illegally. This leads us to some observations on the development of a more efficient policy towards migration both within and into the EU. This is of particular importance in dealing with the extension of the EU's borders to include the candidate countries in central and eastern Europe (CEEC-10). However, enlargement also brings into being a common border with a further set of countries, which leads to even greater migratory pressures.

The remainder of this chapter is divided into five main sections. First, we review recent attempts to develop a consistent EU policy towards immigration. Secondly, we examine some evidence on the main trends in migration. Thirdly, we outline a consistent model of migration and its implications. Fourthly, we present some results from the application of this model. Finally, we discuss the policy options suggested by this approach.

THE EU POLICY BACKGROUND

The European Commission's communication 'On a Community Immigration Policy' was published in November 2000.[1] It identified clearly the changing pressures necessitating a reappraisal of EU immigration policy. First, the advent of the single market with free movement of labour within the EU requires a common approach to immigration regarding its external borders. Secondly, the aftermath of the wars in the former Yugoslavia and continuing ethnic and religious persecution, both in the Balkans and elsewhere, have led to an enormous increase in asylum-seeking – and with it a problem of illegal migration, often exploited by criminal elements. Thirdly, the experience of a period of relatively high and persistent unemployment within the EU has changed attitudes to migration. However, this has disguised the bottlenecks that exist for some specific skills, and demographic projections suggest a considerable tightening of labour markets over the next two decades. Shortages of certain specific skills, especially in the IT sector, require more than nationally based competitive bidding for selected and scarce immigrants.

---

1 European Commission, 'On a Community Immigration Policy', Communication from the Commission to the Council and the European Parliament, COM(2000)757 Final, Brussels, 22 November 2000.

Immigration and asylum were firmly established as areas of Community competence in the Treaty of Amsterdam (1997), leading to agreement on the elements of a common asylum and immigration policy at the European Council in Tampere in October 1999. The key point here is the recognition that individual member states cannot determine their own individual conditions for the admission of third-country citizens if they are supposedly operating in a single unified labour market.[2] However, the development of this EU position has to work with the fact that individual member states have their own historical and cultural differences with respect to immigration, especially concerning migration from specific countries. This affects both the likely pattern of demand for immigration from third countries and the ability of each member state to absorb migrants from different parts of the world.

The basic principles enunciated by the Commission are:

- assessing appropriate immigration levels based on cooperation, exchange of information and reporting. This should review what has happened in previous periods and set out indicative targets tied closely to future labour market needs, while recognizing both existing agreements with countries of origin and the need to absorb new migrants;
- defining a common legal framework for admission based on transparency and rationality, differentiating rights according to length of stay, clear and simple application and assessment procedures and improved availability of information;
- integration of third-country nationals in order to ensure comparable living and working conditions, to fight discrimination and xenophobia and to ensure that this is part of a continuing and lasting process; and
- improving information, research and monitoring of migration flows and patterns, especially relating to the incorporation of information on illegal movements, asylum-seeking etc.

The Tampere Council resolution was concerned primarily with providing a framework for legal migration. This can be seen as essentially providing a common set of rules governing the external influences on the internal labour market of the EU. In this sense it is exactly analogous to the Community's external trade policy, which serves to provide a common approach to trade relations with third countries. The particular problems of illegal immigrants and asylum-seekers raise different questions, relating principally to human

---

2 The conclusions of the Tampere Council meeting recognized 'the need for approximation of national legislations on the conditions of admission and residence of third country nationals, based on a shared assessment of the economic and demographic developments within the Union, as well as the situation in the countries of origin'.

rights and concern over trafficking in human beings and the use of such migrants in illegal employment within the EU labour market. Illegal immigrants are at risk of being exploited because of their (lack of) legal status, often leading them to work at below minimum wages and standards of employment. To a large extent this should be seen as a human rights issue, and not be confused with policies towards legal migration. However, an unfortunate confusion has arisen, which can be exploited by political and media interests, where the term 'economic migrants' features strongly.

Economic migration has become an emotive term applied to those who are seen to be trying to avoid normal migration rules in order to secure economic advantage. However, with the possible exception of strictly political asylum, almost all migration could be regarded as being economic.[3] The main motivation for people to seek employment and/or residence in another region is that the economic returns to them (or their family) are greater in the destination region than in their present location. Allowing this movement to take place can quite easily be shown to be of potential benefit to both the receiving region and the region of origin.[4] It is more important to distinguish between migration that arises from the interaction of labour markets and other market forces in an increasingly integrated global economy and that which arises from essentially non-economic forces such as persecution. The objective for the former is to establish a policy that ensures fair and equal treatment of all according to origin and destination and the skills and other characteristics of the migrant. The latter kind of migration is dealt with through the basic principles of the 1951 Geneva Convention on refugees.[5]

The particular pressure for a review of EU policy on immigration has arisen from the experience of the 1990s. The initial wave of migration from the current EU candidate countries and others in eastern Europe in the early 1990s led to concerns about the long-term implications of free movement for EU labour markets. The expectation was that economic convergence would take a long time and thus would lead to continuing pressures for workers to migrate from poor regions to rich regions. For those countries left outside the enlarged EU such pressures would remain, especially given the aftermath of war and ethnic conflict.

---

3 Indeed, it is quite feasible to include political asylum in an economic framework, taking into account lifetime earnings.

4 We use the term 'region' because the analysis is not just about movement between sovereign states; it also applies to any movement between distinct labour market areas.

5 There is, of course, no perfect distinction between these various types of migrant. One of the basic rights of a refugee is access to work, and acceptance as a refugee may be one way of overcoming failure to gain acceptance as a legal migrant in the labour market. One of the factors which has led to a growth in claims for genuine refugee status is the ambiguous way in which conventional migration rules have been applied. The contention here is that rectifying those rules would lead to reduced pressure of so-called 'bogus' asylum claims.

A guiding principle of the development of EU policy on immigration (and also the policy towards the free movement of labour during accession negotiations) has been that any policy has to reflect and respect the situation in the countries of origin as much as that within the existing EU. The differences in economic status of the candidate countries from that of the existing EU members are feared to imply an enormous continuing pressure for east–west migration that could be threatening to the economies of both the originating and the receiving regions. A further problem is that those states remaining outside the EU may generate increasing migration problems for the newly acceded countries, with which, for historical reasons, many have relatively open borders. Problems of transit or, during any transition period to fully open borders, problems of the 'stockpiling' of hopeful migrants on the western borders of the candidate countries would need to be addressed.

The main objections to uncontrolled migration are that the inflow of less skilled migrants to a region may reduce average incomes, displace local workers from employment and increase the burden on social and welfare services. At the same time the outflow of workers from a region is typically seen to remove the more skilled and able, thereby reducing growth potential. This process is thus seen as a means of perpetuating inequalities between regions and reinforcing a core and periphery structure in the European economy, in which some regions are in a virtuous circle of autonomous economic growth and high income and others are trapped in a dependency situation of low growth and low income.[6]

However, there are certain other factors which need to be introduced to place this in context. First, while the recipient regions fear an influx of migrants taking low-skill jobs, regions of origin fear the loss of higher-skilled, more dynamic residents. Secondly, labour mobility within the EU has typically been argued to be too low to serve as an adequate adjustment mechanism for divergent economic conditions (asymmetric shocks) between different regions, especially in the context of monetary union.[7] Thirdly, the

---

6 See, for example, R. Faini, 'Increasing Returns, Migrations and Convergence', *Journal of Economics*, Vol. 49, 1996, pp. 121–36, and P. Reichlin and A. Rustichini, 'Diverging Patterns with Endogenous Labor Migration', *Journal of Economic Dynamics and Control*, Vol. 22, Issue 5, May 1998, pp. 703–28.

7 Conventional economic theory would argue that labour moves towards higher returns. In the case of an asymmetric shock which reduced labour demand in one region relative to another, labour would move from the lower-demand region to the higher-demand region. This would increase the returns to labour in the lower-demand regions and reduce them in the higher-demand regions, which would correct the imbalance. That this does not happen is frequently put down simply to imperfections in labour markets that prevent labour responding efficiently.

degree of disparity in current economic conditions between the EU and the CEE candidate countries is significantly larger than any experienced in previous expansions of the EU. Fourthly, and most significantly for the case presented here, most migration which does take place is not of a once-and-for-all, permanent nature: migrants frequently move for short periods as a means of enhancing short-term earnings or longer-term earning prospects. Many migrants move on a regular, often seasonal, basis and most migration has to be regarded in the context of family decisions.

The issue of labour mobility within the EU has been addressed in a further Communication from the European Commission on 'New European Labour Markets, Open to All with Access for All'.[8] This is part of the concern within the EU to raise the efficiency of labour markets, which should respond effectively to changes in demand through wage flexibility, occupational flexibility or mobility. Although we are not primarily concerned here with internal mobility, it is important to place consideration of external mobility in the context of the current problems of movement and labour market flexibility within the EU.

A principal concern of the Commission is that various barriers continue to keep labour mobility within the EU at too low a level, although what might constitute an appropriate level of mobility is much less clear.[9] (It is estimated that annual migration between member states amounts to around 0.75 per cent of the resident population and perhaps only 0.4 per cent of resident EU nationals, even if public perceptions are far higher. The most comparable levels of mobility in the United States are on average some six times greater: approximately 2.4 per cent of the population moves between American states on an annual basis.) The potential barriers to mobility in the EU are clear: inconsistent labour market institutions, problems in the portability of pensions and social security rights, the lack of full mutual recognition of qualifications and experience and, above all, a range of social, cultural and language barriers. However, whether the complete removal of such barriers would lead to a dramatic increase in mobility in the EU is much less certain.

The problem of the lack of mobility within the EU was addressed by the High-Level Task Force on Skills and Mobility, which reported in December

8 European Commission, 'New European Labour Markets, Open to All with Access for All', Communication from the Commission to the Council and the European Parliament, COM(2001)116 Final, Brussels, 28 February 2001.
9 For a detailed analysis of this issue, see House of Lords, *Working in Europe: Access for All*, 15th Report of the Select Committee on the European Union, Session 2001–02, The Stationery Office, London, 2002.

2001[10] and whose recommendations fed into the Action Plan[11] proposed to the Barcelona Council meeting in March 2002. The Task Force made a large number of recommendations relating to occupational and geographical mobility, concentrating on the need to improve information and transparency in labour markets, including the provision of basic skills so that the benefits of mobility can be enjoyed by all skill groups. The Action Plan identified eleven actions on occupational mobility and skills development, a further eleven on geographic mobility and three on information and transparency, for completion, in almost all cases, by 2005. The Action Plan made clear the link between factors influencing internal mobility in the EU and the EU's immigration policy.

TRENDS AND PRESSURES IN MIGRATION

In order to structure an analysis of the issues surrounding this search for a common migration policy, it is useful to look at the scale of the problem before outlining a more rational model of migration behaviour and drawing policy conclusions. Our evidence focuses on the economic motives for, and consequences of, migration. The geographical focus is on movement between the EU and the neighbouring states of central and eastern Europe. Within this we need to distinguish between the current CEEC-10 and those remaining outside the EU. The latter include the European states of the former Soviet Union (FSU) except the Baltic states, the states that were formerly part of Yugoslavia (FY) except Slovenia, and Albania. As we shall see, although much interest has focused on the impact of the free movement of labour on entry to the EU, the major pressures actually arise from outside. These pressures affect the existing EU but raise particular problems for the candidate countries.

The analysis suggests a number of key points that need to be taken into consideration. First, it is difficult to substantiate the prospect of a continuing flow from CEECs at the levels experienced in the 1990s, and there is an expectation that migrants from CEECs resident in the EU-15 will stabilize by 2010–20, although there are potential difficulties which might arise from the concentration of migrants into employment in specific sectors or particular regions. This would suggest a parallel to the experience of

---

10 European Commission, Final Report of the High Level Task Force on Skills and Mobility, December 2001, available at *http://europa.eu.int/comm/employment_social/general/index_en.htm*.

11 Communication from the Commission to the Council, the European Parliament, the Economic and Social Committee and the Committee of the Regions, 'Commission's Action Plan for Skills and Mobility', COM(2002)72, European Commission, Brussels, 13 March 2002.

Figure 3.1: Net migration from the CEEC-10 to the EU-8, 1990–97

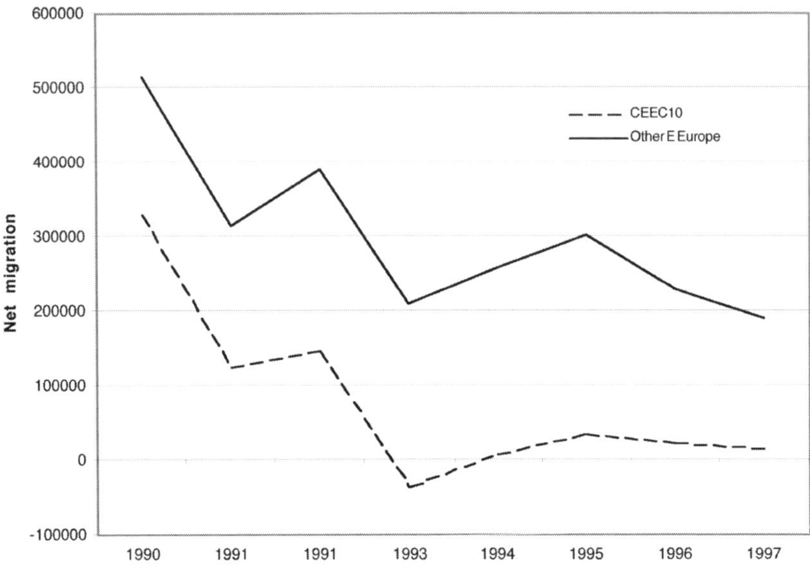

Note: EU-8 = Belgium, Denmark, Finland, Germany, Luxembourg, Netherlands, Sweden, and the United Kingdom.
Sources: Eurostat and OECD.

migration from the south European countries which peaked in the early 1960s and demonstrated little or no response to eventual membership of the EU in the 1980s. Within CEECs, there has been little difference in the overall trend patterns for migration to the EU, but total flows from the non-candidate countries (the FSU and the FY) have continued to run at higher levels than those from the CEEC-10 between 1990 and 1997 (See Figure 3.1).

Secondly, the accession of CEECs provides an important opportunity for the EU to address potential future labour supply problems. It is essential not to lose the potential gains through imposing excessive constraints on the free movement of labour. Labour markets cannot be treated independently of capital and goods markets. However, there is a need for improved information to ensure that there is better matching of potential supplies and demands of migrant labour in terms of skill and destination. Migration to date has often been a haphazard process dependent on inaccurate and asymmetric information.

Thirdly, migration policy should recognize that migration may be not a once-and-for-all relocation but part of a long-term strategic decision within the context of family circumstances. Such migration may have important implications for future capital and trade flows, and this should be borne in mind by those developing migration policy.[12] An important element is the incidence of short-term, seasonal or contract migration. Aggregate flows of migrants do not adequately reflect these differences. Seasonal migration is typically not recorded, but net flows may underestimate the market adjustment potential of total mobility and the characteristics of the migrants involved.

Fourthly, for all EU countries, even the most affected ones – Austria and Germany – the flow of migrants is very small relative to the total population and to the existing stock of migrants. For most CEECs migration is a significant but not overwhelming issue. However, in others migration is a significant problem. Albania is the best-known example of this: by 1998 some 75 per cent of the working population had expressed a wish to work in another country, and between 1994 and 1998 over 40 per cent had in fact done so.[13] In reality, and in marked contrast to the fears expressed in some EU states, such increases in migration flows are likely to be temporary problems. Comparison with the more advanced CEECs, such as Poland, suggests that both the actual and the desired migration rates fall as migrants gain greater experience of working abroad. Furthermore, it is obvious from the Albanian data that most actual movement, even illegal movement, is voluntarily short-term.

Net migration flows from all sources into EU member states remained remarkably constant throughout the 1990s (Figure 3.2 gives data for selected member states). The highest rate of net migration was actually for Luxembourg (not shown in Figure 3.1 but consistently around 10 in 1,000 of its population). Considerable reductions in rates of net in-migration were experienced by Austria, Germany and Greece, the other three countries with relatively higher rates in the early 1990s. This was when they faced the main problems of refugees from war zones immediately after an initial upsurge in movement following the opening of borders during the early stages of transition in CEECs. The main changes were the transformation of Portugal and Ireland from being countries of net out-migration to being net in-migration countries. These changes were related to the improved economic

---

12 Most voters are not aware of the temporary nature of migration; hence, in part, the hysteria that emerges in national media in some countries, notably the United Kingdom.

13 Evidence from a specially collected data set. See H. Papapanagos and P. Sanfey, 'Intention to emigrate and actual emigration: the case of Albania', paper to the European Society of Population Economics Conference, Athens, June 2001.

Figure 3.2: Net migration in selected EU countries

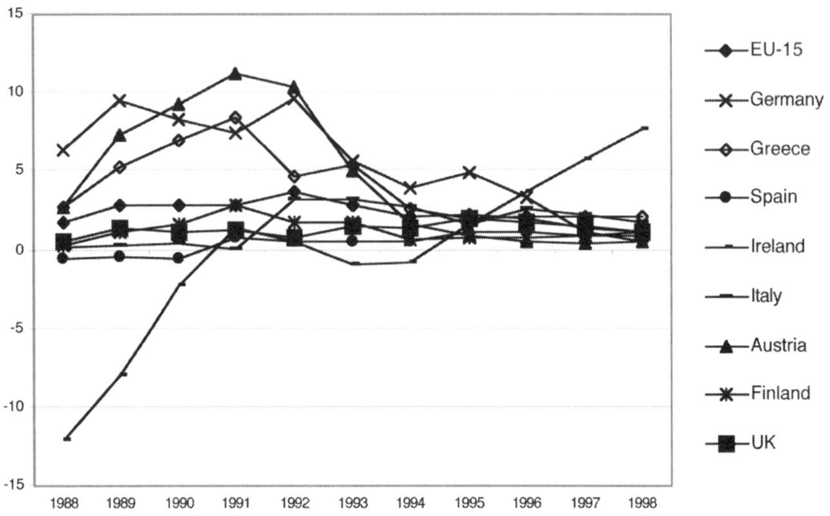

Source: Eurostat.

performance of the two countries, which in turn is an important message for the likely response of CEECs with improved economic performance. Relative to working-age population, however, migration remains fairly low, an average of 0.8 per cent for the EU-15 in 1998, with the highest figure (Luxembourg) being 4.5 per cent and the lowest (Greece and Portugal) just 0.2 per cent.

The contribution of net migration to population growth in the countries in Figure 3.2 is estimated at around 0.18 per cent per annum in the United Kingdom, a little larger than the natural increase.[14] For Germany the figure is 0.25 per cent, against a natural decrease of -0.10 per cent per annum. Stocks of foreign population remain relatively small in most EU states, around 3–3.5 per cent in the United Kingdom, about 6.5 per cent in France and around 8–9 per cent in Germany and Austria. Figures for some of the smaller states are much larger: 34 per cent in Luxembourg (and 19 per cent in Switzerland, a

14 The total change in population is the sum of the natural change in the population (the difference between the birth and death rates of the resident population) and net migration. For many EU countries the natural change in population implied a decrease in the past, but no longer; several now have net out-migration.

Figure 3.3: Migration flows to EU member states, 1998–9

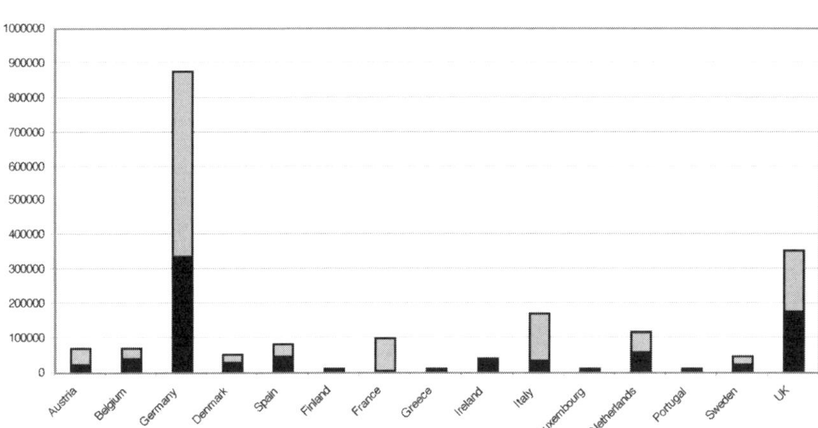

Source: Eurostat.

non-EU state). This translates into an estimated stock of foreign labour in 1997 of about 950,000 in the United Kingdom, compared with 1.57 million in France and 2 million in Germany. The figure for Britain is somewhat larger than in the 1980s, but it remained remarkably constant during the 1990s. The figure for Germany increased by about 25 per cent over the decade from 1987 to 1997, but the stock was actually smaller in 1997 than in 1980.

Sources of immigrants and destinations of emigrants differ substantially between EU member states (see Figure 3.3). Around 40 per cent of migration flows in the EU is internal to the EU, although again there are variations between countries. For the United Kingdom, the CEECs are less important than for many other EU countries: around 50 per cent of migrants in 1998–9 were from the EU; 50 per cent were from third countries, with only around 1.5 per cent of immigrants from CEECs. By contrast, 60 per cent of Germany's immigrants were non-EU, including 16 per cent from CEECs. At the other extreme, only 6 per cent of France's and 22 per cent of Italy's immigrants were EU citizens, and very few immigrants came from CEECs.[15]

---

15 The five largest sources of immigrants into Italy are Albania, Morocco, the Philippines, China and Romania. For France they are Algeria, Morocco, Turkey, China and Tunisia. In both cases these top five sources accounted for 43 per cent of immigrants in 1998.

Figure 3.4: Foreign residents as percentage of population by EU country, 1998

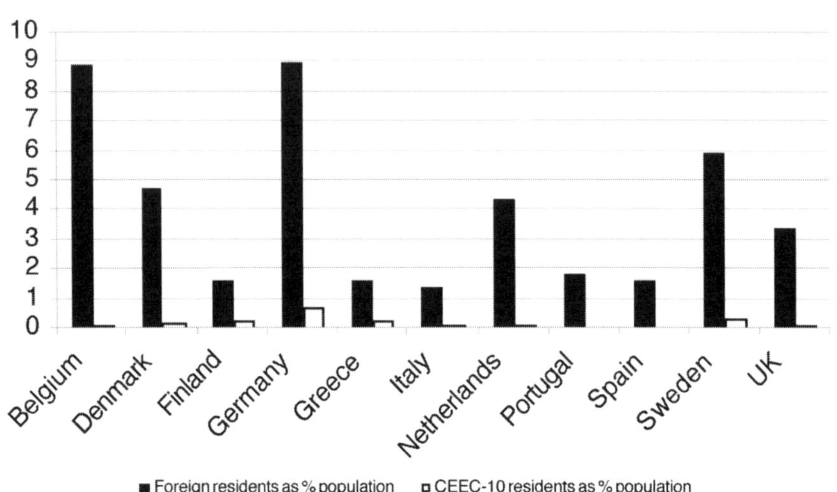

Source: Eurostat.

A recent report by Boeri et al. for the EU estimates that the stock of residents from the CEEC-10 in the United Kingdom at January 1996 was 39,000 (0.07 per cent of the population) and that in Germany in January 1998 it was 554,869 (0.68 per cent of the population).[16] The pattern of the total stock of foreign residents and of those from the CEECs is shown in Figure 3.4. This report estimates likely future trends in migration patterns and stock consequences for Germany on the basis of a plausible econometric model of migration. This suggests a continuing decline of annual net migration from the CEEC-10 to the EU, from an estimated figure of over 200,000 persons in 2002 if migration were uncontrolled to under 100,000 by 2010 and under 30,000 by 2020. This would stabilize the resident population from CEECs at around 2.5 million residents by 2020–30, some 2.5 per cent of the resident population (3.5 per cent of the German population). The corresponding figures for the United Kingdom show a gradual decrease in annual

16 See T. Boeri, H. Brücker et al., *The Impact of Eastern Enlargement on Employment and Labour Markets in the EU Member States*, Report to European Commission, DG Employment and Social Affairs, DIW, CEPR, FIEF, IAS, IGIER, Berlin and Milan, 2000, p. 52.

migration, from around 15,000 to less than 2,000 by 2020, and an increase in the resident population from about 40,000 in 1998 to 170,000 by 2020. For the EU-15 this implies a steady population of about 3.75 million from the CEEC-10 by 2020, just over one per cent of the population.

One further factor of significance is that CEEC migrants are not just concentrated particularly in Austria and Germany (around 73 per cent of the CEEC working-age population resident in the EU, and 80 per cent of those in employment, are in these two countries); they are also clearly concentrated in certain regions within them, which exacerbates the problem of assimilation. In Austria there is a very high concentration in the eastern region of Burgenland (around 6 per cent of the employed population, against a national figure of 1.1 per cent). In Germany the largest concentrations are in the eastern parts of Bavaria (between 1 per cent and 2.5 per cent of the employed population, against a national average of 0.5 per cent). Similarly, London has dominated other regions in the United Kingdom: over 50 per cent of all migrants to the United Kingdom live in London and the southeast, and some two-thirds of all new migrants head for these regions. Around 40 per cent of all EU migrants to the United Kingdom settle in London. It is concentrations such as these that can give rise both to the prominence of the political issue of migration and to associated social problems.[17]

The main states losing population among the CEECs for which any reliable data are available have been Romania and Poland, but migration losses are only on average −0.07 per cent and −0.04 per cent respectively. Substantial migration flows exist between CEECs, especially for the smaller countries such as the Baltic states, where intra-CEEC movement accounts for around 80–90 per cent of the total. Estimates of the 1998 stock of CEEC residents in the EU show that Polish nationals form by far the largest group (over 350,000), constituting nearly half of the total, followed by Romanians (120,000).[18] What is not easy to determine from the more reliable published data is the proportion of movers from the European states of the FSU, in particular those who are not nationals of those countries. There is anecdotal evidence to suggest that many migrants from the Baltic states are ethnic Russians for whom the new order is difficult and for whom return to Russia is also problematic.

17 Note, however, that with the exception of Berlin, concentrations of CEEC immigrants in the new *Länder* of former East Germany, where some of the most prominent political disturbances have occurred, are actually below the national average. Even in Berlin the proportions are only consistent with those found in the main urban areas of western Germany. This, to a large extent, reflects the fact that migrants do respond to the economic pull of employment opportunities.

18 Boeri, Brücker et al., *The Impact of Eastern Enlargement*, p. 54.

What is notable, however, is that some of the CEEC-10 do have significant inflows of migrants, from both the west and the east. Poland, for example, had regular annual inflows of around 8,000 permanent migrants (including returning Polish nationals) in the late 1990s, one-quarter of whom came from Germany, the largest single source. An increasing number, from 3,000 in 1996 to 5,000 in 1998 and 17,000[19] in 1999, entered annually on permanent residence permits, most coming from the FSU, with Ukraine the single main source. These flows match the evidence on cross-border movements for trade, including regular movements by individual traders.[20]

To some extent the perceived problem of migration in the EU has arisen because of the serious problems of the 1990s. First, the instability brought about by the ending of a long period when normal migration between CEECs and the current EU was not possible led to an upsurge in migration between the geographically proximate CEECs – Poland, Hungary, the Czech and Slovak Republics, Romania and Bulgaria (the CEEC-6) – and the EU. Secondly, this upsurge was further and massively distorted by the refugee problem caused by successive wars in the former Yugoslavia. An analysis of flows of migration into Germany from the CEEC-6 and the former Yugoslavia shows a rapid rise in gross inflows of population in the period 1990–93, which was matched within less than three years by an equally large rise in out-migration, such that net migration changed relatively little over this entire period.[21]

We have concentrated thus far on what may be termed normal migration, movements which are captured in official statistics of those moving legally, principally for employment-related reasons. As can be seen, these flows are relatively insignificant in both the total resident population and the total flows of migrants. Asylum-seekers and illegal migrants are a separate question. From relatively insignificant levels the number of asylum-seekers increased rapidly in the 1990s, reaching a peak of around 700,000 in western Europe in 1992 but falling back to around 260,000 by 1997. For the United Kingdom, this rose from a steady figure of between 4,000 and 6,000 in the 1980s to 44,845 in 1991, falling back to 29,645 by 1996 but then rising steeply to 80,315 in 2000 before falling to 71,365 in 2001. Adding dependents increases the 2001 figure to an estimated 92,000 out of an estimated total of

19 This large increase reflected a change in the rules and definitions.
20 See the evidence presented by T. Komornicki, *Potowe Towariowe Polskiego Handlu Zagranicznego a Mredznarodowe Powiazania Transportowe* [Commercial Commodities Flows of Polish Foreign Trade and International Transportation Connections], *Prace Geograficzne* No. 177, Inotytut Geografu i Przestrzennego Zagospodarowania, Polska Akademia Nauk, Warsaw, 2000.
21 Some of this was due to the restrictive conditions under which many refuges were allowed to enter Germany, but the overall impact is clear.

433,300 for the EU as a whole.[22] The United Kingdom had the largest number of asylum-seekers in the EU. Applications from Europe fell in 2000 to 22,880 (28 per cent of the total), being overtaken by those from Asia. Asylum-seeking is certainly a problem that has grown in significance over the past decade and one that it would be unwise to ignore. However, it is related to temporary circumstances in countries of origin, and therefore should not drive overall immigration policy. While clearly a Europe-wide problem, it remains one that is addressed largely by individual member states rather than by the EU as a whole.

Associated with the growth of asylum-seeking has been a substantial rise in illegal immigration. This is a difficult issue on which to find reliable data, but a number of observations are in order. Evidence from work in Albania suggests that illegal migrants are not substantially different from legal migrants in their motivation.[23] Evidence from the US–Mexico border suggests that periods of greater intensity of policing seem to be associated with increasing illegal migration.[24] This arises to a large extent because frustrating potential migrants at the point of entry simply builds up a stock of intending migrants – the motivation does not change; it just takes longer to act out. This situation provides the opportunity for criminal activity to flourish, largely through providing false information to migrants and encouraging them to believe in greater returns from migration, which would more than cover any payments required. Although there is a clear need for reliable information on international movements of persons who are not citizens of a country, there is an indication that excessive enforcement of rules may lead to an increase in attempted illegal movements, often with tragic consequences.[25]

Data on illegal migrants come from a variety of sources, principally relating to those detected attempting entry at a border and those detected working illegally within the country, many of whom may have entered legally but then stayed beyond the limit of their original permission or sought employment without possessing a work permit. Border detection of illegal migrants increased for most EU countries in the late 1990s. In Germany, for example, just under 40,000 a year were detected entering the country, although this number was falling – the figure was 31,000 in 2000. Fines on

---

22 *Asylum Statistics United Kingdom 2001*, Home Office Report 09/02 July 2002.
23 Papapanagos and Sanfey, 'Intention to emigrate'.
24 See G. H. Hanson and A. Spilimbergo, 'Illegal immigration, border enforcement and relative wages: evidence from apprehensions at the US-Mexico border', paper to CEPR workshop on Location and Regional Convergence/Divergence, Louvain-la-Neuve, 1996.
25 It is a matter of regret that the publicity given to this plays into the hands of xenophobic elements who blow the magnitude of the issue out of all proportion and raise and play on the fears of the wider population about alien influences, welfare-scroungers and threats to jobs.

employers for illegal workers also increased, with about 80,000 offences recorded per year. This problem is not restricted to the EU: in 2001 it was estimated that in Poland up to 200,000 foreigners took up work illegally each year, mainly in the informal sector, although border controls only detected around 10,000, and this figure was falling owing to the expectation of better detection.[26]

Overall, however, our main conclusion on migration flows is that there is essentially not a problem which requires major new action in terms of a continuing and rising threat of population flows associated with enlargement of the EU. If we compare the current flow of migrants to those resulting from earlier enlargements of the EU, we find that net outflows of population have been reduced in line with the improved economic performance of the EU countries, Ireland being the most obvious example. The EU needs a consistent policy towards migration, which can be applied at the Union level, to ensure consistent treatment of intending migrants, whatever their point of entry and whatever their intended final destination, and to avoid the temptation of deflecting the perceived migration problem to partner states. The following sections examine first the main causes of migration, which need to be understood as the basis for a consistent policy approach, and then the likely consequences on the economies of the home and destination regions.

A MODEL OF MIGRATION

Economic models of migration are usually based on the so-called 'push–pull model'.[27] This identifies a number of negative 'push' factors in the country of origin that cause people to move away, in combination with a number of positive 'pull' factors that attract migrants to a receiving country. The 'push' factors include elements such as demographic, political and economic hard-

---

26 The majority of these (Romanians, Ukrainians, Afghans, Moldovans, Iraqis, Indians, Vietnamese, Turks and those from Former Yugoslavia are the largest groups) are in transit to western Europe (Poland is one of the main transit routes from India and western Asia and from southeastern Europe) and seek employment while waiting to enter Germany. However, there are also Germans, particularly from neighbouring regions in eastern Germany, working in large-scale projects. There is also organized criminal trafficking and black market activity by Ukrainians overtly involved in trading. See OECD, *Trends in International Migration, SOPEMI* (Paris: OECD, 2001).

27 See D. Massey, J. Arango, G. Hugo, A. Kouaouci, A. Pellegrino and J.E. Taylor, 'Theories of International Migration: A Review and Appraisal', *Population and Development Review*, Vol. 19, No. 3, 1993, pp. 431–66, for a detailed survey of migration literature. For a recent survey specific to the labour market in Europe, see S. Akkoyunlu and R. Vickerman, 'Migration and the Efficiency of European Labour Markets', in J. Brocker and H. Herrmann (eds), *Spatial Change and Interregional Flows in the Integrating Europe – Essays in Honour of Karin Peschel* (Heidelberg: Physica-Verlag, 2000), pp. 157–70.

ship in the origin countries, and the 'pull' factors include the geographic and cultural proximity and the comparative advantages of the destination country, such as higher wages and better working conditions. This is a more comprehensive model than the simplest economic model, which is dependent entirely on differences in wage levels.

Demographic factors are an important driving force in migration. Lower rates of population growth in the EU could lead to a significant shortfall in the labour supply over the next 20 years. Although population growth in most CEECs is also fairly low, higher rates of unemployment could provide a significant incentive for movement.[28] This could put considerable pressure on the economies of the existing EU countries.

Political factors are more complex, and could possibly influence the decision to migrate more profoundly than demographic factors. Impatience, particularly among educated young people, with the slow pace of transition to liberalized markets, and the increase in ethnic tensions within a number of CEECs that remained masked during the communist period could both emerge as major 'push' factors.

Economic factors are the most significant 'push' factors. The slow pace of transition may provoke migratory sentiments in the young, but a speedier transition may result in unemployment, and a weak social security system may provoke mass movements when people weigh gains (higher wages) against costs (unemployment or low wages).[29] For example, GDP per capita in eastern Europe at the end of the 1980s was one-eighth of the average in western Europe, and fell by as much as 12 per cent by 1991. Furthermore, an increase in the unemployment figures in the reformed CEECs resulted in cross-border migration, especially from Poland to Germany. At the end of 1990, nearly 1.2 million Poles were estimated to have become unemployed mainly because of the transition process, which resulted in a decrease in subsidies, budgetary restrictions and a decline in industrial production.

There is still a significant divergence in per capita income between CEECs and EU countries. As Table 3.1 shows, in 2000 the average CEEC GDP per capita was only 38 per cent of the EU average. This, coupled with high unemployment rates in the candidate countries, is the main cause of migration from CEECs to the EU, especially to the border countries of Austria and Germany. However, estimates suggest that over time the

---

28 See T. Bauer and K. Zimmermann, 'Assessment of Possible Migration Pressure and its Labour Market Impact Following EU Enlargement to Central and Eastern Europe: Part 2', *DFEE Research Report RR 139*, Department for Education and Employment, London, 1999.

29 See H. Papapaganos and R. Vickerman, 'Borders, Migration and Labour-market Dynamics in a Changing Europe', in M. van der Velde and H. van Houtum (eds), *Borders, Regions and People* (London: Pion Ltd, 2000), for a detailed analysis of this factor.

Table 3.1: Selected economic indicators of the CEEC-10, 2000

	GDP per capita (PPP adjusted) in euros	Percentage of EU-15	Unemployment (%)
Bulgaria	5,400	24	16.4
Czech Rep.	13,500	60	8.8
Estonia	8,500	38	13.7
Hungary	11,700	52	6.4
Latvia	6,600	29	14.6
Lithuania	6,600	29	16.0
Poland	8,700	39	16.1
Romania	6,000	27	7.1
Slovakia	10,800	48	18.6
Slovenia	16,100	72	7.0
CEEC-10	8,736	38	

Source: European Commission, *Making a Success of Enlargement*, Brussels, 2001.

convergence per capita incomes of various CEEC-10 states will approach at least the per capita income of the low-income EU countries. This will, therefore, ease any migration pressures from accession countries, as they are the most advanced of the CEECs and hence are likely to approach the EU average income relatively quickly. The economic situation in the non-candidate CEECs is, of course, significantly worse, leading to continuing pressures for individuals to migrate in order to survive.

On the other side of the migration model are the 'pull' factors. Labour market effects are by far the most important of these, as there are important reasons for the EU to import labour from the CEECs. The labour market issue is primarily linked to the demographic factors that have already been mentioned. Estimates suggest that the labour force in the EU will contract by 5.5 per cent by 2020 (from 145 million to 137 million). This will have serious repercussions on the EU economies in 20 to 30 years' time, when the ratio of workers to pensioners is almost certain to have fallen significantly.

The other aspect of the labour market effect is that there is a shortage of workers in some key industries. Therefore there is already pressure on domestic authorities from producers to relax restrictions on foreign labour, especially in Germany, where the foreigners may be hired as contract workers for up to six years in the case of IT specialists. This issue has also been raised in the United Kingdom[30] and has been highlighted in a recent OECD study[31] and the European Commission Action Plan.[32]

More significant is migration as part of the dynamic process of labour market adjustment. Migration is not just the permanent movement of labour from one region or country to another involving movement of both workplace and residence. Such migration is at one extreme on a continuum of adjustments that have to be defined both spatially, with respect to workplace and residence, and temporally, with respect to the length of time spent at the new location. Much movement between European labour markets is only short-term, sometimes because of regulatory restrictions but often because of choices made by the migrant. This includes the frequent seasonal movement of workers under specific contracts. At the other end of the spectrum we can observe within the EU the increasing incidence of weekly commuting, reflecting the workplace choices of households with many earners and the constraints of housing markets. We also observe longer-distance conventional commuting, reflecting improved transport into major cities; this is sometimes associated with telecommuting, where people work from home with a computer connected to the Internet and visit their office only two or three days per week. All of these represent examples of people seeking work outside their labour market of residence.

Migration is frequently modelled only as a decision taken by the migrant in terms of (static) differences in earning potential or the probability of unemployment in two regions. But it needs to be seen as part of a long-term, dynamic adjustment in which movement is a response to longer-run expectations in both markets and in which individuals may choose to work for a limited period in another market as part of a process of acquiring new skills or money for future investment or in order to remit earnings home.[33] This movement incurs costs, both the direct costs of moving, including search costs, and the indirect costs of separation from family and possible

---

30 See S. Glover, C. Golt, A. Loizillon, J. Portes, R. Price, S. Spencer, V. Sirinivasan and C. Willis, *Migration: An Economic and Social Analysis*, The Research Development and Statistics Directorate, Occasional Paper No. 67, The Home Office, London, 2001.

31 OECD, *International Mobility of the Highly Skilled* (Paris: OECD, 2002).

32 European Commission, 'Action Plan for Skills and Mobility', Communication from the Commission to the Council, the European Parliament, the Economic and Social Committee and the Committee of the Regions, COM (2002) 72, 13 February 2002.

33 A. De-Coulon and M. Piracha, in 'Self-Selection and the Performance of Return Migrants: The Case of Albania', mimeo (London: Centre for Economic Performance, 2002), have analysed the performance of return migrants to Albania. M. Leon-Lesdesma and M. Piracha, in *International Migration and the Role of Remittances in Eastern Europe*, Studies in Economics 01/13, Department of Economics, University of Kent at Canterbury (revised version of a paper to the European Society on Population Economics Conference, Athens, June 2001), have studied the role of remittances in selected CEECs.

exposure to harassment at the destination. At the level of the family, different members may choose to work in different labour markets as a means of spreading the risks of unemployment. In a process of rapid change, such as during economic transition, labour market expectations will change, and thus people's responses to these expectations will affect their decision to migrate. If people think that life in their own country is likely to improve, they may either postpone a decision to migrate or accelerate it, on the basis that the potential returns to any skill acquisition or financial gain are increased.

Return migration is often interpreted as a failure in information, which has led to migrants taking the 'wrong' decision. However, viewing the decision to make an individual migration move as part of a long-term decision to improve chances in the labour market though better skills makes this movement entirely rational. This is not to deny the problem of imperfect and asymmetric information, and one part of our set of models aims to show that more efficient decisions are taken when these imperfections of information are reduced. Analysis shows clearly that information which enables the better matching of migration flows to labour market needs has a greater positive effect both on migrants' experience and on the destination regions.[34] There is also substantial evidence of short-term seasonal contracted migration (from specific regions to specific employment opportunities), which enables employers to rely on the quality of migrant labour employed (i.e. achieving symmetric information).

Migration is thus part of a dynamic process within the lifetime expectations of workers. In this context, there is evidence that migration is self-selective, i.e. those who migrated would have done better regardless of whether or not they had gone abroad. Therefore, immigrants may be 'more able and more highly motivated' than the natives.[35] For this reason, migration is generally expected to yield welfare gains, especially if the marginal

---

34 S. Akkoyunlu, *European Labour Markets: Can Migration Provide Efficiency? The Polish–German Case*, ESRC, One Europe or Several? Programme Working Paper 31/01, University of Sussex, 2001.

35 See G. J. Borjas, 'Self-Selection and the Earnings of Immigrants', *American Economic Review*, Vol. 77, 1987, pp. 531–53, and G. J. Borjas and B. Bratsberg, 'Who Leaves? The Outmigration of the Foreign Born', *Review of Economics and Statistics*, Vol. 78, 1996, pp. 165–76, for an analysis of the effect of self-selected immigrants on the US labour market; and T. Bauer, P.T. Pereira, M. Vogler and K.F. Zimmermann, 'Portuguese Migrants in the German Labor Market: Performance and Self-Selection', *International Migration Review*, Vol. 36, No. 2, 2002, pp. 467–91, for the effect of self-selection on the German labour market. T. Straubhaar and K. F. Zimmermann, in 'Towards a European Migration Policy', *Population Research and Policy Review*, Vol. 12, 1993, pp. 225–41, show that migration from CEECs to Germany caused the average level of human capital in Germany to increase, whereas the opposite occurred in the sending countries. It has been argued on the basis of such analysis that a selective (or perhaps more accurately 'targeted') immigration policy could be used to attract the highly qualified workers needed in innovative industries.

productivity of labour differs across countries. It has been argued on this basis that if all markets are functioning well, then migration is welfare-improving, not only for migrants but also (on average) for natives. The effects of migration on the labour markets and the regions between which migrants move are considered in more detail in the next section.

THE CONSEQUENCES OF MIGRATION

Migration has positive and negative effects for both the sending and the receiving countries. Both kinds of effect have to be considered, therefore, in order for a migration policy to be effective not only for migrants but also for the economies of the regions involved. Here we discuss important economic consequences from the perspective of sending and receiving countries.

Emigration can provide relatively well-paid employment for both unskilled and skilled workers from CEECs, offering an outlet for domestic frustration with the pace of transition that might otherwise present serious political problems, and it can also produce large inflows of valuable hard currency remittances. At the same time, sending-country governments express concern that emigration deprives their nation of their best human resources, represents a transfer of educational investment from poor to rich countries and leads to abuses or exploitation of their workers. It has been difficult to demonstrate empirically that international migration results in development in the origin countries over the short term. It is not clear that migration does reduce unemployment levels, but it does appear to play an important role in absorbing labour-force growth.

The movement of skilled and highly qualified workers is likely to result in a slowdown of the development process in countries of origin. However, whether emigration constitutes a 'drain' of workers at any skill level sufficient to hinder the development process depends upon the availability of human and other resources to fill the gap. Similarly, because short-term migration may contribute to the acquisition of skills abroad, it may have a substantial long-term beneficial effect. It is more clearly evident, however, that remittances improve the welfare of migrants' non-migrating families and enable a higher level of provision of education and health care for children, which has long-run beneficial effects on future growth. Remittances may have reached very high levels in some countries, anything from 20 per cent to 40 per cent of GDP in Albania, where upwards of 40 per cent of the population has had at least one period of migration.[36] In Poland remittances are estimated to

36 Annual remittances are much higher than annual foreign aid. In 1996, for instance, foreign aid amounted to approximately $200 million, while remittances totalled approximately $370 million. This trend is believed to be continuing.

have increased by over 80 per cent between 1994 and 1998, amounting to over $1 billion by 1998.[37] As well as the generation of current remittances, the accumulation of financial capital for future investment is a major incentive for many migrants to work abroad.[38]

In terms of the receiving countries, studies have shown that international migration has contributed towards human capital formation by influencing natives' accumulation of knowledge.[39] Therefore immigrants have been not only an important source of labour supply but also significant contributors in introducing innovative and dynamic elements in the fields of science and medicine. However, some sectors are more adversely affected by immigration than others and thus the effects of migration on the employment of natives have become a serious and contentious subject of debate in recent years. These effects vary, not only by sector and occupation but also by country and type of migration.[40] For instance, it has been argued that immigration causes negative wage and employment effects in sectors that employ relatively low-skilled workers. The evidence for this is not conclusive. Some empirical studies have shown that such effects are very small.[41] The economic explanation of the absence of wage effects is that migration affects the composition of output rather than wages, i.e. it affects the

37 See Leon-Ledesma and Piracha, *International Migration*.
38 D. Kule, A. Mancellari, H. Papapanagos, S. Qirici and P. Sanfey, 'The Causes and Consequences of Albanian Emigration during Transition: Evidence from Micro Data', *Studies in Economics 00/04*, Department of Economics, University of Kent at Canterbury, published in *International Migration Review*, Vol. 36, No. 2, 2002, pp. 229–39, show that in Albania migration rates are strongly related to migrants' perception of potential advantages in capitalizing on the new liberalized economy.
39 See C.V. Chiswick, 'The Impact of Immigration on the Human Capital of Natives', *Journal of Labour Economics*, Vol. 7, 1988, pp. 464–86, and D. Galor and O. Stark, 'Migration, Human Capital Formation and Long-run Output', in H. Siebert (ed.), *Migration: A Challenge for Europe* (Tübingen, Germany: Institut für Weltwirtschaft an der Universität Kiel, 1994), pp. 59–70.
40 See R.M. Friedberg and J. Hunt, 'The Impact of Immigrants on Host Country Wages, Employment and Growth', *Journal of Economic Perspectives*, Vol. 9, 1995, pp. 23–44; and J.P. Haisken De New and K. F. Zimmermann, 'Wage and mobility effects of trade and migration', in M. Dewatripont, A. Sapin and K. Sekkat (eds), *Trade and Jobs in Europe: Much Ado about Nothing?* (Oxford: Oxford University Press, 1999).
41 D. Card, 'The Impact of the Mariet Boatlift on the Miami Labor Market', *Industrial and Labor Relations Review*, Vol. 43, No. 2, 1990, pp. 245–57, for instance, shows that there is a negligible effect on wages from a large influx of migrants in the Miami area. Also G. J. Borjas, in 'The Economics of Immigration', *Journal of Economic Literature*, Vol. 32, No. 4, 1994, pp. 1667–717, finds no support for the hypothesis that the employment opportunities of US-born workers are adversely affected by immigration. I. Gang and F. L. Rivera-Batiz, in 'Labour Market Effect on Immigration in the United States and Europe: Substitution vs. Complementarity', *Journal of Population Economics*, Vol. 7, 1994, pp. 157–75, estimate that a one per cent increase in migrant labour in Europe will only affect native wages by between +0.02 and −0.08 per cent. More recently, in 'Ethnic Minorities in the UK: Burden or

industrial structure of the receiving country. Thus those sectors that employ immigrants expand, leaving the employment level and wages of natives unchanged, while those sectors that restrict the employment of immigrants shrink, resulting in increased unemployment of natives in that sector without altering wages in a significant way.

The other side of the argument is that cheap, low-quality immigrant labour may lead to a loss of competitiveness, as it induces a slowdown in the adjustment process to higher-quality production. However, declining relative wages for less skilled workers are an incentive for the home population to engage in human capital formation and earn higher wages in the long run. Immigration can increase labour market flexibility and provide incentives to slow down wage growth and thus increase employment. Thus, there is no clear threat to the welfare of indigenous workers from immigration.[42] Moreover, unskilled immigrants increasingly occupy employment opportunities that the indigenous workforce is no longer willing to fill. Furthermore, despite the leakage owing to remittances, immigrants have a relatively high propensity to consume, thereby adding to local demand. In this regard, the entry of unskilled immigrants probably raises EU welfare by more than trade does.[43]

The evidence on the impacts of migration is thus finely balanced. There are costs and benefits to both origin and destination regions. Typically the costs are short-term, and not always those perceived as most important by popular misconceptions of immigrants: by and large migrants do not displace local workers from employment, in contrast to the fears of voters in many states.

TOWARDS AN EU MIGRATION POLICY

The weight of the evidence suggests that migration is a response to economic opportunities and needs to be considered in the context of the dynamic adjustment of labour markets. The past decade is no guide to future expectations of

---

Benefit?', Working Paper No. 2001 14, Institute for Social and Economic Research, University of Essex, 2001, A. Zorlu analysed the wage effects of ethnic minorities in the UK and found both substitution and competition effects occurring simultaneously. Thus there is no clear effect on wages overall. Other recent papers with similar results are J.-S. Pischke and J. Velling, 'Employment Effects of Immigration to Germany: An Analysis Based on Local Labor Markets', *Review of Economics and Statistics*, Vol. 79, No. 4, 1997, pp. 94–604, and N. Gaston and D. Nelson, 'The Employment and Wage Effects of Immigration: Trade and Labour Economics Perspectives', in D. Greenaway, R. Upward and K. Wakelin (eds), *Trade, Investment and Labour: Proceedings of IEA Conference* (Palgrave, 2002).

42 It is possible that relatively recent migrants may be substitutes for previous migrants, as they are likely to move to similar locations in the host country, to have similar skills and to work in similar industries.

43 Haisken De New and Zimmermann, 'Wage and Mobility Effects of Trade', pp. 150–51.

migration within Europe because it involves a period of adjustment to long-term disjuncture in the operation of such markets. Moreover, the evidence points strongly to migration as a short-term response to differentials, not a long-term solution. The danger is, therefore, that interference with market forces produces continuing problems of adjustment and could lead to much longer-term problems of incentives towards illegal migration and the criminal activity with which it is associated than would a more liberal regime.

However, there are some clear indications of ways in which a more active approach to migration could be beneficial. One of the clear problems concerns information: the failure of migrants to gain correct information about opportunities at possible destinations and potential employers to gain adequate information about the skills of migrants. The problems arising from these asymmetries in information, and the benefits from reducing them, can be seen in the growth of seasonal contract movements whereby employers can recruit from the same area and be assured of the quality of the workers.[44]

Policies which aim to match the skill mix of migrants to the needs of destination regions clearly have some merit in this context. They are similar to the points system currently in use in Australia and Canada: a kind of selective immigration policy aimed at fulfilling the needs of particular industries or labour markets. However, there are problems with this system. A points system may fail to take into account possible economic shocks to a country, such as recession. Family reunification under this system can bring in migrants who may not be qualified to fulfil any labour market needs and who may be a burden on the welfare capacity of states. Furthermore, the time lag between identifying the problem sectors with labour shortages and the actual arrival of immigrants can result in a mismatch, with 'wrongly qualified' immigrants.

Germany recently adopted a policy in which bilateral agreements with several CEECs have been signed, whereby people from their own labour force can be hired to work in firms/projects (mainly in the construction sector) in Germany on a contract that should not exceed three years. Wages for contract workers are lower than for German workers because social security benefits are paid according to the rules of the country of origin. This policy has the benefit that administrative costs are lower than under a points system. It clearly defines the relevant sectors so that appropriately skilled workers are admitted; and the quotas can be defined so that migrants can be

---

44 Some 250,000 temporary migrants from CEECs were present in Germany in 1997, of whom 210,000 were seasonal workers, a figure which has grown from under 120,000 in 1991. See Boeri, Brücker et al., *The Impact of Eastern Enlargement on Employment*, p. 60.

used in any EU country in need of a specifically skilled labour force (or skilled labour in a particular sector). Although this policy reduces some of the inefficiencies of points systems, some criticisms, such as time lag and the immigration of wrongly skilled workers, still apply.

An alternative cost-effective policy for the receiving country is one in which work permits are auctioned off either to those wishing to immigrate or, perhaps more practically, to the firms in the host country wishing to employ immigrants.[45] The host country can determine the need for labour for a given time period and then auction off work permits to fulfil that need. All those interested in a job in the host country can participate in such an auction.[46] This would be of particular relevance to migrants from those countries not currently candidates for EU membership. Proceeds from the auction of work permits could be split between the host country (i.e. revenues generated could contribute towards the administration costs associated with setting up an auction and redistribution to natives) and the country of origin, where the funds could be used in the education sector and also in other development-related projects to reduce future emigration pressures. The price at which a work permit could be acquired would set a ceiling on the earnings of the illegal immigration industry, and potential migrants would opt for illegal immigration only if it were considerably cheaper than the legal alternative of acquiring a work permit. Therefore, as long as the auction price of acquiring a permit remains below the costs associated with illegal immigration, such a policy will be efficient not only in attracting 'rightly' qualified people but also in alleviating problems of illegal immigration. In addition, illegal costs are sunk, whereas the work permit fee will be refundable if the immigrant returns to his home country. Therefore, buying a work permit could be considered an investment, especially for the short-term immigrant. Upon repatriation, the refund from the permit, in addition to the retained savings, could be used in the origin country to set up a business or build a home etc., thus benefiting the local economy. For employers, such a policy will be more efficient if permits are transferable across sectors and firms, as this reduces the unnecessary administration costs that could result if migrants had to return to the home country before they could be hired by another firm.

---

45 A variant of this policy has been in use in some Middle Eastern countries since 1974, and has been efficiently tackling the labour shortage problem without any significant adverse effects related to immigration.

46 This includes people already present in the host country who do not have a work permit. Such a model would help to discourage and reabsorb illegal immigration.

CONCLUSION

The potential gross flow of migrants for the EU does not present an overwhelming problem now and will not do so upon enlargement. Enlargement will focus attention somewhat away from the existing EU borders to the new borders farther east, but our judgment is that this is more a question of a shift of emphasis rather than a major new problem. Flows from outside the candidate countries have been greater than those from the CEEC-10, but they are still of a manageable size. The main problems for the future are ones of helping new member states to adjust to a Community-wide immigration policy and dealing with pressures from illegal immigration and asylum-seekers. The migration problems which do exist are more at the microeconomic level of matching potential migrants to labour force needs in the most efficient way.

The evidence available suggests that migrant flows can play a valuable role in helping to improve the flexibility of EU labour markets, which operates mainly through enabling occupational mobility rather than through creating unemployment. Theory suggests that there should be net benefits here as well, especially where individual migration is mainly short-term in nature. Initial results suggest that there are positive impacts on productivity from returning migrants, adding to the beneficial impact of remittances.[47] In addition, labour markets in CEECs seem to be more flexible than in the EU, suggesting that they can absorb market shocks more efficiently.

Migration may also have a positive impact on wage distribution in the home region, as well as on individual wages, not only by raising the mean wage but also by reducing inequality and thus helping to promote greater efficiency. A Community immigration policy thus needs to address mechanisms for identifying migrant flows and preparing for their easy absorption rather than to try to set aggregate quotas or optimal transition periods for free movement.

47 See Leon-Ledesma and Piracha, *International Migration.*

4

EU enlargement and security: turning the inside out

JAMES GOW

There are no simple 'inside and outside' questions, no points of necessary exclusion in the international security environment. This is true, above all, with regard to Europe and its security. The limits of a European security area are not constituted by any well-defined geographical points, but are focused around the spread of values: democracy, the rule of law enforced by an independent judiciary, respect for minorities and a commitment to finding peaceful solutions to conflicts within and across borders. Almost certainly the emergence of a security community must be based around these values. This means that EU enlargement cannot be the end of thinking about stability and security in Europe. Also, European security cannot really be understood without reference to NATO.

Whichever dimension of EU security is involved, there is a logic which means that there is no necessary point at which it stops, or at least there is a very big question about identifying the point at which it stops. Insiders always have to some degree to look to the outside; outsiders have to some degree to be brought into the security structure. However, this cannot all be done at once, and it may not necessarily be possible to have everyone within. In this general perspective, the question must be about where the limits of enlargement in security terms might come, if at all.

There are three main sections to this analysis. The first is about the enlargement of NATO along with that of the EU. In terms of conventional security policy issues, there is a need to be able to work with EU partners not only politically on defence policy but also in operational terms because the development of the EU's Security and Defence Policy (ESDP) is closely linked with the use of NATO assets. Moreover, all the central and east European countries with which EU membership negotiations were concluded in December 2002 were invited at Prague in November that year to join NATO if they had not already done so. There is a whole range of issues regarding complementarity and harmonization that attend this. The second section concerns the nature of the EU as a 'security community' and the issue of borders. The final section looks at questions of categories of 'outsiders' in relation to enlargement.

EUROPEAN SECURITY AND DEFENCE: HARMONIZATION AND THE
DEMANDS OF INCLUSION

At the start of the 21st century there was a strong logic necessitating EU enlargement. That logic was underpinned by the need to increase stability and security throughout Europe. The same strategic logic underpinned the enlargement of NATO as well. EU enlargement is essentially, though not formally, linked to NATO enlargement. There is no possibility of discussing security policy issues concerning the EU – including the creation of a defence capability – without reference to NATO. The key to achieving such a capability is a well-managed relationship with NATO. Membership and complementarity form an important point of interest for current and prospective members of the EU and the North Atlantic Alliance. Relations between the EU and NATO are driven by the latter's assets, as well as by political sensitivities. In the traditional security policy areas of military capability (planning and command, control and communications facilities) the capabilities rest with NATO. Neither the EU as a whole nor any one of its member states will duplicate that which already exists.

Evolution has already occurred within frameworks such as Partnership for Peace (PfP) and the Euro-Atlantic Partnership Council (EAPC), which have become central to redefining both the nature and the practice of security policy in Europe, and therefore to the EU's own security policies (see Box 4.1). The reality of these developments is an organic and *de facto* combined security policy. The focus for this is essentially the Euro-Atlantic Partnership Council. The bonds that are created through this common activity bridge the boundaries between the formal NATO alliance and other bodies, thus changing the nature of the security question and offering a form of genuine security for both those inside and those outside NATO and the EU. Indeed, in 15 or 50 years' time, the Euro-Atlantic Partnership Council might well be the key body, with NATO reduced to a relic of the genesis of the EAPC, perhaps still in existence but no longer the essential part of European security that it has been since its formation in 1949. The key throughout must be the evolution in the use of the assets that exist and that, for now, are associated primarily with NATO.

Evolution in NATO and in the EU is vital not only for the European Union itself but also for the Union's relationship with the United States. Any development should also free the EU to act without the Americans where it might be appropriate to do so. At the same time, notwithstanding the

> **BOX 4.1: PARTNERSHIP FOR PEACE AND THE EURO-ATLANTIC PARTNERSHIP COUNCIL**
>
> Partnership for Peace and the Euro-Atlantic Partnership Council have been important elements in NATO's evolution since the end of the Cold War. Initially, the Alliance formed the North Atlantic Cooperation Council (NACC), which embraced all members of the then Conference on Security and Cooperation in Europe (CSCE). This was a limited, consensus-based framework, mimicking the CSCE's membership of over 50 states. The only thing this arrangement offered that the CSCE did not was the direct involvement of NATO and the possibility of non-members' direct cooperation with the Alliance. But as the NACC was predicated on equality and consensus, whatever one state might want in terms of cooperation, all would need to have. The predictable outcome was little genuine cooperation, which was a source of frustration to many in the former communist countries of central and eastern Europe, as well as to many in NATO.
>
> To deal with these frustrations, PfP emerged in 1994 as a scheme by which members of the NACC could develop variable relationships with the Alliance, on the basis of 1 to 16 (that is, one county to the then 16 members of NATO). This meant that where particular countries and the Alliance sought extensive interaction, this was possible without requiring there to be the same degree of cooperation with all the NACC members. PfP proved to be a great success, fostering considerable activity *vis-à-vis* some countries in central and eastern Europe, as well as with some non-NATO EU countries, such as Sweden and Finland.
>
> The limitation of PfP was the 1 to 16 structure of the relationship (even though this permitted a range of bilateral initiatives that were placed under the PfP umbrella). An example was military cooperation involving the Alliance in the Nordic area, including Sweden, Finland, Latvia, Lithuania and Estonia. This could not really be accommodated by PfP, especially as all involved wanted a share in the planning of, say, joint exercises. Similarly, the involvement of non-NATO countries in NATO's operations in Bosnia and Herzegovina, which otherwise had to be on the basis of all others being invited to join in a plan devised by NATO, needed a framework in which countries making a significant contribution to operations could, as was only reasonable, play their part in planning commitments. The solution here was the development of EAPC at NATO's Madrid summit in 1997: this permitted more variable patterns of cooperation, including multilateral political, strategic and operational decision-making and planning, but only on the basis of countries' voluntary engagement and without any necessity of full Alliance involvement. Thus, there was a significant opportunity for cooperation for those wishing to be involved but no requirement on any party to participate in any particular activity.

determination of the United States to go ahead with its invasion of Iraq despite some of its NATO allies, it is unlikely to be able to dispense with the Alliance over the longer term. It is worth recalling that on 12 March 2002 all the British broadsheet newspapers had the same picture on their front page: President George W. Bush, in the garden of the White House in Washington, surrounded by the flags of all the 17 countries actively participating in the US-led coalition action in Afghanistan. Bush's speech, reported in the associated articles, referred to the 'allies and partners' in a 'joint venture'. Bush expressly noted the flags of the countries operating 'with us'.[1] This was a conscious presentation to the world and, crucially, to the US domestic audience that America was not then acting alone. It was a clear visual and verbal 'thank you' to those countries taking part in the operations. More than this, it symbolized to the US public that Washington was not the 'Lone Ranger' over Afghanistan. Over Iraq, the US publicly showed its appreciation of the 29 countries involved in operations – especially the UK, Australia, Spain and Poland. While the United States has shown that it can act alone militarily, politically this is unlikely to be feasible over a long period of time, in the absence of evident support from partners and allies. The Alliance remains vital to the United States, even if some of its partners are sometimes concerned by an apparent preference for 'coalitions of the willing' and, in particular, a tendency to work with the United Kingdom. Thus Washington is likely to remain engaged with the Alliance, although the character of the Alliance itself will surely change.

The United States needs NATO, and it needs a NATO with a European pillar that is competent and capable of doing whatever needs to be done whenever it needs to be done. NATO is the closest military–political alliance that the United States has or, indeed, could have. It is a military–political organization for which there is no equal in history. It is an arrangement that would never have been recreated had it been allowed to go the way of all other alliances in history and wither away once the purpose of its formation had been removed with the end of the Cold War. Its uniqueness and qualities, particularly in terms of integrated structures and operational procedures, make the Alliance irreplaceable. Although those involved with NATO might only ever mention the problems of getting things to work, it takes little imagination to see how impossible it would be to evolve as far as NATO has done if it had to be created from scratch again.

Moreover, NATO was a relevant asset to America in operational terms, even in an operation such as that in Afghanistan where only limited use was

---

1 See, e.g., *The Times,* 12 March 2002, *The Independent,* 12 March 2002, and *The Daily Telegraph,* 12 March 2002.

made of it. Some of its resources were deployed to US airspace so as to free purely US assets to operate over southern Asia. Some NATO member countries were asked to play a particular role, even though it was not a NATO operation, and there is nothing to suggest that any country refused.

The importance of flexible leadership and use of assets is worth noting in relation to longer-term developments in the European security policy framework. It is especially relevant for the Euro-Atlantic Partnership Council. Whereas the PfP's arrangements outlined above are 19 to 1 (having been 16 to 1), essentially a bilateral relationship between NATO as a collective and one partner country, EAPC created a multilateral framework for planning, decision-making and cooperation. It still left the North Atlantic Council (NAC), the political decision-making body in the Alliance, having to make a decision to release assets, but it gave a range of countries that wished to be involved with NATO an opportunity to be so involved. This is vital for countries such as Finland, Sweden and Austria, which have traditionally had non-participatory, non-aligned or neutral positions and which have got everything they could want from NATO through EAPC without having to cross the line of making a formal commitment to collective self-defence under Article 5 of the Washington Treaty. In each case, while they were closely aligned with NATO in political, security and, increasingly, operational terms, full membership of the Alliance, with a formal commitment to supporting collective self-defence, was a step none was ready to make in the late 1990s. To a considerable extent, planning for the NATO-led Kosovo Stabilization Force (KFOR) deployed in Kosovo after the ending of hostilities was a *de facto* example of EAPC at work. Moreover, this could be an example of how any EU Security and Defence Policy capability might be put into effect, although this is not likely in the near future.

NATO has become a unique club with remarkable and unique assets. It remains an organization for collective self-defence, where relevant – and in this context the United States was very glad to have it decide overnight that the attacks of 11 September 2001 on New York and Washington, DC warranted collective self-defence and make a declaration to that effect for the first time in its history, even if subsequent US actions were based more on cooperation with specific partners. NATO is a club with assets in which all the members contribute in one way or another and in which some of them might want to use some of the assets for particular purposes: Afghanistan is a limited example; Bosnia and Kosovo are more extensive examples. Providing that none of the existing members absolutely objects and vetoes action within the NAC, this is what will happen, and it is the pattern for the future. It is also why a body such as EAPC, linked to ESDP evolution rather than to the NAC, is likely to carry the weight of future armed forces and European security commitments. These developments will take time; how much time remains an open question.

Issues of overlap and complementarity mean that any discussion of EU enlargement needs to have an eye on NATO and vice versa. Yet, inevitably, the two are not identical: NATO enlargement has had different dynamics and many aspects remained up in the air for far longer than was the case regarding the EU, with political priorities in Washington being a determining factor, sometimes appearing to put a limit on NATO expansion but latterly strongly favouring it. The decision at Prague in November 2002 to take in a broad sweep of states – embracing all the central and east European countries expected to join the EU in 2004 except Poland, Hungary and the Czech Republic (which had already joined NATO in 1999), and also Romania and Bulgaria (countries which aspire to join the EU in 2007) – represented a considerable change of approach, especially in Washington. For the EU's enlargement to be effective in terms of its security policy there needs to be a rough parallel between the processes and developments taking place at the NATO and EU levels. Because key assets and resources rest with NATO, any new member state of the EU will have to make a commitment in terms of security and defence that is compatible with NATO.[2] Although, at the time of writing, there was no usable EU force, it was expected that by the time of enlargement in mid-2004 a force with limited capabilities would be ready. The kinds of operation for which such a force might be used include those that will not demand US engagement. This may mean that the operations are likely to be ones that do not demand high-intensity combat.

There will be tough demands on any state acceding to the EU, as there were for Poland, Hungary and the Czech Republic when they joined NATO in March 1999, on the eve of the Alliance's 50th anniversary Washington summit. There were many operational problems, and even some political ones, in integrating those three countries in a limited way. Integration is not easy and it places financial demands on acceding states as well as on existing NATO members and the EU in terms of assistance to the new member states. Enlargement will also place enormous political pressure on the Union and its member states to establish sufficient legitimacy across Europe so as to provide the political coherence necessary to underpin any successful use of armed force. The process of EU enlargement that is already under way will continue the transformation already begun by NATO's expansion. Changing

---

2 Otherwise, new members would join on terms that gave them status and rights without responsibility – a situation in which hypothetically those member states could generate problems and expect others to take responsibility for sorting them out. Of course, each country's capacities determine the contribution it might be expected to make and it is likely that not all states would become involved in each ESDP mission.

the borders of the EU will further change the conceptual and policy boundaries of security in Europe.

THE EU: BORDERS, BOUNDARIES AND FRONTIERS

The essential message of the EU as it has grown from its limited origins (albeit with a vision inspiring it) is that it is a way of ending traditional conflict between states and creating a security community in which the importance of borders is de-emphasized. The achievement has been to remove traditional security and security policy concerns from relations between member states, creating a zone of stability, harmony, political cooperation and, ultimately, prosperity.[3] As a result, there is no reasonable or foreseeable prospect of any member of the EU (or its near neighbours) going to war with another. That logic is one of the elements which carry the imperative to enlarge. The logic is straightforward: if the EU has created security in terms of six, nine, 12 and then 15 states, it can offer the same benefits for 20, 25 or even 30 or more states.

The development of the EU that is most often held to manifest its integration in the field of security is the 'disappearance' of borders.[4] The case of the EU is also relevant to discussions of order and the removal of conditions for conflict in international society. For many observers, the Union's great value is that integration has created conditions in which the statehood and border wars that are the fabric of European history have been woven into a new cloth of peace and security. At its core, this notion builds on the idea that Germany and France no longer go to war to change, for example, the borders of Alsace and Lorraine. Nor do they make claims on behalf of or respond to claims from kin populations on the other side of the border. The pain that was previously caused by the Franco-German border has been dissipated by processes of integration that are deemed to have removed the border – and certainly the border is no longer contested and its significance has changed. It is no longer seen as a reason for war and insecurity; rather, it is seen as providing peace and security. To some extent, a similar case can be made about other borders between member states of the EU, for example between Germany and Denmark. This is another case where the reduced importance of borders as a barrier, coupled with notions

3 This is a 'security community' in the sense identified by Karl Deutsch et al., *Political Community and the North Atlantic Area* (Princeton, NJ: Princeton University Press, 1957). See also Robert Kagan, *On Paradise and Power* (London: Atlantic Books, 2003).

4 James Gow, 'A Revolution in International Affairs?', *Security Dialogue*, Vol. 31, No. 3, September 2001, pp. 293–306.

of regionalization,[5] has altered the conditions for nationalist cross-border communities, helping to defuse tension and reduce support for groups prepared to use violence in an attempt to secure political goals.

The formation of the EU has seen the importance of borders de-emphasized in a number of ways, notably in terms of the four freedoms (of goods, capital, services and labour) that were enshrined in the Treaty of Rome in 1957 and reinforced by the Single European Act of 1986. At the same time the exercise of sovereign rights in a number of areas has been transferred to the Union by individual member states. In part, this is because of the inherent value attached by many to the idea of integration *per se*. It also reflects the reality for all states, that in contemporary circumstances each of them has reached the limit of that which it can achieve and manage on its own.[6]

Although some developments within the EU have reduced the importance of borders between member states, they have not removed borders. The Schengen regime on open borders,[7] originally implemented by seven EU members party to the agreement, has not only shifted the perspective on borders and their importance by removing internal borders but has also created a further, subordinate border between the Schengen EU (plus non-EU Schengen parties) and the remainder of the EU. This is exemplified at any EU–Schengen airport, where passport control operates between different parts of the airport. The Schengen *acquis* is an issue because new members are expected to participate as soon as possible in the Schengen arrangements. This will put increased emphasis on the Union's external borders. This is just one of a range of issues that confirm the continuing importance of borders as the formal and practical markers of inclusion and exclusion.

With enlargement, the external borders of the Union will change and the character of the borders between new and current members will be altered. Given the greater uncertainties about control the farther east one goes, there

---

5 Wolfgang Danspeckgruber, 'Self-Determination and Regionalization in Contemporary Europe', in Wolfgang Danspeckgruber (ed.), *The Self-Determination of Peoples: Community, Nation and State in an Interdependent World* (Boulder, CO: Lynne Rienner, 2002).

6 However, it is wrong to make a leap from this to the judgment that the EU has either ended state sovereignty and borders or removed the responsibility of the individual state for its own security. Security, in fact, continues to be one of the most precious areas of government responsibility.

7 The Schengen Agreement, named after the town in Luxembourg where it was signed in June 1985, originally included just five states, France, Germany and the Benelux countries, which had opted to move ahead of other EC states in removing their internal frontiers. The five signed the Schengen Convention in 1990; the Convention, which came into force in 1995, 'lays down the arrangements and guarantees for implementing freedom of movement' (*http://www.europa.eu.int/scadplus/leg/en/cig/g4000s.htm*). All other EU states apart from the UK and Ireland have subsequently signed up to the Schengen *acquis*, as have two non-EU states, Iceland and Norway.

will be an EU-level responsibility and need to manage borders, those with Ukraine, Kaliningrad (Russia) and Belarus being primary concerns.[8]

This is a central issue because just as the old borders of the EU created a frontier with those countries that have became candidates for membership of an enlarging Union, so the new borders will create new frontiers. A review of the EU's development since the end of the Cold War reveals that some of the Union's borderlands on the continent have become 'frontiers'.[9] To introduce the notion of a 'frontier' is to nuance the discussion of borders. It means not only that the border is relevant for that which it marks in terms of inclusion and exclusion but also that it is a point that can be crossed and can lead to further expansion. This condition highlights the importance of borders of member states that are also borders of the EU in policy and security terms, but it also requires understanding the border conceptually.

The distinction between borders and frontiers is that the latter are somehow going somewhere, suggesting that there is territory already covered but that the limit is perhaps fuzzy and not definitive. It is not a fixed border to be crossed, a line where an individual is on one side of it or the other. Germany in its relations with Poland, especially since the latter's membership of NATO in 1999, offers an example. Both countries have an interest in the border area between Belarus and Lithuania and have looked at ways of managing the movement of people. The European Commission has paid considerable attention to the borders between Poland and both Lithuania and Belarus. The nature of this attention has been to secure the Polish border against illegal activities along and across it, involving organized crime and the smuggling of both humans and goods (including drugs). The reason for assisting in firming up this border is that, as Poland's borders with Germany to the west are made more open, its borders to the east will become those of the Union as whole and will have to fulfil the requirements of the Schengen Agreement. However, when the eastern Polish border becomes that of the EU, it may also become a frontier (Ukraine at least has expressed a desire to accede to the EU).

Another example is provided by Estonia and those parts of the Russian Federation on which it borders. It is not feasible to create there the type of border that Spain has with Morocco at the former's sovereign territories of Ceuta and Melilla, with big walls and barbed wire, fortifications and a large

---

8 For discussion of the cases of Kaliningrad and Ukraine, see respectively Chapter 8 by Christopher Preston and Chapter 5 by Kataryna Wolczuk and Roman Wolczuk in this volume.

9 For a discussion of frontiers and other parts of the lexical set associated with borders, see Noel Parker, 'Integrated Europe and its "Margins": Action and Reaction', in Noel Parker and Bill Armstrong (eds), *Margins in European Integration* (Basingstoke: Macmillan, 2000).

no-man's land, because a key objective in the Baltic region is to carry forward the logic of security through inclusion, cooperation and trade. It is within this logic that further enlargement introduces new frontiers, new points at which the de-emphasis of borders (even if not at the level of Schengen) might be relevant for enhancing security.

Although there have been attempts to create hard borders in terms of formal controls, the strategic logic underpinning enlargement, partnership and the emphasis on broad security and stabilization is that this cannot be done in a meaningful way. In each local situation, there is a frontier that has particular local characteristics. For instance, while Slovenia has been going through association with and prospective membership of the EU, its long-standing arrangements with Italy regarding the mixed cross-border populations have had to be taken into account. In other places, there are exchanges between communities that create local dynamics and imperatives whose logic makes it virtually impossible to fix a hard border. Even where Spain and the EU have tried to do that with Ceuta and Melilla, all that has been achieved is a big impediment that slows down the pace of cross-border activity but does not stop it. On the European continent such borders would surely not be sustainable.

The border between EU candidates and non-candidates is bound to be complex. As noted in the introduction to this chapter, there can be no direct and simple approach to this issue. The strategic and security rationales that underpin both the EU and its enlargement indicate that the EU would be well advised to devise its own equivalent to NATO's PfP. Such an arrangement should be of an 'in-between' type, very different from, say, existing Partnership and Cooperation Agreements (PCAs). It would foster stability by creating a framework for outsiders who wish to have a closer relationship with the Union and for whom the partnership arrangement would make them feel that little bit nearer to being insiders. The essence is to create a partnership arrangement that serves to turn the EU inside out, by bringing the outside at least part of the way in.[10]

---

10 It is unlikely that one simple design can be fashioned quickly to provide for all needs. There must be an overall aspiration and framework, but evolution will more likely be incremental and organic. One of the common problems in many discussions about the Union's deepening and widening, as well as about the possibility of transferring its experience to other contexts (southeastern Europe or the Black Sea region, for example), seems to be the assumption that somehow it was already the way it is now when it began, or at least that the clear template was there. In reality, of course, the history of the EU shows that although some kind of vision was necessary, the Union itself actually emerged one step at a time – from one multilateral agreement on coal and steel to other bilateral and multilateral agreements, and then to the complexities of security and defence policy.

STABILITY AND THE FRONTIERS OF EUROPE: INCLUDING THE EXCLUDED?

Overlapping borders, frontiers, concerns and activity will foster European security at all points of the compass, creating both 'insiders' and 'outsiders'. It is possible to identify five categories of outsider. The first and most important of these comprises the western Balkans: the war-affected lands of what was the Federal Republic of Yugoslavia, including the former Yugoslav Republic of Macedonia, and also Albania, which was not part of the Yugoslav federation. Both NATO and the EU made a substantial commitment to seeking an end to the Yugoslav war. This created such an enormous strategic stake for both Brussels-based organizations that success is vital – and for both, one major measure of that success will be the degree to which these countries emerging from conflict are brought into the fold as partners and, quite probably, eventually as members. There remain issues to be resolved, even if there is no major return to armed hostilities. The prospect of partnership with the EU and of eventual accession, as well as cooperation and partnership with NATO, is vital to carrying forward that process. The strategic stake placed on that region is such that there can be no acceptance of failure. But nor can there be any expectation of early success for NATO or the EU. If they cannot pull it off, both organizations will be fundamentally weakened. Failure would be a sign of their limitations and weaknesses, which would in turn presage a falling away of attachment to the ideas that bind them together. That means making a full and proper commitment to creating polities and societies which are fit for cooperation with and possibly membership of NATO and the EU. A key question is how long these bodies will take to do it, bearing in mind that they can afford to take a very long time but cannot afford to extend the process indefinitely if their credibility is to be retained.

It is important to point out that engagement in the area has not been NATO's only mission since the end of the Cold War; no one should underestimate the importance of Partnership for Peace in terms of security and stability throughout Europe. Without Partnership for Peace, there could have been other Croatias and Bosnias in other parts of Europe. PfP's role was significant as it brought NATO into a relationship with those countries – and with it a political–security connection – and had a stabilizing effect. This, as well as the complementary activities of the EU and OSCE, helped to foster stability in what was an uncertain situation.

This important dimension of partnership is central also to NATO's and the EU's achieving success in their major peace implementation operations in southeastern Europe. Success cannot imply withdrawal: NATO is not going to withdraw; it cannot afford to do so, nor can the EU. However, the point will come when the commitment is transformed from being one of peace implementation, acting against parties obstructing the peace process or stepping out of line, to one of partnership. This conforms with the whole thrust of NATO since the early 1990s. It would be a general benefit if the key mission of the EU were to bring in the war-affected countries of south-eastern Europe and make them partners, worthy collaborators, rather than recalcitrant, awkward, challenging recidivists.

Two other southeast European states, Romania and Bulgaria, both of which are on track for EU and NATO membership, plus a third, Moldova, which does not look likely to become a member of either organization in the foreseeable future, form the second category. Bulgaria and Romania were, as noted, invited to join the NATO Alliance at its Prague summit in November 2002, and the EU has accepted their target date of 2007 for their EU membership. Thus they are now close to being 'insiders'. Although Moldova, a former Soviet territory, is set to remain an 'outsider' it is linked to Romania across a common border, and also shares a focus on the Black Sea. Notwithstanding its internally divided territorial and security situation, Moldova has many characteristics similar to Romania and Bulgaria. It has a security problem with Transdniestr that strongly marks it as a former Soviet state rather than as one of the former communist central and east European states.[11] Because Bulgaria and Romania are to become European insiders and Moldova cannot be included in the same way, Moldova will occupy a peculiar shadowy place: it will simultaneously be linked to an 'insider' but destined to be clustered with a range of other former Soviet states for which there is no obvious opportunity to join the Euro-Atlantic family.

Ukraine constitutes a category of outsider on its own and is perhaps one of the biggest challenges to NATO and the EU. In southeastern Europe the broad way forward is clear: its states are already within the Euro-Atlantic embrace and their status is likely to be transformed into partnership and ultimate membership. The route map regarding Ukraine is far less clear. It is the one country that is regarded as large and important, requiring attention, but for which no defined approach has been found. Its relationship to Russia cannot be ignored, but that relationship should not dominate Western understanding and interpretations of Ukraine and its position. Given its size, human resources, communications, and agricultural and industrial capacity (albeit with a need to modernize), it really ought to be like France or Germany. It is one of the greatest failures of the post-Cold War era that neither the Ukrainians themselves nor outsiders have been, or appear likely to be, able to turn the country round and nurture its potential.

11 For further discussion of the links between Romania and Moldova, see Chapter 6 by Gabriel Partos in this volume.

The European Union, as a security community and in view of its role in fostering stability across the continent, is going to have to consider Ukraine in a special way. This is something Ukraine recognizes in its demands but does little to justify, causing much frustration among EU and NATO representatives. It might well be that only an explicit promise of eventual membership of the EU or NATO, subject to Ukraine's fulfilling the appropriate criteria, would be enough to spur Kiev on to achieve objectives such as improved application of laws that are more or less agreed across the political spectrum. Although there are 'Soviet' sympathies in segments of the population, although the integrated Soviet legacy in some (notably economic) respects cannot be overlooked and although Moscow sometimes casts the shadow of a possessive jilted lover (making Kiev uncomfortable), these elements cannot be taken to define Ukraine. Its underlying orientation is towards the West and towards Europe, even where some legacies of the Soviet era remain and some elements in central and eastern Ukraine still turn politically and socially more to Russia.

It is clear that following the eastward enlargement of the EU and NATO Europe will find a frontier with Ukraine, one that should not become a barrier. Ukraine should not be left as a total outsider, as this would undermine both its internal and its external stability. Thus, there will be no alternative to embracing Kiev and seeking to assure its future as an 'insider-outsider'. Perhaps just as NATO established a special relationship with Ukraine, the EU might arrange a particular partnership arrangement rather than an unambitious PCA. In this context,[12] Britain's Foreign Secretary Jack Straw has introduced proposals for Belarus, Moldova and Ukraine that would offer 'special neighbour' status. While this approach might be embraced by an EU initiative, creating a PCA-plus status for those countries, it is likely that more would be required to accommodate Ukraine's singular status.[13]

The fourth category of outsider state is Russia, with which, given the relative goodwill of President Vladimir Putin, cooperation is possible, notwithstanding the fact that there is a considerable part of Russia lying behind that bright face which may not be so well disposed towards the West for a long time to come. Relations with NATO have been put on a new footing with the creation of the NATO–Russia Council in May 2002, the so-called 'NATO at Twenty', but it is not yet clear whether this will mark a

12 This part of the analysis has benefited from the insightful advice of Clelia Rontoyanni at RIIA.

13 The PCA-plus arrangement might include measures such as greater cross-border cooperation, the setting of conditions for moving towards a free-trade area and perhaps a visa-free zone and engagement with EU scientific, technical and educational programmes. All of these could constitute semi-membership of the EU, in line with the arrangements of the European Economic Area.

fundamental change. Russia will have new borders with the Baltic states, as will the Kaliningrad exclave with Poland. The question of Kaliningrad will probably need to be dealt with jointly, cooperatively and multilaterally as an aspect of Lithuania's prospective accession to NATO.[14]

The NATO–Russia Council provides a significant forum for the type of cooperation that might be required. But if it is to have any real significance over the medium and long term, the problems that dogged its predecessor – the Joint Permanent Council, established in 1997 (ironically, not so permanent) – and most other aspects of Western cooperation with Moscow on security affairs will need to be overcome. There was both a lack of engagement and distrust on Russia's part, with the latter causing the former to some extent. With many in the Moscow security sector still affected by Cold War attitudes, it was often impossible to gain even negative responses to Western initiatives. Sceptical Russian attitudes were strongly affected by a sense of betrayal over Kosovo in 1999. Those attitudes determined Moscow's approach, which saw NATO as no more than a mirror of the old Warsaw Pact and read relations both in and with the Alliance accordingly. Only Washington counted; the other allies were perceived to be mere puppets.[15] Once there was distrust of the United States – which was cemented the moment Moscow realized that the Joint Permanent Council would not give it a real say in what NATO did – this body, as well as broad cooperation on security, evaporated.

In this context, there was significant space for the EU to develop relations with Russia. But whatever small progress was made was transformed by 11 September. The attacks on New York and Washington provided an immediate and somewhat revolutionary catalyst not only in America's perceptions of the world but crucially in its relationship with Moscow. Primarily in the intelligence sphere, there was a breakthrough in contacts and the sharing of information between Moscow and Washington. This put the focus back more than ever on the US–Russia relationship. NATO was a notable context for that relationship, and had some significance in terms of the NATO–Russia Council (although in a sense Moscow sees even that as a bilateral relationship, not as 19 plus 1). As a consequence, especially in the absence of any particular, meaningful or coherent EU policy towards Russia, Brussels has become relatively unimportant for Russia, leaving a major strategic gap for the EU and perhaps also for Moscow. If the EU were to

14 For further discussion of EU–Russian relations, see Chapter 7 by Graeme Herd in this volume; for further discussion of the relationship between Poland, Lithuania and Kaliningrad, see Chapter 8 by Christopher Preston.
15 This analysis is based on a variety of interviews, almost all confidential, with both Russian and Western officials.

deepen and develop its security policy, a strategic partnership with Russia, or at least a strategic initiative towards it, would be needed – and something of this kind would be required simply to deal with the relationship across the new EU–Russia borders established by the Union's enlargement.

The only way in which the EU could establish a mature relationship with Moscow would be through establishing clear boundaries to its scope, and clear and harmonious policies. Otherwise, apart from ensuring further cash injections (which can be expected to come anyway), the EU and its member states (with the exception of some in a NATO context) would not be taken seriously by Moscow. Aspects of a clearly defined agenda might include a commitment to incorporate Turkey eventually and to stake out the EU's role in the Caucasus, making clear to Moscow its major commitment to fostering a stable and secure environment.

The issues of engagement in the Caucasus, and complements to any US or NATO military initiatives there, lead to the final category of countries, the three former Soviet Caucasus countries of Georgia, Armenia and Azerbaijan. The arrival of 290 US military personnel in Georgia at the end of February 2002 as part of an American commitment to train Georgian troops to hunt al-Qaeda-linked groups said to be in the country was a significant marker in the context of the boundaries of European and international security. Until then, these former Soviet states had been regarded as being within Russia's sphere of influence and hegemony: Russian forces were already pursuing Chechen armed groups (associated with the al-Qaeda-affiliated groups), violating Georgia's sovereignty. This was altered by the arrival of US troops. They broke a taboo – troops from a NATO country were trespassing on the ghost of the Soviet Union and the shadow of its Russian successor. Breaking this taboo was an outrage to many in Russia, with ideas of Moscow's near abroad infringed. However, President Putin showed greater cool and diplomacy than others in Moscow by welcoming the initiative to temper international 'Islamist' terrorism, thus giving the signal to others over what the party line should be.[16]

This could mark an initial step towards increasing NATO and EU involvement in Georgia. The strategic logic involved is fairly simple: if

16 The use of 'Islamist' indicates a particular ideology claiming to derive from the teachings of the Prophet Muhammed. It reflects a particularly narrow view of Islam, politics and the world in which modernity is a corrupting force and in which the representatives of modernity – including Muslims contaminated by it – are enemies. This ideology is distinguished from Islam broadly, which, as with other religions or international social movements, has much variety within it. Adoption of the ideology does not necessarily connote a commitment to political violence, such as using terrorist means. Moreover, those who do adopt violent means are only a minority among those who accept this radical version of the faith.

cooperation between US and Russian forces emerged in Georgia, then in order to ensure that a positive relationship is cemented, engagement by the United States would need to continue and be enhanced, including through involvement of its NATO allies and partners as well as through complementary measures by the EU. If this went wrong, then, equally, there would be an imperative to remain engaged, not to concede the Western interest in Georgian security and return to the *status quo ante*, which would be regarded as a victory for forces in Moscow hostile to good relations with the West. Even after enlargement the West's sphere of influence as defined primarily by NATO and the EU will not yet stretch as far as Tbilisi, the Georgian capital. There will ultimately have to be limits of some kind to Euro-Atlantic enlargement, but even when those limits are clear, there will still be a need to foster conditions of peace, security and stability beyond them.

CONCLUSION

There can be no doubt that the same issues of stability and security that impelled enlargement of the EU and NATO will be present across their new borders, wherever they are. Moreover, the EU's reluctance to commit itself to further enlargement means that a prospect which has helped to encourage transition and stability in the more westerly former communist states has been at best only a dim beacon for those farther east. The sense of 'inside' and 'outside', already strong for countries engaged in accession talks with the EU and looking to membership of the Alliance, will be reinforced as the boundary of 'Europe' as a geographical, political and security space moves east. The possibility discussed earlier, of the new border's becoming an open frontier, should be explored. This exploration should take place against the backdrop of the need of those inside both to preserve their internal strength by not spreading themselves too thinly and to protect themselves on the outside by promoting democratic transition, economic and social stability, and security. There can be no simple and direct approach to this issue. But, as argued above, the security rationale and strategic logic that have underpinned both the origins of the EU and its repeated enlargement indicate that political values and security, as well as geography, define the scope and limits of the extension of EU influence; and this process is necessarily tied closely to similar processes for NATO, where the difference is the Alliance's Partnership for Peace Programme. It may well be that the EU will need to devise its own equivalent of this scheme, which fosters stability by creating a framework for 'outsiders' who wish to have a closer relationship with it and to feel nearer to being 'insiders'.

5

Poland's relations with Ukraine: A challenging 'strategic partnership'

KATARYNA WOLCZUK AND ROMAN WOLCZUK

Following the collapse of communism in eastern Europe, Poland was determined to ensure its security by joining NATO and then the European Union. This security doctrine was not focused solely on membership of these key Western institutions, however. In order to avoid ending up as a NATO–EU outpost, Warsaw has also sought to foster the emergence of a friendly and stable neighbourhood on its eastern border, most notably with Ukraine.[1] In more strategic terms, Poland has sought to avoid the emergence of divisions between 'ins' and 'outs' in the EU and the NATO enlargement processes by trying to keep Ukraine involved.

As well as being motivated by security considerations, Poland's interest in and commitment to territories to the east are inspired by long-standing historical ties with these former borderlands (*Kresy*) that had been lost to the benefit of the Soviet Union when Poland's borders were shifted westwards in the settlements which followed the Second World War. As a result, a significant chunk of Poland's national heritage is located beyond its borders, in Ukraine, Belarus and Lithuania. In addition, sizeable Polish minorities are also domiciled there. This symbiotic link with the *Kresy* was encapsulated by the former minister of foreign affairs Bronislaw Geremek, who suggested that 'We are the West with roots in the East.'[2]

For Ukraine, ties with Poland represent a 'way to Europe'. While bilateral ties with Poland are important in themselves, in that close political and social relations are a means of counteracting the overwhelming effects of ties with Russia, they also offer far more ambitious prospects. Policy-makers in Kiev guessed early on that sooner rather than later Poland would be incorporated into the socio-economic system of the West via membership of

---

1 For a more detailed overview of Polish–Ukrainian relations in the context of EU enlargement, see Kataryna Wolczuk and Roman Wolczuk, *Poland and Ukraine: A Strategic Partnership in a Changing Europe?* (London: Royal Institute of International Affairs, 2002).

2 Cited in Roman Szporluk, 'Poland, Europe, and Ukraine's New Geography: "With the Russians or Poles?"', *The Day* (Kiev), 2 February 1999.

NATO and the European Union. Thus, ties with Poland were potentially Ukraine's key to 'entry' into Europe, or so Kiev hoped. Unlike Belarus and Russia, Ukraine declared EU membership to be its long-term strategic objective as early as 1996. The potential for synergy between Ukraine and Poland was apparent as a strategic partnership between the two countries began to emerge in the second half of the 1990s.

This chapter will explore the essential contours of Polish–Ukrainian relations, starting with an outline of the extent to which their troubled history continues to cast a pall over their bilateral relations. It will be seen that despite the significant and noteworthy progress made in improving relations following Ukrainian independence in 1991, the international environment was not, in the main, conducive to the evolution of a strategic partnership. The chapter will also explore the extent to which Poland's aspirations to EU membership effectively placed insurmountable barriers in the way of partnership, most particularly in the form of the Schengen Agreement. The self-inflicted nature of Ukraine's marginal status makes the contrast between Poland as a potential insider and Ukraine as an outsider with little prospect of EU membership all the more stark. Despite Poland's best efforts, Ukraine was unwilling or unable to implement the kind of political and economic reforms that would have made it a credible contender for membership of the European 'clubs'. (Indeed, in many respects, Ukraine went backwards in terms of reform in the 1990s.) However, in conclusion it will be argued that in the longer term, Poland's opportunity to shape the EU's eastern policy may compensate for its inability to influence the pace of Ukraine's domestic transformation.

STRATEGIC PARTNERSHIP: DESPITE OR BECAUSE OF HISTORY?

Poland has a strong emotional attachment to its *Kresy*. It was, after all, the *Kresy* which spawned pre-eminent Polish cultural figures, including two romantic poets, Juliusz Slowacki (in Ukraine) and Adam Mickiewicz (in Belarus), and the twentieth-century writer and Nobel prize winner Czeslaw Milosz (born in Lithuania). Ukraine in particular features prominently in Polish historiography. Despite the myth of Ukraine as an idyllic land of freedom and tolerance, Poland's ties with it are marred by a long history of conflict. More recently, in the early twentieth century the territories of today's southeastern Poland and western Ukraine were the scene of violent clashes between Poles and Ukrainians as the two peoples struggled for control over the historically mixed territories. Against this backdrop, in 1991 the fostering of close interstate relations between Poland and Ukraine seemed unlikely:

Until recently, everything divided them: national aspirations, territorial claims, national stereotypes and memory of the wrongs done to each other. It is of no consequence which of these peoples, at which moment in history, was more to blame for that state of affairs. Their history made conflicts inevitable.[3]

Nevertheless, while the changes on the European continent between 1989 and 1991 have inspired Polish elites to establish relations with independent Ukraine on new, more amicable terms, at the societal level memories continue to set the peoples against each other. In Poland a negative stereotype of Ukrainians prevails which continues to influence Polish national mythology, especially at the popular level. The postwar loss of the *Kresy* resulted from Soviet collusion with the West in an act of geopolitical *Realpolitik*. Yet it is Ukrainian nationalists, driven to eradicate the presence of Poles on Ukrainian territory, who remain the main villains in Polish eyes. The memories of wartime atrocities perpetrated against Poles by Ukrainians run deep in Poland.[4] The image of the Ukrainian as the mortal enemy of the Pole has been perpetuated in vivid accounts of suffering inflicted on the innocent Polish population by the ruthless Ukrainian Insurgent Army in the latter years of the war. Half a century later, manifest anti-Ukrainianism in the southeastern city of Przemysl demonstrated the continued difficulties of ethnic coexistence between Ukrainians and Poles following the eradication of multiculturalism which took place in Poland after the war. Similarly, across the border in western Ukraine, Poland's cruel domination and harsh policies *vis-à-vis* Ukrainians in the years leading up to the Second World War were not forgotten. Indeed so vivid were those memories that Polish demands in the 1990s to restore sites that form the backbone of the Polish cultural heritage in this region were met with fury by Ukrainians. This was despite the efforts of Kiev to attenuate the more vocal elements in Lviv, a key city in former Poland and the birthplace of Ukrainian nationalism. In sum, real reconciliation has yet to take place at the societal level.

Despite these difficulties, the Polish political class was eager to leave the past behind and open a new chapter in Polish–Ukrainian relations. 'Ukraine as an ally' turned into a paradigm for the Polish intellectual and political elites and came to form the basis for Polish foreign policy towards the East in the second half of the 1990s. However, in the first half of the decade things were less clear-cut between the future allies.

---

3 Antoni Z. Kaminski and Jerzy Kozakiewicz, *Polish-Ukrainian Relations 1992–1996: Report* (Warsaw: Centre for International Relations at the Institute of Public Affairs, 1997), p. 5.
4 For an overview of the difficulties in the Ukrainian–Polish historical reconciliation see Wolczuk and Wolczuk, *Poland and Ukraine*, pp. 29–46.

THE POLISH–UKRAINIAN STRATEGIC PARTNERSHIP

Until 1994–5, Poland's relations with Ukraine were characterized by declarations and formalities rather than by a real commitment to partnership.[5] Poland was just too concerned with instability emanating from the east and with the potential Russian response to a genuine Polish–Ukrainian *rapprochement* to put relations with Ukraine at the top of its list of priorities. However, by 1995 Poland's internal and external environments had changed sufficiently to allow it to pay more attention to ties with Ukraine, especially as Warsaw's prospect of NATO membership started to gain credibility.

Developments in and around Ukraine greatly facilitated this task. Ukraine ceased to be a pariah in the international community following its accession to the Non-Proliferation Treaty and the signing of the Trilateral Agreement (along with Russia and the United States) in 1994. Ukraine also considerably attenuated its opposition to NATO enlargement, the trade-off being that Warsaw helped to ameliorate Kiev's relations with Western institutions.

All of the above was highly desirable to Poland. As far as Warsaw was concerned, Ukraine's marginalization was hardly in Poland's interests, as it merely increased the likelihood that Ukraine would again gravitate towards Russia. It is this which explains Poland's 'special' interest in Ukraine. In the words of its President, Aleksander Kwasniewski, 'It is Poland's joint responsibility to strengthen the sovereignty, independence and economic development of Ukraine.'[6] Warsaw thus sought to develop an *Ostpolitik* that put Ukraine at the heart of what Poland was trying to achieve along its eastern border – a stable, friendly, *pro-European* neighbourhood. The high point of the strategic partnership was probably reached in summer 1997, when, thanks to close cooperation between the two states, Poland received an invitation to join the North Atlantic Alliance while Ukraine signed a Charter on a Distinctive Partnership with the Alliance.[7] If anything, after this success Warsaw became even more intent on 'dragging' Ukraine westwards (i.e. trying to 'Europeanize' Ukraine and bring about its membership of Western institutions), in line with its aim of avoiding ending up as the bulwark of Europe.

---

5 Roman Wolczuk, 'Ukrainian–Polish Relations between 1991 and 1998: From the Declaratory to the Substantive', *European Security*, Vol. 9, No. 1, Spring 2000, pp. 127–56.

6 *Gazeta Wyborcza* (Warsaw), 16–17 January 1999.

7 The significance of the Charter was to avoid Ukraine's isolation as NATO and Russia drew closer together. However, two prime issues stand out. First, it moved the two sides' relations beyond the standard Partnership for Peace programme, thereby institutionalizing Ukraine–NATO relations at a higher level. Perhaps more importantly, the Charter was designed to reinforce relations between the two parties at a time when NATO–Russia relations were themselves becoming more institutionalized. See Roman Wolczuk, *Ukraine's Foreign and Security Policy 1991–2002* (New York and London: RoutledgeCurzon, forthcoming 2003).

Political, economic and security cooperation

The main way in which Warsaw sought to Europeanize Ukraine after 1997 was by institutionalizing its political relationship with Ukraine, as a means of sharing its own experiences of an ostensibly successful transformation. A plethora of bilateral institutions was created, although few of them lived up to expectations. The Consultative Committee of the Presidents of Poland and Ukraine has been by far the most active of these institutions. The Polish–Ukrainian Inter-Governmental Coordinating Council for Inter-Regional Cooperation (set up in 1993 and expanded in 1999 to include transborder cooperation) was overwhelmed by the task of coordinating no fewer than 17 bodies on the Ukrainian side and nine on the Polish side, all of which deal with border issues; it was dormant until 2002. Another initiative, the Polish–Ukrainian Forum, established as a means of strengthening contacts between Polish and Ukrainian political parties, cultural and civic associations and community groups, took two years to convene after the idea was accepted in principle in 1994. At the time of writing it had failed to fulfil its mission.[8]

In autumn 1998, Bronislaw Geremek, the Polish foreign minister, announced the creation of the Standing Polish–Ukrainian Conference on European Integration.[9] The Conference sought to support Ukraine's aspirations for participation in European integration and to share with Ukraine Poland's experience of transformation. By 2001 four meetings had taken place. In the field of military cooperation, the creation of a joint Polish–Ukrainian battalion (POLUKRBAT), which was subsequently deployed in former Yugoslavia, was a highly symbolic act in the light of the animosity that had prevailed between the two societies within living memory. This will be examined in more detail later.

In contrast to political and military cooperation, economic ties have not developed strongly. Ukraine is only Poland's ninth largest trading partner (in 2001, their trade was worth $1.48 billion, $1 billion of which came from Polish exports),[10] first, because of Poland's efforts to redirect its trade towards the West and, secondly, because of Ukraine's protracted economic crisis, which massively diminished its attractiveness for any foreign investors. The expansion of economic ties has been largely confined to informal cross-border trade. Indeed, so successful has been this shuttle trade by 'tourists' from the east that it contributed to Poland's being listed among the world's top ten tourist destinations in 1997.[11]

---

8 Kaminski and Kozakiewicz, *Polish–Ukrainian Relations 1992–1996: Report,* p. 39.
9 Speech by Polish Foreign Minister Bronislaw Geremek, at Polish European meetings, Polish Robert Schuman Foundation, Warsaw, May 1999.
10 *Elektroni Visti* (Kiev), 4 June 2002.
11 For further discussion of shuttle trade, see Chapter 2 by Alan Smith in this volume.

Regional and cross-border cooperation

In addition to state-level ties, regional and cross-border cooperation has been growing steadily since Ukraine's independence, although it is still regarded by Poland as insufficient. This is hardly surprising, as such ties had to be built from scratch after the collapse of the Soviet Union. Direct cross-border contacts between Soviet Ukraine and Poland had been virtually non-existent: they were prevented by an 'iron curtain' which existed even between states *within* the Soviet bloc. In order to kick-start cross-border cooperation, two major initiatives were undertaken: the Bug Euroregion, which also involved Belarus, and the Carpathian Euroregion, which also comprised Romania, Slovakia and Hungary.[12] The Euroregions did not live up to initial expectations in terms of fostering Polish–Ukrainian links, mainly because of a lack of finance. Nevertheless, they were beneficial in that they contributed, for example, to the establishment of direct links between regional and local government bodies, thereby helping to eliminate the legacies of hostility and communist-era isolation. Other forms of cooperation included academic exchanges and the proposed establishment of a Polish–Ukrainian university in Lublin, modelled on the German–Polish university, Viadrina, in Frankfurt on the Oder.

In the non-governmental sector, Polish NGOs have been keen to utilize their expertise and act as 'guides' for Western NGO initiatives in Ukraine. In contrast to Poland where it is already established, Ukrainian civil society is weakly developed and hence is deemed to be a priority. A key development in this regard is the Poland–America–Ukraine Cooperation Initiative (PAUCI). It is funded by the US government and aims to promote cross-border ties, especially in business and local government.

In addition, at the popular level Ukrainians and Poles have taken advantage of the newly gained freedom of movement, which was denied to them under communism. In 1997, the volume of traffic across the Polish–Ukrainian border reached nearly 16 million people. The numbers dropped to 9.5 million in 1998 as a result of the deleterious effects on Ukraine of the economic crisis in Russia, although they subsequently recovered somewhat. These figures reflected the economic interdependence which resulted from the opening of the border and which was driven by the substantial price and wage disparities between the economies on either side of the border. It is estimated that 95 per cent of border crossings have an economic purpose.

---

12 Euroregions are institutional forms of transborder cooperation designed to benefit communities living in border region areas. Benefits include support for regional development, trade and economic development, protection of the environment, cultural cooperation, promotion of tourism and education and so forth.

International 'advocacy'

In addition to numerous bilateral initiatives, Poland has acted as Ukraine's 'advocate' in international organizations and institutions such as the EU, NATO, the Council of Europe and the Central European Initiative. For example, prior to the EU's Helsinki summit in December 1999, Poland lobbied for a stronger commitment from the EU to Ukraine than that offered in the Union's 'Common Strategy on Ukraine'. Indeed, the latter is seen in Warsaw as an inadequate and misconceived instrument. Poland has been quite vocal in this regard, with Kwasniewski joining Ukraine's President Kuchma in criticizing the West's policy towards Ukraine.[13] Not only has Poland been Ukraine's advocate in the West, it has also shown itself to be willing to act as the ambassador of the West in Ukraine. It is claimed in Poland that during the various political crises which have engulfed Ukraine since 2000 – for example, the Gongadze affair, in which Georgiy Gongadze, a journalist who was highly critical of the regime, was killed, allegedly with government involvement, and the reformist prime minister Yushchenko was removed from office – President Kwasniewski has a mandate from Germany and France to act as their spokesman with the Ukrainian president.

Poland's sense of importance in this matter is particularly buoyed up by the coincidence of its own and US interests in Ukraine – in acknowledgment of Ukraine's geopolitical importance for stability in Europe, the country was certainly one of Washington's top international priorities before the events of 11 September 2001. Common interest in Ukraine is also cited as one of the reasons for Poland's commitment to strong US engagement in Europe, primarily through NATO.

Inevitably, Poland's advocacy of Ukraine has impacted on its relations with Russia in that it was perceived to have interfered with the latter's interests in the 'near abroad'. In a reversal of policy of the early years following the collapse of the Soviet Union, Poland has come to subordinate relations with Russia to those with Ukraine. (However, since the election of a left-wing government in Poland in 2001, this Ukraine-first policy is being increasingly questioned.[14]) The most explicit example of this has been Warsaw's shared interest with Kiev in the construction of the Odesa–Gdansk oil pipeline for the transportation of Caspian oil, something which is contrary to the interests of Russia. Indeed, in 2000 Poland refused a Russian proposal to construct a gas pipeline across Poland bypassing Ukraine, on the

13 *Gazeta Wyborcza* (Warsaw), 16–17 January 1999.
14 See *Rzeczpospolita* (Warsaw), 8 July 2002.

grounds that it would harm Ukraine's economic interests. Although Poland, somewhat disappointed by Ukraine's ambivalence on the issue, owing to conflicting domestic interests, subsequently softened its stance, it continued to insist that Ukraine's interests must be taken into account if the pipeline were to be built. However, in another twist to the long-running saga, in 2002 Russia offered Ukraine incentives to 'come on side', probably in an effort to split the two partners.

LIMITS TO THE STRATEGIC PARTNERSHIP

Although positive declarations continued to be made on a regular basis, with the Polish and Ukrainian presidents keen to display *bonhomie*, after 1997 Poland became increasingly exasperated with Ukraine's recalcitrance in implementing meaningful reform and frustrated with its own inability to influence Ukraine. Inevitably, these difficulties reverberated in Kiev's relationship with the EU, which in turn meant that the latter became progressively less amenable to any proposals from Warsaw for Brussels to soften its line on Kiev. Each of these points will now be examined in more detail.

EU policies towards Ukraine

In institutional terms, by 2002 relations had developed little beyond the partnership and cooperation agreement (PCA) signed in 1994 but only ratified by the EU member states only in 1998. Yet Ukraine failed to adhere even to the demands of the relatively undemanding PCA. Indeed, it pursued a series of actions contrary to the conditions of the PCA (and contrary to the rules of the WTO, with which the PCA's conditions were harmonized). For example, Ukraine effectively reneged on its commitment to reduce protectionist measures when it introduced unjustified certification requirements for certain goods, as well as new tariffs and excise duties. The EU did not accept Ukraine's defence, that it introduced such measures to cope with its ongoing economic collapse and that massive under- and unemployment necessitated protection of the few domestic sectors that were still producing. From the EU's standpoint, relations with Ukraine were floundering because of Kiev's continued failure to introduce measures necessary for a functioning market economy: liberalization of prices and trade remains a distant goal and barriers to market entry and exit remain prominent. Property rights, laws and contractual obligations are far from transparent.

Ukraine's failure to appreciate the implications of the demands of the PCA and its rejection of the need to abide by laws and agreements to which it had voluntarily subjected itself have cost it dear.[15] As has been pointed out, 'Ukraine's political leaders have sometimes acted as if they could achieve integration by declaration, or simply by joining and participating in international organisational and political clubs rather than by undertaking concrete structural changes.'[16] Ukrainian policy-makers also miscalculated the damage a reversal of liberalization would do to Ukraine's wider objectives, namely membership of key international institutions such as the EU and the WTO. This in itself reflected flawed strategic reasoning, as accession to the WTO was seen as an end in itself rather than as part of a comprehensive economic policy, something which Ukraine still sorely lacked.[17] Thus Ukraine's insistence on an association agreement with the EU, which would suggest that the country was advancing along the road towards EU membership, remained an empty wish. Indeed, this was demonstrated prior to the Helsinki summit of 1999, when it became evident that Ukraine was not perceived as a potential candidate for membership. Instead, it was offered the insipid benefits of a 'Common Strategy on Ukraine'. As Ukraine's domestic political situation deteriorated in 2000 with the death of Georgiy Gongadze and the fall of the reformist Yushchenko government, it became clear that the EU's decision to maintain the status quo regarding Ukraine had been justified.

Difficulties in Polish–Ukrainian relations

By 2000, Warsaw had become acutely aware of its limited ability to facilitate the 'Europeanization' of Ukraine – it just did not have the means to influence Ukraine strongly enough. As the Polish analyst Zdzislaw Najder pointed out, the policy pursued towards Ukraine 'is mainly one of rhetoric … [as] the means at our disposal are very limited'.[18] The nature of the relationship was deeply unbalanced, particularly in terms of costs and benefits of expectations.[19] In crude terms, Poland was probably more concerned about Ukraine than Ukraine was about Poland.

There were a number of reasons for this imbalance. For a start, while western Ukraine was westward-looking, this was less true of central Ukraine

15 Oleksandr Pavliuk, *The European Union and Ukraine: The Need for a New Vision, Policy Paper Based on the Study on the Current State and Prospects of Relations Between the European Union and Ukraine* (Kiev: East–West Institute, 1999), p. 12.

16 James Sherr, *Ukraine's New Time of Troubles*, G67 (Camberley: Conflict Studies Research Centre, 1998), p. 12.

17 Ibid., p. 11.

18 'Polish Policy vis-à-vis Ukraine and How it is Perceived in EU Member States', transcript of a debate, Centre for International Relations, Warsaw, *Reports & Analyses*, Number 2/00, p. 7.

19 *Rzeczpospolita* (Warsaw), 8 November 2001.

and eastern Ukraine, which were oriented more towards Russia. In addition, Ukraine lacks the type of ties with Ukrainians in Poland that Poland has with its brethren in Ukraine. Furthermore, according to Najder, Polish–Ukrainian issues were not of symmetrical importance – Ukraine's strategic partnership with Poland mattered to a narrow political elite and to the politically aware in western Ukraine. Poland's objectives of 'Europeanizing' Ukraine mattered to the whole of Poland, a country which prided itself on its abhorrence of the Soviet Union and in particular of Russia, notwithstanding the pragmatism of Poland's foreign policy in the first years following the collapse of the Soviet Union. Ukrainian independence mattered, as it helped to preserve Poland's independence from Russia, but Poland had no correspondingly profound role in the eyes of Ukraine. In other words, 'Poland's future is tied to the future of Ukraine; the Ukrainians rarely suggest that their fate is tied to the fate of Poland', even if Poland could help to give Ukraine an *entreé* into Europe.[20] It is regarded as noteworthy in Poland that, whatever happens, Ukraine will have a safe western border, from which no threat is likely to emanate. Poland does not have the same feeling of comfort, believing that, despite being in NATO, it remains vulnerable to instability from the east.

In addition, Poland's relations with Ukraine, and its eastern policy generally, are complicated by two dilemmas. The first dilemma derives from the fact that in the successor states of the former Soviet Union, Russia remains the most important country and that the EU's relations with Ukraine seem to be conducted through the prism of relations with Russia. Adopting a similar Russia-first approach would give Poland the benefit of becoming a more credible partner in the formation of policy about relations between West and East and perhaps enable it to fulfil its aspirations to be 'a bridge between the East and West'.[21] Yet it is Ukraine's proclaimed European choice which makes it an obvious key partner for Poland, in contrast to Russia and Belarus, which do not voice such aspirations. It is for this reason that Poland's political class believes Ukraine's choice should be given proper recognition. However, this diversity of European aspirations among its eastern neighbours challenges and indeed undermines Poland's policy. This is because Poland has to reconcile two conflicting aims: '[the] first of them is a need for normalization of relations with Moscow. The second, in turn, is the need to support the further enlargement of NATO and EU, something which conflicts with the interests of Russia.'[22]

Poland's second dilemma, further compounding the situation, is the fact that although it remains focused on Ukraine, 'the pro-western orientation of

20 Ibid.
21 *Unia i Polska* (Warsaw), 10 July 2000, p. 19.
22 Idem.

Ukraine has never been met with open arms by Western leaders … it is not worth endangering relations with Putin'.[23] It is realized in Poland that its support of a pro-Western Ukraine is not necessarily looked upon favourably in the West. The Polish foreign policy elites are thus fundamentally at odds with those in the EU who maintain that there is no danger if Ukraine becomes more pro-Russian, as long as Russia itself remains stable. Poland has been forced to confront the fact that its advocacy of Ukraine's membership has not been well received in the EU and that it even risked damaging Poland's own EU aspirations. 'One may actually get the impression that Poland is ready to sacrifice its own strategic interest of EU membership to drag somebody [who] is actually unwilling to change or reform himself forcibly to the West.'[24]

In sum, by the end of the first decade of Ukrainian independence Polish opinion-makers had grown disillusioned with Ukraine, and there was the additional problem that Poland's aims *vis-à-vis* Ukraine conflicted with its aspirations *vis-à-vis* the EU. Nor was it evident how it could influence Ukraine, although it was becoming clear to Warsaw that if Poland were to facilitate the 'Europeanization' of Ukraine, it would have to do so via the EU, after having joined the Union's institutions. This would entail the combining of its eastern policy with its policy towards the EU.

POLAND'S ACCESSION TO THE EU: LONG-TERM OPPORTUNITIES
TO 'EUROPEANIZE' UKRAINE

Poland hopes that among the benefits of membership of the EU will be the possibility of influencing the formation of the EU's *Ostpolitik*, most of all in relations with Ukraine (this is a reciprocal process, in that the EU is already limiting the scope of Poland's own *Ostpolitik*). For example, accession will allow Poland to play a fuller role in defining the Common Foreign and Security Policy (CFSP) of the EU, in which Poland hopes to enjoy the support of other central and east European states that also have an interest in closer ties with Ukraine.

In a document published by the Polish Ministry of Foreign Affairs in June 2001, the Polish government reiterated its 'desire to contribute to the future Eastern policy of an enlarged European Union' on the understanding that 'there is every justification for enhancement of cohesion and coordination of EU external policy in respect of both the countries which will be sharing the EU's eastern border, as well as other states in the post-Soviet

---

23 Ibid., 14 May 2001, p. 23.
24 'Polish Policy *vis-à-vis* Ukraine', p. 4.

space'.[25] More specifically, the document stated that Poland views PCAs as inadequate for conducting relations with the EU's neighbours to the east after the Union's enlargement. It advocated supplementing them with 'direct neighbourhood instruments geared to solving specific problems'.[26] In anticipation of direct borders with countries such as Belarus and Ukraine, the EU began to develop a new, comprehensive policy towards its prospective new neighbours, as evidenced by the Communication from the Commission in March 2003.[27]

In addition, Warsaw hopes to help shape the European Security and Defence Policy in ways that would incorporate Ukraine. For example, Poland's joint battalion with Ukraine, POLUKRBAT, established on the basis of NATO standards and interoperability with the Alliance, could eventually form an important component of the European capability for out-of-area operations (within the scope of the Petersberg tasks adopted by the Western European Union in 1992, which comprise humanitarian and rescue activities, peacekeeping tasks, crisis-management and peacemaking). Indeed, the battalion has already served as a part of the Kosovo Stabilization Force (KFOR). In May 2001, Bronislaw Komorowski, the Polish defence minister, suggested to the EU that the Polish brigade, which will serve in the EU's rapid deployment force (to be operational in 2003), might include an entire Ukrainian battalion. However, until it joins the European Union, Poland's main difficulty lies in the gap between 'the declared foreign policy aims of the [Polish] government and its dialogue with the European Commission on the eastern dimension of CFSP'.[28]

SCHENGEN: A SHORT-TERM SETBACK IN THE PROJECT OF 'EUROPEANIZING' UKRAINE?

In the immediate future, however, Poland needs to deal with some potentially negative consequences for its relations with Ukraine in its preparations for EU accession. One of the institutional requirements of membership that

25 Ministry of Foreign Affairs, 'The Eastern Policy of the European Union in the run-up to the EU's enlargement to include the countries of Central and Eastern Europe – Poland's viewpoint', Warsaw, 2001, p. 7. A more detailed set of proposals was contained in the so-called 'non-paper'.

26 Ibid., p. 11.

27 'Wider Europe – Neighbourhood: A New Framework for Relations with Our Eastern and Southern Neighbours', Communication from the Commission to the Council and the European Parliament COM (2003) 104 Final, Brussels, 11 March 2003.

28 Zdzislaw Najder, 'Porozumienie w Schengen a Wschodni Sasiedzi Polski' [The Schengen Agreement and the Eastern Neighbours of Poland], in Jan Stanislaw Mis (ed.), *Polska Droga do Schengen. Opinie Ekspertow* [The Polish Road to Schengen: Experts' Opinions] (Warsaw: Instytut Spraw Publicznych, 2001), p. 76.

Poland had to adopt was the Schengen *acquis*, which stipulated the introduction of a visa regime for Ukrainian citizens. As a result, it is on the border between Poland and Ukraine that divergence between Warsaw's policies and the EU's policies *vis-à-vis* Ukraine have been apparent.

In preparation for membership, the applicant countries have undertaken the massive task of adopting the *acquis communautaire* of the EU. The export of the Schengen *acquis* has proved to be particularly problematic because of its nature. It aims to minimize risks to the internal security of the member states stemming from the abolition of internal border controls by adopting measures such as visa requirements, asylum policies, external border controls, and police and judicial cooperation.[29] However, by focusing on ensuring its 'internal security' the EU has decided to secure its external border irrespective of the impact this will have on the pattern of relations between states in central and eastern Europe. From the perspective of the EU, the external border is not only the frontier of the zone of internal security but also the interface with non-members such as Ukraine. As recently as 1999, some Polish officials hoped that visas would not have to be introduced for Ukraine. Only after being 'informed' of the political sensitivity of the issue for the member states did Polish officials bow to the inevitable. Thus, when Poland presented its position on the Justice and Home Affairs *acquis* in 2000, Polish negotiators did not ask for a transitional period. Under pressure from Brussels, in early 2002 Warsaw announced that Poland would introduce visas for Russia, Ukraine and Belarus in July 2003.

Yet Poland remained fearful that the construction of the Schengen 'paper curtain' on its eastern border would damage its efforts to 'Europeanize' Ukraine. Not only will the new Schengen border severely hamper any further intensification of ties between the two countries but the closure of the border after 10 years of openness, following 45 years of a closed, Soviet-style border, will also lead to Ukraine's exclusion at a time when its European choice remains subject to some doubt. Warsaw is afraid that, as a result, pro-Western forces in Ukraine, unable to justify a Western orientation, will be weakened. The effective closure of borders will fuel the already growing disillusionment with the West in Ukraine. For Ukrainians the promise of freedom at the end of the Cold War has been replaced by the prospect of a new 'round' of exclusion from Europe.

Undoubtedly, the introduction of a visa regime between Poland and Ukraine will spell the end of central and eastern Europe as a 'unique area of

---

29 Horst Krenzler and Kataryna Wolczuk, *EU Justice and Home Affairs in the Context of Enlargement*, Policy Paper No. 4, The Robert Schuman Centre for Advanced Studies, European University Institute, 2001, p. 3.

liberalized movement of people'.[30] In the decade after the fall of the Soviet Union, the region witnessed a remarkable spurt of a specific pattern of short-term migration that subsidized the income of citizens engaged in cross-border trade and casual employment. However, after Poland enters the EU, or, indeed, after the imposition of a visa regime, this type of economic activity will become more difficult. It is conceivable that those Ukrainians who finally manage to cross the western border and get into central Europe may simply continue onwards. Poland, cut off from the east, might cease to be a middle zone and instead become simply the periphery of the Union.[31]

The creation of a new dividing line in central and eastern Europe may also jeopardize the hard-won harmony between formerly antagonistic neighbours and could reverse the efforts to reduce socio-economic disparities between them. According to the Polish government, 'One of the most essential problems … is the asymmetry of economic and administrative development and of the actual condition of the infrastructure on both sides of the border, which can possibly fuel the widening of the developmental disproportions between the nations concerned and endanger the area's fragile economic and social equilibrium.'[32] In particular, Poland is fearful that the 'Schengen border' may come to symbolize a sharp division between the winners and losers in European integration. This fear is exacerbated by the potential for a negative spiral effect: keeping Ukrainians out, without opportunities to earn a living through short-term migration, would only increase the socio-economic gap between 'insiders' and 'outsiders' in the 'new Europe'. In turn, this would lead to an increase in migratory pressures, potentially leading to ever more rigorous measures to control population flows from Ukraine into the EU.[33]

In order to mitigate the impact of the wholesale imposition of Schengen standards on the Polish–Ukrainian border, Warsaw intended to introduce cheap and easily accessible visas (including multiple-entry ones) for Ukrainian citizens. In fact, driven by the belief in the benefits of the easy movement of people, in January 2003 Poland went as far as agreeing to offer free visas for Ukrainian citizens (Ukraine was to maintain a visa-free regime for Polish

30 Claire Wallace, 'The New Migration Space as a Buffer Zone?', in Claire Wallace and Dariusz Stola (eds), *Patterns of Migration in Central Europe* (Basingstoke, Macmillan: Palgrave, 2001), p. 82.

31 Dariusz Stola, 'Two Kinds of Quasi-Migration in the Middle Zone: Central Europe as a Space for Transit Migration and Mobility for Profit', in Wallace and Stola (eds), *Patterns of Migration in Central Europe*, pp. 101–2.

32 Ministry of Foreign Affairs, 'The Eastern Policy of the European Union', 2001, p. 9.

33 Grzegorz Gromadzki, 'Konsekwencje Polityczne Umowy z Schengen – problemem dla calej rozszerzonej Unii' [The Political Consequences of the Schengen Agreement – A Problem for the Whole Enlargement of the Union] in Jan Stanislaw Mis (ed.), *Polska Droga do Schengen i Opinie Ekspertow*, p. 42.

citizens). Ensuring easy access to visas is an immense undertaking. In 2002 over 12 million people, mostly Ukrainians, crossed the Polish–Ukrainian border. It has been estimated that the introduction of visas will reduce cross-border traffic by 40 per cent. Even if that were the case, Polish consulates in Ukraine would have to issue tens of thousands of visas daily. At present, the sparse Polish consular network in Ukraine is grossly inadequate for such an undertaking, lacking the necessary financial resources, personnel and organizational preparedness. Compounding the financial situation for Poland is the fact that while the beefing up of the security infrastructure of the border is essentially financed by the EU, any investment designed to improve the traffic flow through border crossings has to be financed by cash-strapped Poland. Despite these problems, Warsaw recognizes the benefits of imposing the Schengen regime on the Polish–Ukrainian border. The introduction of Schengen procedures will bring to an end 'undesirable practices' on both sides of the border, which is renowned for its long queues, inefficiency and corruption. At present, Polish border guards, when admitting Ukrainian citizens to Poland, exercise often arbitrary decision-making power, something which breeds a deep sense of humiliation among Ukrainian travellers. Thus the visas will introduce greater transparency and predictability for Ukrainians crossing the Poland–EU border, even if they will be inconvenient in terms of time and cost.

The consequences of introducing a visa regime for Ukraine will be felt in Poland as well as in Ukraine. 'Bazaar' trade makes an important contribution to the income of Poland's impoverished southeastern provinces, thus helping to offset the growing regional economic disparities within Poland. But as these border provinces have come to realize the importance of trade with the east for their economic situation, Warsaw is having to face up to internal discontent: while it is intent on EU membership, some in the eastern regions are in favour of maintaining an open border with Ukraine *in preference* to membership of the EU.[34] Warsaw counters that informal, 'suitcase' trade is a side effect of the economic discrepancies between Poland and Ukraine and that as such it will disappear once Ukraine emerges from its economic collapse. Nevertheless, Warsaw lacks a strategy about how to counterbalance the negative consequences of the loss of trade for the eastern provinces. It hopes that after accession EU structural funds will pour in and offset the worst effects of closing the border.

Poland is also faced with the problem of how to maintain links with the approximately 200,000–300,000 Poles who live in Ukraine. The links they currently have with Poland, which are vital for their cultural as well as

34 *Unia i Polska* (Warsaw), 1 May 2000, p. 7.

physical survival, will be hindered by the visa regime. In anticipation of this problem, the idea of a 'Polish Card' (*Karta Polaka*) was conceived. It was intended that the card would confer on the bearer (who would be a person of Polish extraction) the right to simplified border crossing and to free access to health services and educational facilities in Poland. However, given that throughout the former Soviet Union there are up to 2,000,000 people of Polish extraction who would have been entitled to this card and that such a huge number would place an unsustainable burden on the threadbare Polish budget, the proposal was rejected by the Polish parliament, the *Sejm*, in 2000.

CONCLUSION

Notwithstanding lingering animosities and tensions at the societal level, especially in the ethnic borderlands, Poland and Ukraine proclaimed a 'strategic partnership' in the 1990s. For Poland strong ties with Ukraine were important on a number of levels. On the one hand, by drawing Ukraine into the 'European orbit' Warsaw hoped to bring a degree of stability to the state on its eastern border. At the same time Poland sought to strengthen ties with its forcibly relinquished territories, where much of Poland's cultural heritage lies, along with a significant Polish minority. Poland very much depended on its knowledge and understanding of Ukraine conferring on it some form of 'competitive advantage' with the EU. This, it was hoped, might in turn reinforce its membership credentials.

Warsaw also hopes that this competitive advantage can be utilized to influence the EU's eastern policy. In particular, Warsaw will endeavour to eliminate the incongruence between the promotion of 'internal security' and the pursuit of the Common Foreign and Security Policy. (In order to reduce threats to the internal security of the Union, the CFSP has as one of its objectives the fostering of cooperation with and stability in the EU's eastern neighbours.) Currently, the contradiction between the two EU projects is most glaring on the border between Poland and Ukraine.

Poland's contribution to the resolution of this contradiction is a matter for the future. In the meantime, the adoption of the Schengen *acquis* will profoundly reshape relations with countries that do not join the Union at the same time as Poland. Poland as a candidate state must confront the challenge of being required to adopt policies it regards as counter to its vital interests. It alone has to deal with the consequence of the fact that member states' preoccupations with the threat of crime and immigration overshadow the role of the border regime in Poland's relations with neighbours. While the European Commission is aware of the problem, there is little support in the member states for reconsidering the issue.

As for the future, Polish officials believe that as the prospect of conditional accession remains a key EU foreign policy tool, the EU should offer it to Ukraine. Warsaw is of the view that the prospect of membership would help to accelerate domestic transformation in Ukraine and lead to greater stability in the region. Unlike Belarus and Russia, Ukraine's European aspirations, even if mainly declarative, offer the EU scope for influence. As things stood in mid-2003, however, Poland was being left alone to plough its own furrow.

Poland's eastern policy dictated that it support Ukraine's independence and thus that Ukraine be 'dragged to Europe at any price'.[35] The lack of an EU policy towards Ukraine meant that the latter had little incentive to move beyond mere pro-European declarations. Although 'from the point of view of Poland as a future member of the EU, the most important thing is that eastern enlargement of the European Union should not reinforce the eastern border as the border of contrast and civilizations and political systems', the EU clearly does not appear to share this concern.[36]

35 Jerzy Giedoyc, *Polityka* (Warsaw), 24 January 1998.
36 Eva Feldmann and Bartlomiej Sienkiewicz, 'Issues of Pan-European Security in the Framework of Direct Neighbourhood – a Polish Perspective', in Iris Kempe (ed.), *Beyond EU Enlargement, Vol I: The Agenda of Direct Neighbourhood* (Gütersloh: Bertelsmann Foundation Publishers, 2003), p. 243.

6

Hungarian–Romanian and Romanian–Moldovan relations

GABRIEL PARTOS

During the decade after the collapse of communism in Europe and the subsequent break-up of the Soviet Union, Hungarian–Romanian and Romanian–Moldovan relations were considerably affected and, in some ways, shaped by the different speeds with which each of these three countries was integrating into Euro-Atlantic institutions. From the beginning, Hungary was in the vanguard of central and east European (CEE) countries that were on their way to 'rejoin Europe'; Romania brought up the rear. Farther to the east, Moldova had barely started to mobilize itself for the march towards Europe even a decade after achieving independence in 1991.

As the 21st century began, Hungary, already a NATO member since March 1999, felt confident that it would be included in the first wave of former communist-ruled countries to join the European Union. Budapest had been spearheading the demands for a new round of EU enlargement, which, in its case, was most likely to take place in 2004, barely a decade and a half after the dismantling of the one-party state.

Although engaged in formal accession talks with the EU, Romania was quite some way behind Hungary. Bucharest was hoping, perhaps a little optimistically, that it might become a member in 2007. It was also lobbying hard, and ultimately successfully, in the run-up to NATO's summit meeting in Prague in November 2002 to be included among the countries that the Alliance was planning to invite to join it in its second wave of post-Cold War enlargement. Having been a serious candidate for membership as far back as the Madrid summit of 1997, Romania hoped to demonstrate by its inclusion in NATO that it had a firm place in Euro-Atlantic structures even while it was still waiting in the queue for eventual EU membership.

* I am very grateful to Geoffrey Edwards, Paul Nicolopulo, Helen Pickering and Camilla Soar for their valuable comments on an earlier draft of this article, and to Edith Adler, Ben Crampton, Petru Clej, Brigid Fowler, Károly Grúber, Oana Lungescu and Elizabeth Teague for their help and advice.

Meanwhile, Moldova remained not only a long way behind the central European states but also in limbo. Its Partnership and Cooperation Agreement (PCA) with the EU was no substitute for a guaranteed process of accession. In the absence of a realistic chance for closer integration with Europe in the foreseeable future and remaining dependent on Russia for its energy supplies, Moldova began to turn back towards Moscow – a process that was accelerated by the return to power of the Communist Party after the elections of 2001. At the same time, Moldova, through its breakaway Transnistria (Transdniestr) region, continued to play unwilling host to Russian troops whose withdrawal, scheduled for the end of 2002, failed to take place on time.

These vastly different levels of integration with Europe, and the West in general, were already presenting a number of problems in bilateral relations between Budapest and Bucharest on the one hand and between Bucharest and Chișinău on the other. As Hungary was knocking on the door of the EU while Romania remained in the waiting room and Moldova seemed destined to be shut out perhaps for a generation, there was a danger that a new dividing line was about to be drawn across Europe. As a result, it was increasingly likely that the existing differences between these three countries would be further increased and accentuated. Access to EU funds could be expected greatly to benefit the new members, leading to a likely increase in living standards denied to countries that remained outside. The eastward shift of the Schengen regime would lead to the creation of hard borders, including, where required, the imposition of visas, thereby making the movement of people and goods across these three countries more restricted than at any time since the end of the Cold War. Co-national communities stuck on the wrong side of the border had long been one of the key factors in bilateral relations for all these states. Now there was a danger that the sizeable Hungarian minority in Romania and the majority in Moldova, linked by the closest linguistic and cultural affinities to Romanians, would feel themselves more isolated from their kin-states, from neighbouring countries and from the European mainstream than before. All these problems, actual and potential, presented policy-makers in Budapest, Bucharest and Chișinău with fresh challenges to which the recent history of their bilateral relations provided few, if any, useful answers.[1]

---

1 For historical background to Hungarian-Romanian and Romanian-Moldovan relations, see R. J. Crampton, *Eastern Europe in the Twentieth Century – and After*, 2nd edn (London: Routledge, 1997); Joseph Rothschild, *Return to Diversity: a Political History of East Central Europe since World War Two* (Oxford: Oxford University Press, 1989); Stephen Fischer-Galati, *Twentieth Century Romania*, 2nd edn (New York: Columbia University Press, 1991); Charles King, *The Moldovans: Romanians, Russia and the Politics of Culture* (Stanford: Hoover Institution Press, 2000).

Hungary and Romania

With the Trianon Treaty of 1920, the Western powers gave their blessing to Romania's newly acquired control of Transylvania, which had previously belonged to Hungary. During the inter-war years Hungarian-Romanian relations were clouded by Hungary's overt revisionist ambition to regain Transylvania and by Romania's equally strong determination to keep control of its territorial gains. Romania sought security through its alliance with Czechoslovakia and Yugoslavia, the Little Entente, which had been established under French sponsorship. Hungary had no powerful allies until a resurgent Germany under Hitler's rule began to put into practice its own revisionist policies in the mid-1930s.

Alliance with Nazi Germany helped Hungary recover northern Transylvania in August 1940 in the face of stiff opposition from a by then equally pro-German Romania. Ultimately, Hungary's enduring ties with Germany led to the loss of the recovered territories after Romania had abandoned Hitler and joined the Allies in 1944. Bucharest's political dexterity was rewarded by the Paris Peace Treaty of 1947, which restored the Hungarian–Romanian border that had been established at Trianon.

As Hungary and Romania both came within the Soviet sphere of influence and communist rule was established, long-standing bilateral disputes were swept under the carpet. Just as Budapest and Bucharest had sought to outbid each other in their devotion to Hitler's war objectives, so in the early years of communist hegemony the two sides competed eagerly to be regarded as Stalin's best disciples in central Europe. Any public dispute between the two sides would have been impermissible. In the meantime, there were also some notable improvements (within the strict constraints of one-party rule) in the conditions of Romania's ethnic Hungarians in the early 1950s.

However, these achievements, which included the establishment of an autonomous Hungarian region in Transylvania and a Hungarian-language university in Cluj, were gradually whittled away as Romania began to adopt a more nationalist policy and a more independent line from Moscow from the late 1950s onwards. Even if the Hungarian minority institutions established at the height of Stalinism were more for show than for real, their abolition starting in the 1960s had a strong symbolic message both for Romania's ethnic Hungarian community and for the Hungarian authorities across the border. This was all the more so because both communist protocol and later the signing of the Helsinki Final Act (1975) effectively made existing borders sacrosanct. As a result, the position of the Magyar minority in Romania became the touchstone of Hungarian–Romanian relations. With the fate of

Romania's ethnic Hungarians taking a turn for the worse, there was a cooling in relations between the two countries that had not previously been matched among nominal Warsaw Pact allies, apart from during brief periods of crisis.

By the late 1980s Hungary was playing host to over 30,000 mainly ethnic Hungarian refugees from Romania; it was another unprecedented experience in relations between two Soviet bloc countries.[2] The refugees had been escaping President Nicolae Ceauşescu's increasingly dictatorial regime and the general pauperization that followed a disastrous economic policy. As the edifice of communism was being dismantled peacefully, brick by brick, in Hungary and then was brought crashing down in a violent revolution and *coup d'état* in Romania at the end of 1989, relations between the two countries were badly in need of a fresh beginning.

Romania and Moldova

Before Moldova's emergence as an independent state in 1991, its relations with Romania were either part of Romania's internal affairs or a subplot to the story of Bucharest's relationship with Moscow. Known as Bessarabia and part of the medieval Moldavian principality, the region between the rivers Prut and Nistru (Dniestr) had passed from Ottoman Turkish control to a much more direct form of rule under Russia in 1812. After the First World War Bessarabia was reunited with the rest of Moldavia, as it was then known, as part of the newly enlarged Romanian state. However, the Soviet Union refused to accept the loss of this region and, in the aftermath of the Molotov–Ribbentrop Pact, it issued an ultimatum in June 1940 for Romania to cede Bessarabia (and northern Bukovina, the region between the northern parts of Transylvania and Bessarabia). Bucharest complied with the Kremlin's demands but retook the territories a year later when it joined Germany's invasion of the Soviet Union.

As the tide of war turned, Bessarabia was recaptured by the Red Army in 1944 and was reincorporated into the Soviet Union as one of its 15 republics. However, its outlet to the Black Sea in the south and lands in the north were transferred by Stalin to Ukraine, while a narrow strip of land to the east of the Nistru, with a majority Slav population, was added to historical Bessarabia. The result was to sow the seeds for Moldova's post-independence woes: a separatist Transnistria, inter-ethnic tensions and serious doubts over the small, landlocked country's economic viability.

---

2 Gabriel Partos, 'Romania', in Alan Day (ed.), *The Annual Register: A Record of World Events, 1988* (London: Longman, 1989), p. 127, and the same entry for the 1989 edition (London: Longman, 1990), p. 126.

During the Stalin era the territorial dispensation imposed at the end of the Second World War remained unchallenged. However, as Romania adopted a more nationalist form of communism from the late 1950s onwards, Bessarabia's annexation by the Soviet Union began to be questioned, albeit in a largely implicit way. Meanwhile, contacts between Romania and Soviet Moldavia (the Moldavian Soviet Socialist Republic) had to go via Moscow. Even in the areas of culture, language and the arts, severe restrictions were placed on direct links.

Relations improved somewhat after President Ceauşescu went to Chişinău in 1976 on what was the first visit to Soviet Moldavia by a Romanian head of state. Subsequently, there was a gradual easing of curbs on cultural links between Soviet Moldavia and Romania – a process that accelerated during the period of glasnost inaugurated by the then Soviet leader Mikhail Gorbachov in the second half of the 1980s.

Following the end of communist rule in Romania and Soviet Moldavia, thousands of people from both sides of the river Prut staged a demonstration, known as the Bridge of Flowers, in May 1990 to celebrate the victory of democracy. Just over a year later, in August 1991, Soviet Moldavia proclaimed its independence as Moldova, a decision that would receive international recognition after the Soviet Union disappeared at the end of that year. Moldova's independence introduced a whole range of questions as to the nature of the relationship between what most people in Romania, and many in Moldova, regarded as the 'two Romanian states'.

THE CHALLENGE OF EUROPE

As the communist era drew to a close in central and eastern Europe, Hungary was in pole position to exploit the emerging opportunities for integration with the West. Apart from Yugoslavia, which was about to descend into more than a decade of conflict and chaos, Hungary had the most open economy in the region and the closest trading links with Western countries. It was also the first country (with the exception of soon-to-be-extinct East Germany) to hold fully free elections, which went ahead in March 1990, and to complete the process of democratization. Hungary was the first CEE state past several milestones along the path to integration: it acceded to the Council of Europe in 1990; submitted a formal membership application to the EU in 1994; was among the initial five CEE states that opened formal accession talks with Brussels in 1998; and joined NATO (along with the Czech Republic and Poland) in 1999.

Romania's progress towards Europe was much more hesitant and painful. Emerging from more than two decades of Ceauşescu's increasingly despotic rule and the bloody uprising that overthrew it, President Ion Iliescu and the other ex-communist functionaries who took some of the key posts in the new administration seemed reluctant to put their pro-European rhetoric into practice. Their commitment to democracy and the rule of law appeared to be in doubt when they encouraged violent demonstrations by miners as a way to deal with their political opponents in 1990–91. Meanwhile, their embrace of the market economy remained half-hearted as they dragged their heels over privatization.

It was only in the mid-1990s that a more comprehensive pro-Western change of mentality could be perceived. Romania had been the first country to sign a Partnership for Peace (PfP) agreement with NATO in 1994. Three years later the newly elected centre-right administration under President Emil Constantinescu went out of its way, ultimately unsuccessfully, to have Romania included among those countries that NATO's Madrid summit was to invite to join the Alliance. But the relatively slow pace of reform meant that on key aspects of integration with the West, Romania continued to lag behind Hungary. Bucharest was admitted to the Council of Europe in 1993, applied for EU membership in 1995 and became part of a second wave of ex-communist (and other) countries to open formal accession talks with the European Commission in 2000.[3]

Hungary and Romania

Ceaușescu's fall was accompanied by the sudden emergence of Hungarian-Romanian solidarity as the two nations each celebrated the dawn of democracy. In Romania's case that process had been set in motion in December 1989 by protestors in Timișoara who were trying to protect the local ethnic Hungarian Reformed Church minister László Tőkés from the secret police. In the wake of Ceaușescu's overthrow timely Hungarian emergency aid for impoverished Romania helped to bolster the improvement in bilateral relations.

The flowering of Hungarian–Romanian friendship turned out to be short-lived as the immediate euphoria over the end of communist rule wore off. Within months relations settled back into the more usual routine of mutual incomprehension, suspicions and, among some of the public,

---

3 For reviews of Hungary's and Romania's relations with the EU and NATO, see Bennett Kovrig, 'European Integration', in Aurel Braun and Zoltan Barany (eds), *Dilemmas of Transition: The Hungarian Experience* (Lanham, MD: Rowman & Littlefield Publishers, 1999), pp. 253–71; David Phinnemore, 'Romania and Euro-Atlantic Integration since 1989: A Decade of Frustration?', in Duncan Light and David Phinnemore (eds), *Post-Communist Romania – Coming to Terms with Transition* (Houndmills, Basingstoke: Palgrave, 2001), pp. 245–69.

hostility. Riots in Târgu Mureş in March 1990 in which three Hungarian-speakers were killed turned out to be an exception to the otherwise largely non-violent, but often cold, inter-ethnic relations within Romania. However, newly legalized radical nationalist groups did their utmost to stir up or maintain anti-Hungarian sentiments. There were relatively few positive changes in the position of Romania's Magyar community in the early 1990s, apart from two by-products of Romania's new democracy: the establishment of the Democratic Union of Hungarians in Romania (DUHR), a political party representing the interests of ethnic Hungarians, and the easing of travel restrictions between the two countries.

From Budapest's perspective, the key to better relations with Bucharest was the Romanian authorities' treatment of their country's Hungarian minority. A lack of any substantive improvement in the ethnic Hungarians' conditions was also reflected in the absence of any positive shift in bilateral relations in the first half of the 1990s. The two countries failed to reach agreement on an interstate treaty in time for the Paris Conference on the Pact on Stability in Europe in March 1995. Yet Brussels had presented the conclusion of such an agreement as something of a precondition for negotiating accession to an EU that was reluctant to import active disputes over territorial claims or minority issues from the candidate countries. One reason, it seemed, for the failure to sign a Hungarian–Romanian treaty (along with nearly 100 other bilateral or multilateral agreements) was the remoteness of the prospect of EU membership for Romania.

However, attitudes in Bucharest were already changing. As the Iliescu administration began to adopt a much more firmly pro-European position, it threw the ultra-nationalist and neo-communist parties out of the governing coalition in 1995–6. The parting of the ways with the arch-nationalists was designed to present a more acceptable face to the international community. It was prompted more specifically by the prospect of NATO enlargement – a process in which Romania stood a better chance of inclusion in the medium term than in the EU's eastward expansion. With the anti-Hungarian factions out of office, it also became possible for the administration to conclude the long-delayed treaty with Hungary in September 1996. The two sides pledged, *inter alia,* to 'mutually support each other's efforts aimed at integration with the European Union, NATO and the Western European Union'.[4]

The treaty heralded a new chapter in Hungarian–Romanian relations. Within months President Iliescu's post-communist administration, with its

---

4 Gáspár Bíró, 'Bilateral Treaties between Hungary and its Neighbours after 1989', in Ignác Romsics and Béla K. Király (eds), *Geopolitics in the Danube Region – Hungarian Reconciliation Efforts, 1848–1998* (Budapest: Central European University Press, 1999), p. 369.

mixed record on promoting better inter-ethnic relations, was replaced by a centre-right government. For the first time in Romanian history the new broad-based coalition included elected representatives of the country's ethnic Hungarians. The DUHR was given several ministerial portfolios, among them the newly created post of State Secretary for Minorities. The DUHR was partly transformed from being a single-issue pressure group with local administrative experience in Hungarian-populated areas into a party with a stake in governing the whole of Romania. Ethnic Hungarians were no longer viewed by the political elite merely as a problem; they were seen as part of the solution.

President Constantinescu was determined to project a new image of Romania designed to fit in better with the 'European' values of democracy, ethnic tolerance and opposition to discrimination. Romania's leaders realized, and frequently reiterated, that the road to Europe and the West would lead through Hungary.

That argument gained even greater credence following NATO's invitation to Hungary in 1997 to join the Alliance and the opening of Budapest's EU accession talks in the following year. As Hungary's integration with Euro-Atlantic institutions deepened, Budapest's voice was heard more audibly in Brussels. In 1999 Hungary formally acquired a say in NATO's decision-making; the time was approaching when that would become the case in the EU as well.

In those conditions, Bucharest was fully aware that it would need Budapest's support over a whole range of issues related to Romania's integration process. The reverse side of the coin was that Hungarian opposition to Romania's endeavours could further delay the already slow progress of Romania's attempts to join NATO and the EU. Whether it was a question of lifting the Schengen visa requirement for Romanian citizens, lobbying for Romanian membership of NATO or starting Romania's EU accession talks, Hungarian help or, at the very least, acquiescence was seen as an important factor by both Bucharest and Budapest. The key to unlocking the door to a more positive Hungarian attitude was improving the conditions of the ethnic Hungarians in Romania. The inclusion of the DUHR in the governing coalition was just the first step in that direction. It was accompanied by a range of reforms, including improvements in Hungarian-language educational provisions.

The sea change in the Romanian government's thinking on the minority issue was reflected in its relations with Hungary. Within months of the centre-right government's taking office, the long-delayed reopening of the Hungarian consulate in Cluj took place. It was followed soon after by the establishment of a Romanian consulate in Szeged. That consulate was inaugurated in the presence of President Constantinescu, who in January 1998 paid the first official visit to Hungary by a Romanian head of state.[5] For its part, the new centre-right administration that took office in Hungary in 1998 made clear that it wanted to help its neighbours in the integration process. As the then foreign minister János Martonyi put it, Hungary's 'national policy interest is for the countries inhabited by ethnic Hungarians to become … successful EU member states'.[6]

Although the prospect of the Iliescu administration's return to office caused some concern among Hungarian politicians, the defeat of the centre-right in the elections of November–December 2000 did not signal a revival of the heavily criticized minority policies of the early 1990s.[7] On the contrary, the ethnic Hungarians' position remained strong, as the new prime minister, Adrian Năstase, needed the DUHR's support in parliament in order to secure the survival of his centre-left minority government. Although no longer enjoying the benefits, or shouldering the responsibilities, of being in the central government, the DUHR continued to exert considerable influence. In some areas it secured greater concessions from Prime Minister Năstase's government than it had achieved while in government as part of the fractious centre-right coalition during the previous four years. Among the benefits that emerged in 2001 was the right of minorities to use their mother tongue for official purposes in districts where they made up more than 20 per cent of the local population.[8]

Romania's ultra-nationalists continued to question and at times actively oppose the policy of improving relations with Hungary. The strength of their challenge was demonstrated when the radical nationalist Greater Romania Party emerged from the elections of 2000 as the second strongest political force and its leader became the challenger to Ion Iliescu in the second round of the presidential elections. However, the limits of the nationalists' strength were clearly demonstrated when the other parliamentary parties resolved, whether in government or in opposition, to isolate the GRP.

The 'status law'

The most serious, albeit temporary, setback to the improvement in Hungarian-Romanian relations at the start of the 21st century came not from

5 Gabriel Partos, 'Persistent Diplomacy', *War Report*, No. 58, February–March 1998, pp. 62–3; Associated Press (AP) news agency, 1639 GMT, 27 January 1998.
6 *Népszabadság*, 29 October 1998.
7 Mediafax news agency, 1600 GMT, 4 October 1999; *Agence France Presse* (AFP) news agency, 1010 GMT, 25 May 2000.
8 AP, 1810 GMT, 2 February 2002 report on a marriage ceremony in Hungarian being declared legal.

the usual sources – Romanian nationalists or the Bucharest authorities, which were at times eager to appease them – but from the Hungarian government. For much of 2001 the two countries were at loggerheads over Hungarian legislation, passed in June of that year, which had been drafted to provide a range of benefits, and a special status, for ethnic Hungarians living in neighbouring countries.[9] These benefits, which came into force on 1 January 2002, included the payment of bursaries to ethnic Hungarians who sent their children to Hungarian-language schools. More controversially, they also stipulated various rights that ethnic Hungarians would enjoy in Hungary itself: easier entry into the labour market (up to three months' employment every year), subsidized travel and access to university education and health care.

Hungary justified the 'status law' on various grounds, but the main reason given for the legislation was EU-related. Budapest said it was concerned that Hungary's early accession to the EU would accelerate the steady stream of ethnic Hungarians who were leaving their country of birth in search of a better life in more advanced Hungary or in the West.[10] Officials quoted surveys suggesting that a high proportion of ethnic Hungarians, around 25 per cent, would seriously consider moving to Hungary once it was inside the EU.[11] In terms of numbers, this was most likely to involve the Magyars of Romania – a country that was well behind Hungary in the EU membership stakes and that had much lower living standards. (Yugoslavia and Ukraine, both of which were worse off than even Romania, were also expected to generate further ethnic Hungarian migration. However, their combined Magyar population of around 500,000 is less than one-third of Romania's.)

Prime Minister Viktor Orbán's government, which was becoming increasingly nationalistic in outlook as the parliamentary elections of April 2002 approached in Hungary, was determined to ensure that age-old ethnic Hungarian communities would not disappear from their land of birth. By offering them temporary benefits in Hungary through opportunities for work, education and travel, his government hoped that many of those who were considering uprooting themselves and their families would instead

---

9 Formally known as 'The Law on Hungarians Living in Neighbouring States', the 'status law' is available in English on the website of the Hungarian government's Office for Hungarians beyond the Borders, *www.htmh.hu/law.htm*. For a comprehensive discussion of the law in a comparative context, see Brigid Fowler, *Fuzzing citizenship, nationalising political space: a framework for interpreting the Hungarian 'status law' as a new form of kin-state policy in Central and Eastern Europe*, Working Paper 40/02, ESRC One Europe or Several? Programme, University of Sussex, Falmer, Brighton, 2002.

10 Hungarian foreign ministry spokesman Gábor Horváth, quoted in Eugen Tomiuc, 'Hungary: Status Law Causing Dispute with Neighbours', Radio Free Europe/Radio Liberty (RFE/RL) website, *www.rferl.org/nca/features/2001/10/04102001123954.asp*.

11 *The Economist*, 7 April 2001; *International Herald Tribune*, 20 June 2001.

return to their home regions in the neighbouring countries. There they would be able to make good use of the new skills, qualifications, professional contacts and savings that they had acquired while in Hungary by finding or creating employment. While the 'status law' was being drafted, one survey suggested that its enactment would encourage 80 per cent of ethnic Hungarians to stay in their country of birth; another indicated that half of those who might otherwise consider moving to Hungary would not now do so.[12] Opposition figures, particularly from the liberal Free Democratic Party, argued that such benefits might prove counterproductive because the opportunities that short-term work or study in Hungary would create were more likely to encourage some of the visiting ethnic Hungarians who had profited from them to stay on in Hungary.[13]

Reactions in Romania (and in Slovakia which has a large number of ethnic Hungarians) were almost uniformly hostile to the 'status law'. Three main criticisms were levelled against the Hungarian government's policy. Romanian politicians argued that it amounted to ethnically based discrimination, that it involved an infringement of Romania's sovereignty and that the legislation had not been preceded by proper consultations with the Bucharest authorities.[14] In brief, the 'status law' was 'un-European'. The Romanian claims evoked considerable resonance among various European organizations that were uneasy about one or another aspect of the Hungarian legislation. The very fact that Romania appealed to European institutions about its disagreement with Hungary was in itself a fresh departure. Previously it had usually been Hungary that had tried to internationalize its disputes with Romania in an attempt to bring greater pressure to bear on Bucharest to improve its treatment of the Hungarian minority. Romania's initiative was indicative of its now firmly established European commitment. It was also symptomatic of the fact that the balance of forces between Budapest and Bucharest had shifted. When Hungary first began to look for international assistance in its dispute with Romania over the position of the ethnic Hungarian minority during the final phase of Ceaușescu's rule, Bucharest had been largely impervious to outside pressure. Even in the early 1990s, when Romania's EU membership seemed a very remote prospect and Bucharest's commitment to full integration with the West remained tentative, international efforts to influence Romanian policy had had only limited success.

12 *Heti Világgazdaság*, 2 December 2000; Zsolt Németh, quoted by Reuters news agency 1639 GMT, 25 May 2001.
13 *Duna TV*, 22 January 2001 on CD-ROM, BBC Monitoring 2001 (BBC, 2002); *Heti Világgazdaság*, 27 January 2001, quoted in Klara Kingston, 'The Hungarian Status Law', in *RFE/RL East European Perspectives*, Vol. 3, No. 17, 3 October 2001, p. 2.
14 President Iliescu, quoted by AFP, 1313 GMT, 25 April 2001; Prime Minister Năstase, quoted by AFP, 1609 GMT, 22 December 2001.

However, the scope for outside influence over Bucharest began to expand from the mid-1990s as Romania joined the Council of Europe and gradually committed itself to a much more integrationist path. In its attempt to catch up with Hungary and other leading candidates for EU and NATO membership, Bucharest became much more sensitive to outside criticism. From 1997 onwards, following NATO's invitation to Hungary to join the Alliance, Romania also grew concerned that Budapest (even without having a formal veto on potential new members) would be able to influence both the decision over Romania's future NATO membership and the timetable relating to it. Meanwhile, Hungary's position *vis-à-vis* Romania was further strengthened by its marked economic success in the second half of the 1990s and beyond. As Hungary's GDP increased by one-third in the six years from 1996,[15] it became an increasingly important trading partner as well as a market for Romania's excess labour in both the formal and informal economies.

Hungary's policy also began to be affected by its own considerable achievements in the political and economic transition process. Through its enactment of the 'status law', Budapest was now adopting a more assertive attitude both in relation to its neighbours and, to a limited extent and in an indirect way, towards the EU. Part of the reason was Prime Minister Orbán's wish to demonstrate to the more nationalist constituency in Hungary that joining the EU was not incompatible with taking action to assist ethnic Hungarian communities across borders. On the contrary, Hungarian politicians argued that the European integration process would help to bring about the elimination of borders and lead to the reunification of Hungarians who had been divided after Trianon. From the Hungarian perspective this was a modern, 'European' alternative to the old policies of territorial revisionism of the inter-war years. As Orbán put it, the law was designed to 'unify the nation across the borders'.[16]

Viewed from Romania, however, it was seen as a possible first step towards returning to the old policies in a new guise. Prime Minister Năstase retorted that his country refused 'to be a testing ground for some people … who, because of revisionist nostalgia, are looking for all sorts of alternative formulas that are not authorised at a European level'.[17] Ioan Rus, the Romanian minister of the interior, argued that Budapest was seeking 'co-sovereignty' over Transylvania while aiming 'to "Magyarize" the population by encouraging people to claim they were Hungarian for economic reasons'.[18]

15 The Economist Intelligence Unit, *Hungary Country Report* (London: EIU, 1996–2001).

16 Reuters, 0953 GMT, 20 June 2001.

17 AFP, 1341 GMT, 28 July 2001.

18 AFP, 1117 GMT, 29 October 2001. See also Fowler, *Fuzzing Citizenship*, p. 24 for different Hungarian and Romanian interpretations of the sovereignty issue.

The international community was generally slow to wake up to the impending dispute between Hungary and Romania and to other implications of the 'status law'. Among the first steps taken by the EU was to persuade Hungary to exclude Austria from the provisions of the proposed legislation because they would have gone against the EU's principles of non-discrimination. The law was then passed in the face of strong criticism from Bucharest. During the six-month period leading up to its entry into force on 1 January 2002, there were intense bilateral discussions as well as engagement by various European bodies.

The matter was referred to the Council of Europe's European Commission for Democracy through Law, the Venice Commission. Its ruling took exception primarily to two aspects of the Hungarian legislation.[19] One was the provision of services to co-ethnics living in another country unless they had the consent of that country. The implication was that Hungary was obliged to reach a deal with its neighbours. The other aspect was the empowerment of non-governmental organizations (NGOs), in this case political parties representing ethnic Hungarians, to recommend applicants to be considered by the Hungarian authorities as qualifying for the proposed benefits. According to the Venice Commission, that provision implied that these NGOs had been given quasi-administrative powers without the approval of the countries in which they were operating. In subsequent regulations introduced by the authorities in Budapest these provisions were watered down.

The Council of Europe was not alone in trying to resolve the problems that arose from the enactment of the 'status law'. The Organization for Security and Cooperation in Europe (OSCE) also got involved through Rolf Ekéus, its High Commissioner on National Minorities, who acted as a mediator. The OSCE's concern was partly motivated by the possibility that the Hungarian example might set a precedent in potentially more dangerous areas, in particular for Russia and ethnic Russian populations in some of the former Soviet republics. Unease felt over aspects of the Hungarian legislation was reflected in a statement issued by Ekéus which was implicitly critical of Hungary's endeavours:

> Protection of minority rights is the obligation of the State where the minority resides … Although a state with a titular majority population may have an interest in persons of the same ethnicity living abroad, this does not entitle or imply in any way, a right under international law to exercise jurisdiction over these persons.[20]

19 *Report on Preferential Treatment of National Minorities by their Kin-State*, adopted by the Venice Commission, Document CDL-INF, Council of Europe, Strasbourg, 22 October 2001.
20 'Sovereignty, responsibility and national minorities: a statement by the OSCE minorities commissioner', 26 October 2001, *www.osce.org/news/generate.php3?news_id=2095*.

Perhaps even more importantly, the EU also made its apprehensions public after a lengthy period during which it had been pursuing quiet diplomacy. For the EU the emerging Hungarian–Romanian disagreement was precisely the kind of dispute it did not want, because of the danger that it would further complicate an already complex enlargement process. It had earlier hoped that the bilateral treaties concluded at the time of the 1995 Paris Stability Pact Conference (or in the case of Hungary and Romania the treaty concluded in 1996) would exclude a recurrence of this kind of friction between two would-be members of the EU.[21]

Brussels was also irritated by the lack of prior consultation on the part of the Budapest authorities. That was reflected in the EU's insistence, at a relatively late stage, that Austria be removed from the list of countries covered by the 'status law'. Continuing EU concern over the Hungarian legislation was highlighted by the Commission's annual progress report on the candidate countries, published in November 2001. Previously it had contained the most praise and least criticism for Hungary. This time the report made clear that the EU harboured various misgivings about the 'status law', noting that 'some of the provisions … apparently conflict with the prevailing European standard of minority protection'.[22] The report went on to recommend that Hungary should reach an agreement with its neighbours to comply with the findings of the Venice Commission. Looking ahead to the medium term, it noted that the law would have to be amended, 'at the latest upon accession', because it was 'currently not in line with the principle of non-discrimination…'.[23]

The mixture of advice, recommendation, criticism and, at times, pressure from various European institutions contributed to the successful resolution of the Hungarian–Romanian disagreement after six months of talks. At the end of 2001 the two prime ministers signed an agreement that spelt the end of the most intense phase of the dispute. Its most important stipulation made the Hungarian labour market equally accessible to all Romanian citizens, regardless of their ethnic background. Subsequently, under pressure from the opposition, which claimed that Hungary's labour market would be flooded with job-seekers from Romania, Budapest introduced a quota on foreign labour, to match the available vacancies in the country.[24] However, by then the strains between the two sides had largely been removed. Moreover, the replacement of the increasingly nationalist Orbán administration by a

21 Gáspár Bíró, 'Bilateral Treaties between Hungary and its Neighbours', p. 360.
22 See the EU website, *www.europa.eu.int/comm/enlargement/report2001/hu_en.pdf*, p. 91.
23 Idem.
24 Eugen Tomiuc, 'Romania: Bucharest to Closely Monitor Law Granting Benefits to Ethnic Hungarians,' RFE/RL website, *www.rferl.org/nca/features/2002/01/16012002090020.asp*.

Socialist–Free Democrat coalition after the elections of April 2002 heralded an improvement in relations between Budapest and Bucharest.

Romania and Moldova

In the decade after Moldova declared its independence, Romania's relations with the 'other Romanian state', as many Romanians viewed Moldova, were increasingly affected by Chişinău's failure to make any breakthrough in its integration with Europe. Indeed, at times Moldova seemed stuck in a no-man's land between what had once been the old East and the old West, between Russia and the EU.

Initially, Moldova's poor performance was not through lack of commitment to the European ideal. On the contrary, the first post-independence government was a strong advocate of joining 'Europe' after nearly five decades of the republic's semi-isolation as part of the Soviet Union. For the administration of President Mircea Snegur, whose nationalism took a firmly pro-Romanian turn, the logical way of initiating the process of moving towards the West was through forging closer ties with Bucharest. History pointed in that direction: during the inter-war years Romania, which at the time included Bessarabia, had been France's ally; even during the Ceauşescu era Bucharest had distanced itself from the Soviet Union in order to court western support and investment.

At the beginning of the 1990s Chişinău was eager to demonstrate that it was turning its back on the Soviet legacy and moving in the direction of Romania and the West. Decisions such as the reintroduction of the Latin script in place of Cyrillic emphasized the closest possible similarity between Romanian and Moldovan (as Moldova's language was defined in a referendum). Likewise, the adoption of a history curriculum that followed the Romanian model not only indicated Moldova's rediscovery of its shared past with Romania but also implied that a return to these historical roots could one day lead to a common future. With Bucharest moving slowly but surely towards Europe, such a future held out the prospect that Chişinău could also belatedly clamber onto the bandwagon of integration.

However, if Romania's road to Europe was rocky, Moldova's appeared at times virtually impassable. Moldova's break with the Soviet Union, and even more its rapprochement with Romania, was opposed by the Russian-speaking Slav minority, which accounted for over a quarter of the population. In Transnistria, where Slavs formed a majority, a separatist administration was established in 1991 under Igor Smirnov. Its control was cemented after fighting in 1992, which was ended only by the intervention of Russian troops. Ten years later Transnistria's separatists remained defiant and over 2,000

Russian troops were still deployed in the region. Moscow had promised to withdraw its forces by the end of 2002, as required by the OSCE's Istanbul summit of 1999. But as there were no signs of an imminent Russian withdrawal, the meeting of OSCE foreign ministers in Porto in December 2002 extended the timetable for the pull-out by 12 months and made it dependent on the 'necessary conditions' being in place.[25]

Transnistrian separatism was only one of several obstacles that were holding back Chișinău from being able to embark on the journey towards integration with western Europe. Moldova's economy was in a parlous state – the legacy of a Soviet past that had seen its access to the Black Sea taken away and given to Ukraine. There was little industrial capacity, and much of that was concentrated in Transnistria. The economy was largely agricultural, and its main markets in the former Soviet Union had collapsed in the early 1990s. Last but not least, Moldova was heavily dependent on Russian energy. Any shortfall from that source could be made up only partially from Romania.

As Moldova's economy went from bad to worse while the confrontation over Transnistria festered, Chișinău's foreign policy orientation gradually began to change towards a more pro-Russian approach. It was also affected by the realization that Romania's integration with the West, although a steady process, was unlikely to produce any substantive early results. Meanwhile, relations with the EU remained relatively limited, owing to geography, Moldova's lack of economic competitiveness and a shortage of potential political sponsors. There were few signs that Brussels would be willing to forge a close relationship. There was little the EU could do beyond providing what was essentially first aid to bandage up the former Soviet republic's much-damaged finances.

As part of its change of foreign policy orientation, from the mid-1990s Chișinău began to take steps to repair the damage in its relations with Moscow. The initial, post-independence anti-Russian rhetoric was toned down and official contacts with the Kremlin became more frequent, leading to improved ties between the two countries. Meanwhile, the initial phase of post-independence enthusiasm for the Romanian connection was beginning to cool, partly because Romania itself was barely able to cope with its own enormous problems of transition. Moreover, the pro-Romanian forces were considerably weakened by their increasing fragmentation as they splintered into different political parties. The process of policy realignment was greatly accelerated by the electoral success in February 2001 of the Party of

25 Vladimir Socor, 'The OSCE and "Federalization" Failing in Moldova', in electronic news bulletin provided by *www.moldova.org*, 30 January 2003, pp. 1–3.

Communists of the Republic of Moldova (PCRM). This was the first occasion anywhere in the world that a communist party had won an absolute majority of the votes in a nationwide free election. Subsequently, parliament elected the communist leader, Vladimir Voronin, president of Moldova. During the election campaign Voronin had mooted the idea that Moldova might apply to join the Russia–Belarus Union. Although that idea was subsequently put on the back burner, the shift in Chişinău's foreign policy direction was not in doubt. President Voronin became a regular visitor to Moscow in the hope that the Kremlin would help to guarantee more plentiful, and cheaper, energy supplies to Moldova and put pressure on the Transnistrian separatists to make them accept a deal that would grant the region autonomy but not independence.

Meanwhile, relations with Bucharest were not making much progress after the signing of a treaty by the two countries in April 2000. Eight years in the making, the agreement was a compromise between Romania's wish that it should be a 'fraternal' treaty between two states representing different parts of the same nation and Moldova's insistence that it should be 'regular' in every respect, i.e. a document that had been agreed by two fully independent states. In the end it was described as enshrining 'privileged relations' between the signatories. Instead of Bucharest's preference for the formula of the 'two Romanian states', the furthest the treaty went in acknowledging the special ties between Romania and Moldova was to mention their 'community of culture and language'. While once again recognizing Moldova's independence, Romania did not commit itself to anything that might rule out the possibility of reunification at a future date. For Moldova the signing of the treaty was a way of promoting its acceptance into the Stability Pact for Southeastern Europe. For Bucharest it was yet another way of improving its international image as a responsible administration that was willing to accept a sensible compromise, even in complex matters, so as to remove any possible obstacles on the way to its accession to NATO and the EU.[26] It was another matter that two years after its signing, the treaty had still not been ratified.

Moldova's relations with Bucharest took a turn for the worse when Romania cancelled Prime Minister Năstase's planned visit to Chişinău in October 2001 after a Moldovan official had accused Bucharest of interfering in his country's affairs. There was further tension when Moldova expelled the Romanian military attaché in March 2002 after accusing him of involvement in anti-government demonstrations. Romania retaliated by declaring the Moldovan deputy head of mission in Bucharest *persona non grata*. With

26 V. G. Baleanu, *In the Shadow of Russia: Romania's Relations with Moldova and Ukraine*, CSRC Research Paper G85, Royal Military Academy Sandhurst, Camberley, 2000, pp. 18–19.

President Voronin accusing Bucharest of orchestrating the demonstrations as part of a wider 'Romanian ideological intervention in Moldova', bilateral relations reached their lowest point since Moldova's independence a decade earlier.[27] For its part, Prime Minister Năstase's government was doing its best to keep out of the worsening dispute between the Moldovan administration and the pro-Romanian nationalist protesters, pursuing a low-key policy towards Moldova. Its policy, as in its relations with Hungary, was to continue to avoid doing anything that might jeopardize its chances of being invited to join NATO at the eagerly awaited Prague summit.

By the time the expulsions took place, protesters had already succeeded by way of demonstrations in forcing the Moldovan government to withdraw two controversial initiatives: the reintroduction of Russian as a compulsory language in schools and the adoption of a Moldova-based history curriculum in place of the Romania-centred syllabus introduced at the time of independence. The proposed measures, which for many Moldovans served as a reminder of the Soviet era, helped to reinvigorate (at least for a time) the heavily fragmented pro-Romanian nationalists, first and foremost the Christian Democratic People's Party (CDPP). It was primarily these demonstrations and Chișinău's decision to put a temporary ban on the CDPP's activities for organizing unauthorized public meetings that reawakened Europe's interest in Moldova. Western diplomatic pressure led to the ban being rescinded. Meanwhile, Chișinău also heeded advice from the Council of Europe and withdrew plans to return to the Soviet-era structure of municipal government and hold early elections on that basis.

Moldova's responsiveness to Western criticism indicated that the reorientation of its foreign policy towards Russia was not an outright rejection of the European option, such as that evinced by President Alexander Lukashenka of Belarus. On the contrary, Moldovan leaders, including President Voronin, repeatedly stressed that they wanted their country to serve as a bridge between Russia and Europe. Even though joining the EU remained a distant dream, Chișinău continued to seek the help, and abide by the decisions, of various European institutions.[28] After Moldova postponed controversial municipal elections on the advice of the Council of Europe, the Council, through its Parliamentary Assembly, was soon of help again: it found a way to defuse the three-month-old anti-government protests when in April 2002

---

27 'Moldovan–Romanian Relations Sink to their Lowest Point,' in an electronic news bulletin provided by *www.moldova.org*, 19 March 2002, p. 4.

28 Viorel Cibotaru, 'The Foreign and National Aspects of Moldova's Strategic Foreign Policy', in Igor Munteanu and Trevor Waters (eds), *Highway or Barrier? The Republic of Moldova's Integration into Euro-Atlantic Structures*, CSRC Research Paper G96, Royal Military Academy Sandhurst, Camberley, 2001, p. 3.

it recommended, among other things, a moratorium on the proposed changes to Moldova's educational system.[29]

Moreover, Moldova's communist leaders understood that the European option could be pursued effectively only through improved relations with Romania – a point Voronin spelt out shortly after his election when he committed himself to forging even better relations with Bucharest than his predecessors had achieved.[30] It was another question whether he could honour that commitment while introducing policies that embittered Moldova's pro-Romanian political forces. The indirect result was a deterioration in relations with Romania in the year after the PCRM gained power.

TRADE AND INVESTMENT

Hungary and Romania

In the decade following the end of the communist era Hungary emerged as a regional economic success story. Hungary's growth outstripped its neighbours' rate of development. It became the largest CEE recipient of foreign direct investment. By contrast, Romania, slow to embark on reforms, lagged behind. Initially, trade between Budapest and Bucharest was hit by the two countries' early (and, in Romania's case, longer-lasting) difficulties in the transition from a planned to a market economy. It was also affected by both countries' attempts to reorient their exports to the West, primarily to the EU.

Bilateral trade began to expand considerably in the second half of the 1990s, particularly when Romania further liberalized its economy after it had joined the Central European Free Trade Agreement (CEFTA) in 1997. (CEFTA, with Hungary as one of its founding members, had been set up five years earlier in order to stimulate trade across the region in the face of difficulties in breaking into the tough EU market.) Bilateral growth continued, even though Bucharest resorted on some occasions to temporary protectionist measures against Hungarian wheat and flour exports. Over a five-year period, trade between the two countries increased two-and-a-half times, from $472 million in 1997 to $1,126 million in 2001. Hungary became Romania's most important trading partner among the CEFTA countries and was Romania's eighth largest export market.[31]

---

29 Moldpress news agency, Chişinău, 29 April 2002.

30 BASA Moldovan news agency, 1608 GMT, 12 March 2002.

31 For trade figures, see Hungarian Ministry of Economy and Transport, *www.gm.hu/gyorsmenu/statisztikak/htm/020408/usd/RO_30_1.htm*; Tamás Réti, 'Comparison of the Hungarian and Romanian economies from the perspectives of regional economic cooperation', posted on website *www.eu-enlargement.org/attachments/ 745FB0AF-46AA-11D4-A2D8-0050DA76D265.DOC*.

As Hungary became a strong regional economic actor, it began to invest in neighbouring countries. Much of Hungary's capital exports to Romania, where it was the eleventh largest foreign investor, was concentrated in Transylvania, owing to the region's proximity to Hungary, its relatively advanced and flexible economy and the fact that it was home to the majority of Romania's ethnic Hungarians. At times, Budapest tried to play down the Hungarian connection so as not to offend Romanian nationalist sensitivities. However, business links, particularly between small and medium-sized enterprises, were often easier to establish or to extend for people on the two sides of the border who shared the same language and network of contacts. From time to time, Romanian officials suggested that they would prefer, as Foreign Minister Mircea Geoană put it, 'a geographically even distribution of Hungarian investment' that would not discriminate in favour of Transylvania.[32]

Romanian nationalists, in turn, repeatedly accused Hungary of pursuing political objectives through economic means. Corneliu Vadim Tudor, Chairman of the Greater Romania Party, saw the dangers of the involvement of the Hungarian oil company MOL in building petrol stations in Romania. 'If the entire fuel stock is in the hands of Hungarian investors,' Tudor said on the eve of Prime Minister Radu Vasile's visit to Hungary in 1999, 'the Romanian army's tanks, military vehicles and armoured vehicles could get into the hands of foreign investors in the event of a military conflict.'[33] During periods of tension in relations with Hungary, even Romanian government officials repeated claims with a similar message, albeit in more moderate language. Interior Minister Rus went as far as to argue on one occasion that 'Hungary wants to control Transylvania economically' as part of its endeavour to 'federalize' the region and seek 'co-sovereignty' over it.[34]

For its part, Hungary dismissed Romanian accusations that political considerations lay behind its encouragement of trade and investment links. When Romanian nationalists argued that Hungary was being guided by ulterior motives in proposing that a planned motorway linking the two countries should go through Cluj, the main city of Transylvania, Zsolt Németh, the Hungarian state secretary for foreign affairs, responded that such thinking was 'paranoid' and devoid of any understanding of 'the principles of the functioning of the economy'.[35] In any case, the Romanian accusations were undermined by the fact that many of the Hungarian

32 *Népszabadság*, 24 March 2001.
33 *Duna TV*, 1700 GMT, 7 February 1999, in *BBC Summary of World Broadcasts* (SWB), Part 2, Former Yugoslavia, Balkans and Central Europe, EE3455, p. C5, 9 February 1999.
34 AFP, 2022 GMT, 29 October 2001.
35 *Duna TV*, 1700 GMT, 7 February 1999, in *SWB*, Part 2, EE/3455, p. C6, 9 February 1999.

investors were, at least in part, foreign-owned. Moreover, with Hungary's expected early accession to the EU, the national character of its capital investment in Romania was likely to be further diluted.[36]

Romania and Moldova

Although in the economic sphere Romania continued to lag well behind the other EU accession countries, compared with Moldova it was relatively advanced. This was hardly surprising given that Moldova entered the 21st century with the lowest GDP in Europe and was ranked 26th out of the 27 former communist-ruled countries of Europe and the Commonwealth of Independent States (CIS) in a survey of human development carried out by the United Nations Development Programme. Average wages in 2002 amounted to $30 a month, less than a third of Romania's already low level of $100 a month.

As Moldova struggled to stave off economic catastrophe, Romania offered a helping hand. However, Moldova also suffered from insufficient energy resources. In the late 1990s Bucharest stepped up energy deliveries, to roughly 20 per cent of Moldova's needs, as Chişinău became increasingly indebted to Russia, in particular over natural gas supplies. But Romania itself repeatedly halted electricity supplies to Moldova in a dispute over unpaid bills.[37]

In the decade after the break-up of the Soviet Union, Romania emerged as Moldova's second largest trading partner. However, their bilateral trade was modest by most standards: barely $100 million in 1999. In any case, Romania was still a long way behind Russia, which continued to be a major provider of natural gas and oil to energy-poor Moldova and remained a key market for Moldova's farm produce. Because it was part of the former Soviet economic space and continued to rely so heavily on Russian and Ukrainian sources of energy, Moldova remained closely tied to the CIS economies. By contrast, even 10 years after Moldova's proclamation of independence and of its desire to join Europe, the EU accounted for only a third of Chişinău's trade. Meanwhile, the per capita EU assistance Moldova received in the decade up to 2000 was less than half of what had been disbursed to Romania (21 euros as against 52 euros).[38]

The low level of trade with the EU was symptomatic of a general failure to take advantage, admittedly in Moldova's case in a very difficult situation, of the opportunities presented by post-Soviet-era independence. Although the Partnership and Cooperation Agreement Moldova concluded with

36 Réti, 'Comparison of the Hungarian and Romanian economies'.
37 AP, 1918 GMT, 15 November 1998 and 1501 GMT, 25 April 2000.
38 *Le Monde Diplomatique*, January 2002, p. 7.

Brussels in 1994, which entered into force in 1998, provided for a gradual approach towards bringing Moldova into line with EU legislation on a single market and establishing a free trade area, in practice during the 1990s Chişinău made little progress in creating a business-friendly legal and administrative framework. As a result, even after Moldova joined the World Trade Organization in 2001 it was still not judged ready by Brussels to start negotiations on a free trade area.

Romania itself had concluded a free trade agreement with Moldova in 1994. Four years later the two countries joined Ukraine in launching an ambitious plan to set up a special economic zone, the Lower Danube Euroregion, with shipping, port, oil pipeline and refinery capacities free of corporation tax, value-added tax and excise duties.[39] Bucharest's various free trade arrangements would have to be reviewed on Romania's accession to the EU, with the potential of dealing another heavy blow to Moldova's beleaguered economy. However, as Romania was not expected to join before 2007 at the earliest, this tentative schedule appeared to provide sufficient time for Moldova to negotiate its own free trade agreement with Brussels.

DEFENCE AND SECURITY

Hungary and Romania

Even in the first half of the 1990s, when Hungarian–Romanian political relations were less than satisfactory and trade was at times stagnating, military ties between the two countries were largely unaffected by problems in other areas. A shared concern over the wars in the former Yugoslavia and the lack of a security umbrella to protect either country were among the main factors that encouraged cooperation rather than rivalry between Budapest and Bucharest in the defence area. From 1994 onwards membership of Partnership for Peace provided a constructive framework for expanding bilateral links as part of a broader movement towards integration with NATO. Starting in 1994, Hungary and Romania concluded several agreements on notifying each other about troop movements near border areas, expanding the exchange of information and increasing the number of reciprocal military inspections. The despatch of a Hungarian tank unit to Turda in 1996 was the first time since the Second World War that Hungarian troops had taken part in joint exercises on Romanian soil.[40]

---

39 Russian Public TV, 0800 GMT, 23 October 1998, in *SWB*, Part 1, Former Soviet Union, SU/3368 D/1, 27 Oct 1998.

40 V. G. Baleanu, *Romanian-Hungarian Relations: from Mutual Misunderstanding to Irrational Rationality*, CSRC Research Paper G71, Royal Military Academy Sandhurst, Camberley, 1999, pp. 36–8.

Hungarian–Romanian defence relations were not entirely trouble-free. In 1998 a Romanian mountain corps rifle unit, en route to take part in PfP exercises in Slovenia, was held up at the Hungarian frontier because of an apparent misunderstanding over how long in advance the Romanian side should have applied for permission to cross the border.[41] There were also lengthy delays over implementing plans to set up joint peacekeeping units.

The race for NATO membership, an unequal contest because Hungary was well ahead of Romania in the transition process, was also a source of strain in the two sides' security relations. Bucharest was worried about being left behind, and in 1996 Gheorghe Tinca, the Romanian defence minister, warned that Hungary's accession to NATO before Romania might 'start an arms race between the two countries'. No such thing happened when Hungary joined NATO in March 1999, for the simple reason that it was not in the interests of either side. Meanwhile, at the time of Hungary's accession some Hungarian politicians implied that Budapest's membership of NATO meant it would have an important say in determining when Romania itself would be able to join the Alliance. As Prime Minister Orbán put it in 1999, 'NATO and the EU would consult Hungary ... because Budapest knows Romania best.'[42] The implication of this and similar arguments was that Romania needed to do more to satisfy Hungary's demands over improving conditions for Romania's ethnic Hungarian community. But this was a double-edged sword: by asserting, and perhaps overplaying, its role within NATO in relation to Romania's future membership, Budapest was laying itself open to possible accusations from Bucharest that a failed accession bid in 2002 would be due in part to Hungarian obstructionism. That might in turn produce negative consequences for Romania's Magyar community, as the Romanian prime minister, Radu Vasile, among others, made clear quite early on. That point was understood by Hungary's socialist opposition leaders and, gradually, by the more nationalist governing coalition.[43] As a result, Hungarian official rhetoric changed somewhat in the years after Hungary joined NATO, its purpose being to reassure rather than to cause anxiety in Bucharest. In the end, the decision of the NATO summit in Prague in 2002 to invite Romania to join the Alliance resolved this particular problem.

41 Romanian Radio, Timişoara, 1200 GMT, 24 November 1998, in *SWB*, Part 2, EE/3394, p. B4, 25 November 1998.

42 V.G. Baleanu, *Romanian-Hungarian Relations*, p. 38.

43 Hungarian Radio, Budapest, 0700 GMT, 5 February 1999, in *SWB*, Part 2, EE/3453, p. B4, 7 February 1999.

Romania and Moldova

Although an early adherent to PfP, Moldova showed no signs of wishing to join the race for NATO membership during the decade after independence. Instead, it continued to steer a middle course between the West and Russia in the defence sphere, with a pronounced shift back towards Moscow after the PCRM gained power in 2001. Security was one of the key elements in this process. Moldova's leadership hoped that by fostering good relations with Russia, it could persuade the Kremlin to pull its forces out of Transnistria and to put more pressure on the Tiraspol regime, representing Slavonic-speaking nationalists, to give up its separatist agenda.

However, Moldova was keen to exploit some of the benefits of closer cooperation with NATO, and with Romania, on a bilateral level. During the latter half of the 1990s Chişinău concluded a number of cooperation agreements with Bucharest, notably in military transport and anti-aircraft defence and for setting up a joint peacekeeping unit. It also agreed to joint participation with Romania in PfP training projects.[44] Subsequently, even the newly formed communist government under Prime Minister Vasile Tarlev made it clear that rather than scale back its cooperation with NATO, it wanted to expand its activities within PfP. That was particularly the case in the field of peacekeeping operations. Moldova also continued to benefit from NATO's assistance in civil emergency planning and in the destruction of anti-personnel landmines and munitions under way since 2001.[45]

BORDERS

Hungary and Romania

For many people one of the immediate benefits that came with the collapse of communism was the opening up of borders between most CEE countries. Even in cases where visa-free (or even passport-free) travel had been allowed during the communist era, a range of petty restrictions, police or secret police vigilance as well as elaborate customs inspections had made cross-border travel relatively complicated. In the years after 1989 people in much of the region got used to a new freedom to move across borders. Yet it seemed that some of these freedoms would be taken away once the first wave of EU members from the region joined the Schengen regime. After enlargement, with the EU's 'hard' borders shifting eastwards and southwards, the Hungarian–Romanian border seems likely to become one of the first. For several years before its expected accession in 2004, Hungary, along with

44 V.G. Baleanu, *In the Shadow of Russia*, p. 17.
45 NATO website *www.nato.int/docu.update/2001/0514/e0515a.htm.*

other first-wave applicants, has been busy tightening its border controls as part of its preparations for membership. The expectation is that once it joins the EU, it will probably take no more than about two years before Hungary has in place all the sophisticated border controls and information systems that are part of the Schengen regime.

True, the abolition from 1 January 2002 of visa requirements for Romanians visiting Schengen countries removed perhaps the biggest potential obstacle to continued easy access to Hungary. It was a policy Budapest had advocated for several years.[46] Hungary's relief was immense: there would have been a high political price to pay for any Hungarian government that might have been forced to impose a visa regime on the ethnic Hungarians of Romania sometime after 2004. Even after the defeat of Prime Minister Orbán's government in the April 2002 elections, the issue continued to have a strong emotional resonance in Hungary.

Allowing visa-free travel between Hungary and Romania to continue had an economic as well as political advantage: the continuation of small-scale cross-border trade, legal and illegal, which was particularly beneficial for the poorer Romanian economy. The regions along or near the border profited most from access to a different market on the other side of a porous dividing line. Over many years Romanians had taken advantage of the higher prices for their produce, the higher wages for their labour, the abundance of locally produced Western-quality goods and a stable hard currency that were all available in Hungary. Meanwhile, Hungarians were making the most of cheap labour, food and less sophisticated mass-produced products from Romania.

Some of these benefits were almost certain to disappear with the imposition of more stringent border controls. Although a better-policed border and customs regime was aimed primarily at stopping the trade in drugs, illegal migrants and large-scale contraband, it would also almost inevitably make it more difficult to smuggle relatively small quantities of other goods across the border. Part of that trade was likely to continue through the exploitation of loopholes and part of it was going to be shifted into the open economy with its higher costs, but another part would almost certainly be forced out of business once its very informality and low costs could no longer be sustained. One way to tackle this problem was to use some of the available EU funds not only to tighten border controls but also to make them more efficient. It has been argued that through more advanced technology and the better training of border guards it might be possible to reduce waiting times at

46 The Hungarian foreign minister János Martonyi was quoted as calling for Romania's removal from the visa blacklist. Mediafax Romanian news agency, 30 July 1999, in *SWB*, Part 2, EE/3603, p. B3, 3 August 1999.

borders and even to speed up the circulation of people and goods without compromising security.[47]

Romania and Moldova

Even though Romania's progress towards accession had been relatively slow, the prospect of its eventual EU membership had a marked impact on its relations with Moldova. As part of the deal that ensured Romania's removal from the Schengen visa blacklist, Bucharest was required to tighten up its border controls, for example by upgrading equipment and introducing more sophisticated computer systems.

Perhaps the most tangible and, for many Moldovans, the most painful of these measures was the introduction from 1 July 2001 of the requirement for Moldovans to have passports when travelling to Romania. Apart from the bureaucratic formality of acquiring a new passport – many Moldovans had not obtained replacements for their old Soviet-era travel documents – the new requirement was a heavy burden both for the Moldovan administration with its empty coffers and for many impoverished Moldovan citizens. Bucharest stepped in to lighten that burden with a $1 million subsidy to enable about 60,000 Moldovans, mainly students and those living near the border, to purchase new passports, normally costing more than the average monthly national income, at a quarter of the usual price.[48]

There would be worse to come for Moldova, however, if Romania's EU accession were to lead to its imposition of a visa regime on Moldovan citizens. The cost and the bureaucracy involved in this would be serious obstacles to many Moldovans who might want to travel to Romania. Because of the parlous state of Moldova's economy, by the turn of the 21st century many of its people had come to rely extensively on work, trade and business opportunities in Romania. With two-thirds of Moldovans being Romanian-speakers, there were no language barriers to their activities. Moreover, since independence they had been helped by the lack of formalities or administrative costs involved in crossing the border with Romania. Thus Moldovans feared that the approach of Romania's EU membership would transform this situation. In the years leading up to its accession, Bucharest was likely to come under even greater scrutiny on account of its border provisions than the first-wave EU candidates.

The best that Bucharest and Chișinău could hope for in the medium term was the abolition of Schengen visa requirements for Moldovan citizens.

47 Heather Grabbe, *Profiting from EU Enlargement* (London: Centre for European Reform, 2001), p. 51.
48 Rompress website, 0933 GMT, 2 July 2001; AFP, 1449 GMT, 15 August 2001.

Although by the late 1990s Moldova was already a major source of illegal labour – and in many cases its citizens were victims of the white slave trade[49] – its relatively small population of 4.5 million was seen as a factor that would make the lifting of the visa requirement for Moldovans a manageable issue. This was reinforced by the fact that many of those looking for work were not going further than Romania. However, lifting the visa requirement for Moldovans was likely to create resentment in countries in a similar situation, the EU's other 'future eastern neighbours' – most notably in Ukraine with a population that was over eleven times the size of Moldova's.

In the meantime, many Moldovans began to prepare themselves for Romania's future EU membership by taking out Romanian citizenship. Estimates of the number of Moldovans who had been granted Romanian citizenship by the end of the 1990s, that is in less than a decade, were in the region of 200,000–300,000. However, it was difficult to ascertain the accuracy of these figures because under Moldovan law, dual nationality is allowed only where there is a relevant bilateral agreement in force; and in the case of Romania at the time of writing there was no such arrangement. All the same, the numbers were sufficient to encourage several candidates during Romania's presidential elections in 2000 to take their campaign to Moldova.[50] For much of the time Moldova tried to ignore this embarrassing 'virtual flight' of its citizens. However, when Romania opened eight new offices in order to process a backlog of applicants in 2000, Moldova temporarily closed its state archives, to prevent its people acquiring the documents required for obtaining Romanian citizenship.[51]

CONCLUSION

At the start of the 21st century the EU's eastwards enlargement began to turn into a medium-term reality for Hungary and into a strong, although longer-term, prospect for Romania. For Moldova it remained a distant dream. This presented a range of challenges for Budapest, Bucharest and Chişinău, as well as for the EU, in their attempts to prevent the emergence of a new 'Iron Curtain' between the prospective EU insiders and those destined to be left outside for the foreseeable future.

The expected time-lag of at least three years between the likely respective accession dates of Hungary and Romania was almost certain to create some difficulties in bilateral relations over the new border regime. However, the

---

49 *Victims of Trafficking in the Balkans* (Vienna–Geneva: International Organization for Migration, 2001), pp. 12–27.
50 AP, 1600 GMT, 19 November 2000.
51 AP, 1802 GMT, 15 March 2000.

problems appeared to be manageable. True, tougher controls would have to be instituted on the Hungarian–Romanian border until Romania could join the Schengen regime, and Hungary would benefit for several years from EU funds that would not be available to Romania. Nevertheless, there were various ways in which the widening of the gap between the two countries could be partially reversed at least, notably through greater investment in the Romanian economy by Hungary's increasingly successful companies. A more prosperous Hungary, the expected outcome of Budapest's EU accession, would be able to provide greater opportunities both for Romania's producers and for its labour force.

Meanwhile, the political rapprochement between Budapest and Bucharest, which was another by-product of the two countries' determination to meet EU and NATO conditions for membership, was also expected to help accommodate some of the problems that had previously often cooled and, at times, poisoned bilateral relations. By early 2002 the dispute over Hungary's 'status law' seemed to have been consigned to the past. With Romania's Hungarian minority acting more and more as a bridge between the two countries, there was a growing likelihood that Budapest would act as an advocate for, not an opponent of, Bucharest within the EU.

The real dividing line appeared to lie farther to the east, on the Romanian–Moldovan border. Moldova's likely exclusion from the EU for perhaps a generation carried with it the danger of consigning the former Soviet republic to another lengthy period on the periphery of Europe. Moldova's fate was in no way unique: it was only one of the EU's 'future eastern neighbours', which included the much larger Ukraine, not to mention Belarus.

For Bucharest the problems facing the 'other Romanian state' were clearly a major headache. Solidarity with the Moldovans, whom many within Romania traditionally regarded as fellow Romanians, was one reason for that concern – the more so as links between the two countries and their citizens were likely to be more difficult to foster as they end up on different sides of the EU's Schengen borders. In such conditions, Bucharest's hopes for building up a special or 'privileged relationship' with Chişinău would suffer a severe setback. The idea of bringing about the closest possible integration with Moldova, so as to overcome the legacy of its separation from Romania during the Soviet era, would be extremely difficult to pursue across the emerging 'hard' borders. Moreover, such borders were bound to be costly to police, as many of Moldova's economically desperate people were expected to continue to try to cross into Romania in search of a better life.

The solution to these and similar problems seemed to lie, at least in part, in increased funding for projects that would help Moldova's longer-term integration with Europe. Over the years leading up to its own EU member-ship, Romania might be able to generate an increasing share of the resources needed to help Moldova. However, the bulk of the funding would need to come from Brussels. It would also be for the EU to find a way to ease or abolish visa requirements for Moldovans, so that their access to Romania, and the vital link it represented for many of them, would not be made too difficult. With the approach of the next rounds of enlargement in 2004 and, tentatively, 2007, the EU is destined to play an increasingly crucial role in bilateral relations on and around its periphery.

7

Russia and the European Union

GRAEME P. HERD

'Complex and dynamic processes are going on in Europe today. European structures are being transformed and the role of big European organizations and regional forums is changing. In this context, the importance of our relations with the European Union is indubitably growing. To be sure, we do not set ourselves the goal of joining the EU, but we should seek ways of cardinally promoting cooperation and improving its quality.' – President Vladimir Putin to the Russian Foreign Ministry Board, 26 January 2001

RUSSIA'S EUROPEAN PATH?

Russia–EU relations have hitherto been underestimated, as the NATO agenda dominated relations between Russia and the West.[1] But whereas a NATO-centric approach dominated Russia's relationship with Europe in the past, relations with the EU will define Russia's European policy in the future. The policy issues and dilemmas raised by the expansion eastwards of the European Union are much more profound, deep-seated and far-reaching for Russia's security and stability in the new century than those arising from NATO's enlargement. Thus, the extent of Russia's cooperation with the EU will play a critical role in shaping its relationship with the European security order and hence stability in Europe. A Russian Federation in outright conflict with and isolation from such an order would fatally undermine both

---

* The views expressed in this article are those of the author and do not necessarily reflect the official policy or position of the George C. Marshall European Center for Security Studies, the United States Department of Defense, the German Ministry of Defence, or the United States and German Governments. My grateful thanks go to Clelia Rontoyanni, Sergei Medvedev, Igor Zevelev and the editors for their invaluable comments on earlier drafts and to Mary Ellen Haug of the Marshall Center Research Library for helping me with references. All errors of fact and weaknesses of interpretation are mine alone.

1 Yuri Borko, 'The European Union's Common Strategy on Russia: a Russian View', in Hiski Haukkala and Sergei Medvedev (eds), *The EU Common Strategy on Russia: Learning from the Grammar of CFSP* (Helsinki: The Finnish Institute for International Affairs, 2001), pp. 117–43.

its own integrity and legitimacy and those of the European security order and the transatlantic security community; Russian cooperation with the EU will transform the quality of European stability and security. What then are the key dynamics within the political, economic, military and societal security sectors that are driving the Russia–EU relationship in the new century?

In the early 1990s Moscow's ability to manage the policy agenda arising from the collapse of the Soviet Union was complicated by a psychological disorientation among the elite and a lack of leadership and direction at the centre. Russian identity, always contested, was stretched to breaking point between two strategic orientations – the nationalists and communists, who supported Eurasianism, and the emergent democratic factions, which formed the liberal-Atlanticist school. Neo-imperial, autocratic and revanchist impulses, which fed off reformed communist and national-patriotic sentiments, competed for controlling influence against the desire to 'return to Europe' and Westernize according to the prevailing Euro-Atlantic dynamic seen in central and eastern Europe through market-democratic transition and then consolidation.[2] Both Europe and Asia represented existential threats to the opposing camps, with few prepared to argue that Russia was both 'a part of Europe and apart from Europe'.[3]

The Russian Federation, buttressed by a federal treaty in February 1992 and by a new constitution in December 1993, began slowly to formulate a 'European policy' and to establish a relationship with the EU. It signed a partnership and cooperation agreement (PCA) with the EU in June 1994 (ratified in December 1997), but both partners concentrated on a largely economic agenda.[4] The emergence and elaboration of Russia–EU relations in the 1990s can partly be attributed to geopolitical change and partly to the impact of new EU member states. As non-aligned states, Finland and Sweden were instrumental in developing EU policy within eastern Europe and they were particularly keen to facilitate the shift towards a 'soft security' agenda in this region. The European Council in Vienna in December 1998 endorsed the Northern Dimension.[5] This Finnish initiative aims to

2 Andrei P. Tsygankov, 'From International Institutionalism to Revolutionary Expansionism', *Mershon International Studies Review*, Vol. 41, No. 2, November 1997, pp. 248–53; Jeffrey Surovell, 'Western Europe and the Western Alliance: Soviet and Post-Soviet Perspectives', *Journal of Communist Studies and Transition Politics*, Vol. 11, No. 2, June 1995, pp. 155–97.

3 Vladimir Baranovsky, 'Russia: A Part of Europe or Apart from Europe?', in *Europe: Where Does it Begin and End?*, Special Issue of *International Affairs*, Vol. 76, No. 3, July 2000, pp. 443–58.

4 D. Allen, 'EPC/CFSP, the Soviet Union, and the Former Soviet Republics: Do the Twelve Have a Coherent Policy?', in E. Regelsberger et al. (eds), *Foreign Policy of the European Union: From EPC to CFSP and Beyond* (Boulder and London: Lynne Rienner, 1997), pp. 219–35.

5 'A Northern Dimension for the Policies of the Union', European Commission, COM (1998), 589 Final, 25 November 1998.

coordinate economic, environmental, societal and political cooperation in northern Europe (comprising the five Nordic states, the three Baltic states, Poland, Germany and the Russian Federation); it has already had an important impact in shaping Russia's role and policies within the region. At the Cologne summit in June 1999, the EU unveiled a Common Strategy of the European Union on Russia, with the aim of promoting 'a stable, democratic and prosperous Russia, firmly anchored in a united Europe, free of dividing lines'.[6] Russia responded in October of that year with the elaboration of 'The Medium-term Strategy for the Development of Relations between the Russian Federation and the European Union (2000–2010)'.[7]

Western scholars and policy-makers and policy practitioners have generally characterized Russia–EU relations by two key features. First, there is a lack of interest and understanding by the publics (shared to some extent by the elites), which is reflected in opinion polling and interviews with foreign policy elites.[8] Secondly, Russia–EU interaction is set within a declaratory and aspirational framework of 'closer cooperation', 'mutual understanding', and a 'balance of interests'. Thus, lip-service has been paid to the abstract benefits of partnership, buttressed by a limited understanding of the impact of enlargement.[9] By the Cologne summit in 1999, Russia's rhetoric of cooperation was beginning to be matched by a greater awareness of EU policy-making and enlargement strategy.[10] This awareness of the EU's political, economic, military/defence and societal security sectors and pillars was reflected in Russia's channelling of greater human and capital resources into relations with the EU and its gradual switch from prioritizing bilateral relations between itself and individual EU states to an acknowledgment of Russia–EU negotiations *per se*. There was also a greater awareness of the

6 A. Stent, 'American Views on Russian Security Policy and EU–Russian Relations', paper prepared for the IISS/CEPS European Security Forum, Brussels, 14 January 2002, p. 2. See *http://www.eusec.org/stent.htm*. See also H. Haukkala, 'The Making of the European Union's Common Strategy on Russia', Working Paper No. 28 (Helsinki: The Finnish Institute of International Affairs, 2000).

7 *Diplomatichesky Vestnik*, November 1999, pp. 20–28.

8 Margot Light, John Löwenhardt and Stephen White, 'Russian Perspectives on European Security', *European Foreign Affairs Review*, Vol. 5, No. 4, December 2000, pp. 489–505, report that some of the foreign policy elite interviewees lacked 'even elementary knowledge about the EU'.

9 Timofei V. Bordachev, 'The Russian Challenge for the European Union: Direct Neighbourhood and Security Crises', in Iris Kempe (ed.), *Beyond EU Enlargement, Vol. I: The Agenda of Direct Neighbourhood for Eastern Europe* (Gütersloh: Bertelsmann Foundation Publishers, 2001), pp. 47–64. See also V. Baranovsky, *Russia's Attitudes towards the EU: Political Aspects*, Finnish Institute of International Affairs, Programme on Northern Dimension of CFSP, No. 1, Helsinki, 1993.

10 See 'A Common Strategy of the European Union of 4 June 1999', *Official Journal of the European Communities*, L 157/1, 24 June 1999.

impact of EU enlargement on Russia's relationship with its near neighbours, particularly Belarus and Ukraine. This was underscored by Russia's support for a multipolar world, as outlined by the Russian National Security Council in June 2000 in the Foreign Policy Concept of the Russian Federation.[11]

The presidency of Vladimir Putin has also redefined the relationship between Russia and the EU by placing it on a new footing, through the recognition that Russian bilateral relations with key EU states, particularly Germany, cannot be separated from the context of Russia–EU relations – a mutually reinforcing dynamic had emerged that promoted a correlation between the strength of Russia's bilateral relations with individual EU member states and its relations with the EU as whole, and vice versa. As Putin himself has noted, 'It is impossible to view the relations between Russia and Germany now beyond the context of Moscow's relations with the European Union. Germany is one of the centres of European integration.'[12] While Putin has projected the sort of rhetoric of commonalities and shared interests that characterized the Yeltsin years, it is apparent that Russia–EU relations have also begun to address the realities of challenges and obstacles generated by 'practical integration'. For this reason, by 2003 they were at a crossroads. It remained to be seen whether they could be deepened and consolidated constructively through greater cooperation and within an increasingly institutionalized framework or whether they would be shaped by obstacles and antagonisms. When discussing the relationship the central question is not whether Russia will join the EU. As Mikhail Zadornov, the former Russian finance minister has noted, it would take at least '20 or 30 years of hard work' to join the EU; and many would deny it was even a prospect.[13] In the short and medium term, certainly, the prospect of Russian membership of the EU is not on the policy agenda. The real question is, what will be the nature and quality of the relationship between Europe's largest state and the EU?

11 See, for example, V. Pozdniakov and S. Ganzha, 'New Countries on the EU's Doorstep', *International Affairs* (Moscow), Vol. 45, No. 3, 1999, pp. 55–63; V. Likachev, 'Russia and the European Union: A Long Term View', *International Affairs* (Moscow), Vol. 46, No. 2, 2000, pp. 116–26.

12 ITAR-TASS News Agency, Moscow, 10 April 2002. 'In the view of some EU officials, however, Russia has come to master using EU complexity for its purposes, playing various levels of the organisation off against each other – the Commission and the Council, the Presidency, foreign ministry and EU bodies.' Dov Lynch, 'Russia Faces Europe', *Chaillot Papers*, No. 60 (Paris: Institute for Security Studies, European Union, May 2003), p. 78.

13 Ekho Moskvy News Agency, Moscow, 3 July 2001. *Country Strategy Paper 2000–2006, National Indicative Programme, 2002–2003, Russian Federation, European Commission*, 27 December 2001, Brussels.

POLITICAL SECURITY: INTERGOVERNMENTAL VERSUS FEDERAL?

Russia and the EU have very different attitudes towards the state, regions, federation and subsidiarity, and this makes one issue particularly difficult to solve. The question of Kaliningrad demonstrates the apparent intractability of these obstacles to closer political cooperation between Moscow and Brussels and the limited extent to which they can reach 'technical' solutions.[14] Putin has argued that Kaliningrad is the 'pilot project' of their ability to cooperate. As a result, Moscow carried on intense negotiations with the EU over the status of this region, and in January 2002 the Russian state Duma passed a resolution 'On State Policy of the Kaliningrad Region'. This instructed the Security Council to complete the formulation of Russian policy in the near future.[15] Kaliningrad and the issues of power supply to the region, visa regimes and fishing dominated the 28 May 2002 EU–Russia summit, with Russia pushing for 'non-visa or privileged status for the region's residents for crossing the borders of the states [Poland, Lithuania, Latvia, Estonia] entering the EU'.[16]

The elaboration and implementation of EU policies towards Kaliningrad is largely dependent on Russian, Polish and Lithuanian cooperation. Lithuania is linked to Kaliningrad through joint participation in the envisaged 'Baltic Euroregion', the 'Neman Euroregion' (linking Lithuania with Kaliningrad and Belarus) and the 'Saule Euroregion' (linking key Kaliningrad towns with Lithuanian, Latvian and Swedish ones). More concretely, on 10 February 2000 Russia and Lithuania submitted a list of joint project proposals to the EU Commission (the 'Nida Declaration') for consideration by the Northern Dimension Action Plan. These proposals, including one for transport modernization, environmental protection and cross-border cooperation, were approved by the EU at the Feira summit in June 2000 and represent the emergence of regional and sub-regional interdependence.[17]

Despite these initiatives, a successful 'integration' of Kaliningrad into the EU is contingent on a reduction in Moscow's sovereignty over this region, entailing a possible growth of autonomy and even separatism within what will become an EU enclave.[18] The geopolitical issues raised by Kaliningrad

14 Editors' note: for a fuller discussion of this issue see Chapter 8 by Christopher Preston in this volume.

15 ITAR-TASS News Agency, Moscow, 16 January 2002.

16 BNS News Agency, Kaliningrad, 1 March 2002.

17 David Gowan, *How the EU Can Help Russia* (London: Centre for European Reform, London, December 2000), p. 34.

18 Igor Leshukov, 'The Regional-Centre Divide: The Compatibility Conundrum', in James Baxendale, Stephen Dewar and David Gowan (eds), *The EU and Kaliningrad: Kaliningrad and the Impact of EU Enlargement* (London: Federal Trust for Education and Research, 2000), pp. 127–42.

have generated political opposition within the Russian Federation and highlighted the conceptual gaps that still need to be bridged. Nikolay Tulayev, representative of the Kaliningrad region to the Council of the Federation, has, for example, described a report by the Parliamentary Assembly of the Council of Europe, which suggested that discussion should be held on transforming the Kaliningrad region into a subject of European legislation, as 'an encroachment upon Russian sovereignty'.[19]

At the tenth annual EU–Russia summit, held in Brussels on 11 November 2002, both sides reached a political agreement on transit from the Russian Federation to the Kaliningrad region. As of 1 July 2003, when Poland and the Baltic states are required to meet Schengen Treaty border control standards, 'facilitated transit documents' (effectively, cheap or free single- or multiple-entry transit visas) may be issued to Russian citizens to allow land transit between Kaliningrad and the rest of the Russian 'mainland'. A feasibility study on a high-speed non-stop train service providing a rail corridor through Lithuania is also being considered.[20]

Former First Deputy Foreign Minister Aleksandr Avdeyev noted in 2000 that 'The endurance of our relations with the EU will be tested by the work on the agreements on ensuring unrestricted relations between the Kaliningrad region and the rest of Russia and also on the creation of favourable conditions for the development of this region of Russia's external economic relations.'[21] In January 2001 the Russian Ministry of Foreign Affairs went further, suggesting that the regional policies of the EU might serve as a useful model for Moscow's management of the foreign relations of its constituent parts. Clearly, the EU–Russia agreement needs to be long-term, and should treat Kaliningrad as just one aspect of the relationship rather than as a test case or pilot project which, if resolved, will signal cooperative Russia–EU relations on all other issues. The very uniqueness of Kaliningrad means that the cooperative framework designed to ensure its integrity and stability within EU borders does not create a template that is transferable to the rest of northwestern Russia. Moreover, tensions in Lithuania's relations with the EU resulted from this agreement, as some MPs argued that the Schengen Treaty itself would have to be changed so as to allow Russian transit and that the agreement belittled Lithuania's sovereignty and its diplomatic service.[22] Some sections of the Russian press declared: 'Putin Surrenders Kaliningrad'.[23]

19 BNS News Agency, Kaliningrad, 26 April 2002.
20 'Joint Statement on Transit between the Kaliningrad Region and the Rest of the Russian Federation', Tenth Russia–EU Summit, Brussels, 11 November 2002.
21 Interfax News Agency, Moscow, 14 December 2000.
22 *Kaunas Diena*, Kaunas, 12 November 2002.
23 *Gazeta.ru* website, Moscow, 11 November 2002.

Although the November 2002 EU–Russia summit reached agreement on the issue of Kaliningrad, it also highlighted a further outstanding and long-term point of conflict: EU objections to Russia's violation of human rights in Chechnya. Russia, particularly under the Putin presidency, has consistently rejected the charge that it is suppressing liberty in Chechnya, arguing that it is an internal matter upon which Russia does not accept EU advice.[24] Although the EU has toned down criticisms following Putin's firm support for the international anti-terrorist coalition and the Chechen rebels' siege of a theatre in Moscow in October 2002, Danish criticisms of Russia's Chechen policy drew an angry response from Russia. As a result the venue for the EU–Russia summit was changed from Copenhagen to Brussels.

ECONOMIC SECURITY: AN ASYMMETRIC RELATIONSHIP?

EU enlargement raises a number of economic challenges that the Russian Federation must meet, including the economic viability of Kaliningrad after the imposition of the Schengen border regime and of Russia's exports in the face of the EU tariffs and trade priorities that newly acceding states will be required to implement. The Russia–EU–WTO nexus also has an impact on Russia's Baltic policy and relationship with Ukraine. Many of the overtly political issues of contention between Russia and the EU gain currency because of the interrelationship between policies on political issues, economic consequences and Russia's sovereignty. The resolution of each of these specific issues and the nature and timing of their solutions will impact on the quality of Russia–EU relations.

Russia's trade turnover with EU countries amounted to 40 per cent of its total trade in 2001, outstripping intra-CIS economic relations, and this was predicted to rise to 55 per cent after EU enlargement to Poland and the three Baltic states. As Gowan notes, the trade relationship is asymmetric given that only 3 per cent of the EU's external trade is with Russia. However, this 3 per cent constitutes 21 per cent of the EU's natural gas and 12 to 15 per cent of its oil and oil products (the core of the 'Energy Dialogue'). Thus although it may appear that 'Russia does not matter as much to the EU as the EU to Russia', it is clear that each is of strategic importance to the other.[25]

In November 2001 Deputy Prime Minister Ilya Klebanov noted that

24 Deutschland Radio, Cologne, 12 November 2002.

25 David Gowan, *How the EU Can Help Russia,* p. 7. Note that the EU is also the leading source of foreign direct investment (FDI) in the Russian economy, while capital flows in the other direction are insignificant in terms of total FDI into the EU. See also 'The EU's Relations with Russia: EU-Russia Trade', updated May 2002: *http://www.europa.eu.int/comm/external_relations/russia/intro/trade.htm* and *http://europa.eu.int/comm/energy_transport/en/lpi_en_3.html#ref.*

cooperation with the EU was critical to a breakthrough in Russia's democratic rebuilding and to the modernization of the Russian economy by 2015. Russian Prime Minister Mikhail Kasyanov has rejected full EU membership in the short term, but has called for economic *sobornost*, or 'togetherness', through a joint EU–Russia economic area modelled on the European Free Trade Association.[26] In early 2002 the EU Trade Commissioner Pascal Lamy produced an upbeat assessment of Russia–EU relations, noting that Russia was becoming a priority track for the European Union's economic policy in the years ahead. When asked how economic relations between Russia and the EU were developing, Lamy observed that there were three basic directions in this process: the implementation of measures provided by a long-standing agreement on partnership and cooperation; negotiations currently being held on Russia entering the WTO; and the establishment of a unified economic area in the future, which was expected gradually to assume a more definite shape.[27] As interstate borders within the Schengen area become increasingly transparent, legislation becomes harmonized and the single currency is introduced, economic relations with the EU are set to become of critical importance to the Russian Federation. The gas and energy sectors and cross-border infrastructure issues will dominate the agenda in the economic sphere. After the EU's enlargement Russia will be able to deal with one bloc rather than a number of different currencies, border regimes and transit legislation.

However, such a rosy picture fails to note the actual, potential and still latent points of economic contention between Russia and the EU. President Vladimir Putin has stressed the potentially negative impact of 'virtual divisions' within Europe that transcend the territorial: 'There are economic barriers, organizational barriers, administrative barriers – all kinds of barriers.'[28] As a result, the real danger arises that the border with the CIS could evolve into the economic and bureaucratic equivalent of the Berlin Wall, rather than Vladimir Putin's preferred 'gates into a democratic country'.[29] Such a border, also described as an 'epidemic faultline', would separate EU states and potential members (those with the realistic possibility of adopting EU rules, regulations and the *acquis communautaire*) from the Russian Federation.[30]

---

26 *Der Standard*, Vienna, 4 July 2001, p. 2.

27 Interfax News Agency, Moscow, 12 January 2002.

28 Phoenix TV, Berlin, 19 June 2000.

29 Interfax News Agency, Moscow, 29 November 2000. Some analysts warn of the emergence of a *de facto* 'silver' or 'paper curtain' or a cultural divide (where modernity is differently perceived). Such a barrier could also be characterized as the 'digital divide': the adoption of e-commerce and Internet and mobile phone access linked to third-generation (3G) technology is generally slower in the east owing to outdated telecommunication infrastructures and financial systems.

30 René Nyberg, 'Russia and Europe', *European Security*, Vol. 8, No. 2, Spring 1999, pp. 15–21.

Tariff and transit costs, combating organized crime, the implementation of Schengen border regulations and Russian access to the EU's common market are all issues that still have to be managed.[31] Putin himself has warned that if the EU integrates former Soviet republics, namely the three Baltic states, too speedily, this could 'endanger economic stability all over Eastern Europe', with the potential of undermining Russia's trade relations in the region.[32] Although Russian foreign ministry spokesman Aleksandr Yakovenko described the EU's eastward enlargement as 'a natural integration process', he added that it should not negatively influence Russia's economic relations with new EU members.[33]

Moreover, as one analyst has noted, 'Sharing geographical borders with Russia, Belarus and the Russian exclave of Kaliningrad, and having had strong institutional links with Moscow during the years of annexation, the Baltic States are perceived as an inevitable "door into Europe" for criminal networks in the CIS seeking to extend their activities westwards.'[34] Although the worst criminal excesses of the Yeltsin years have been ameliorated, it is worth noting the impact criminality can potentially have on the integrity of the state. Within the Russian Federation, the effects of such a rapid growth of criminal influence upon federal governance are multifaceted. The moral authority and legitimacy of the federal system have been brought into question, as federal and regional power structures have been 'colonized' by criminal groups. The very nature of criminal activities – tax exemption, money-laundering and embezzlement of state funds – all weaken the resources of the state, thereby limiting its ability to fulfil its federal functions and administrative responsibilities within the regions as well as reducing its legitimacy. One expert has commented that 'Privatization, banking, a media run by advertising, stock markets: all these elements of capitalist economies are now controlled to a large degree by criminal enterprises, as are too many politicians who stand as people's deputies.'[35] Criminal activities also distort the transition to the market economy and the international standing of the state, in turn threatening Russia's political and economic integration and

31 Heather Grabbe, 'The Sharp Edges of Europe: Extending Schengen Eastwards', *International Affairs*, Vol. 76, No. 3, July 2000, p. 519.
32 BNS News Agency, Tallinn, 16 June 2000.
33 ITAR-TASS News Agency, Moscow, 24 January 2001.
34 P. Rawlinson, *Russian Organised Crime and the Baltic States: Assessing the Threat*, ESRC 'One Europe or Several?' Programme Working Paper 38/01, available at *http://www.one-europe.ac.uk/pdf/w38rawlinson.pdf.*
35 Phil Williams (ed.), *Russian Organised Crime: The New Threat?* (London: Frank Cass, 2000), p. 9; CSIS Global Organized Crime Project, 'Russian Organized Crime', *CSIS Panel Report*, 1997 p. 104 – *www.csis.org/goc/taskruss.html.*

potentially affecting its relations not just with the EU but with the rest of the world.[36]

In June 2002 Russian First Deputy Minister for Economic Development and Trade Mikhail Dmitriyev stated that 'Russia still has serious problems with the European Union, which hampers dynamic development in Russia's relations with [it]. So far, the European Union has not recognized Russia as a country with a market economy.' The EU did not accept that Russian export prices (for certain goods, e.g. steel) reflected production costs at market prices, and took anti-dumping measures against certain Russian producers and categories of goods. In Russian eyes, these measures were unjustified and discriminatory. Prime Minister Kasyanov protested in 2001 about ostensibly discriminatory EU measures against Russian steel, metal products and furs and also about what he called 'the silent effort to prevent the export of Russian nuclear fuel to the EU'.[37] Russia and the EU subsequently agreed terms for deliveries of Russian steel for the following three years. Maksim Medvedkov, deputy Russian Minister of Economic Development and Trade, reported that a general agreement on the steel trade for 2002 had been agreed at talks in Paris on 6–7 February 2002.[38]

Russia also has disagreements with the EU over its negotiations for admission to the WTO. The objections within Russia to WTO membership are strong and the anti-WTO lobby quite powerful and vociferous (as evidenced by the 2003 May Day demonstrations in Moscow). More substantively, Russian officials have complained that WTO members (including the EU) are demanding more concessions from Russia than from countries that joined the organization earlier. The main requirement for Russia is to bring its laws into compliance with WTO regulations before joining (rather than upon accession), and this requirement has seriously complicated negotiations for admission.[39] As its largest trading partner as well as its principal investor, the EU has insisted that it is not creating any barriers to Russia's accession to the WTO, while noting that Russian subsidies to domestic gas consumers effectively subsidize Russian exporters and therefore are particularly problematic for the country's accession. Richard Wright, head of the European Commission delegation in Russia, has called on Russia to bring its

36 Mark Galeotti, 'Crime, Corruption and the Law', in Mike Bowker and Cameron Ross, *Russia after the Cold War* (London and New York: Longman, 2000), pp. 135–50. As *The Economist* noted, 'Far from "civilising" the wreckage of the Soviet economy, economic transactions between Russia and the West are running the risk of corrupting the western side, if only by forcing it to wink at practices that would be outlawed in more established economies.' 'Fuelling Russia's Economy' and 'Russia's Organized Crime', *The Economist*, 26 August 1999, p. 13 and pp. 17–19 respectively.
37 ITAR-TASS News Agency, Moscow, 24 April 2001.
38 Interfax News Agency, Moscow, 11 February 2002.
39 Interfax News Agency, Moscow, 31 October 2001.

domestic gas prices into line with world prices; currently they are one-sixth of them.

On 1 November 2002 the EU officially recognized Russia as a market economy and made appropriate amendments to European anti-dumping legislation in order to reflect its new status. This should address some EU reservations with regard to Russia's bid for WTO membership, thereby removing a bone of contention between Russia and the EU. Market status should increase trade flows between them. Critical to the increase in trade will be the development of transport corridors into and around Russia.

Russia's export trade will impact on its role as a European bridge into Asia and on its relationship with the Baltic states. The pan-European transport corridor number two, 'Berlin–Warsaw–Minsk–Moscow', will be extended as far as the Volga river and the Urals, linking in Nizhni-Novgorod and then Ekaterinburg. According to the Russian transport minister Sergey Frank, 'This turns the Trans-Siberian main line into a complex of railways and motorcar highways', integrating it into 'European cargo flows', with St Petersburg as the 'Western window' of the Trans-Siberian trunk line and as one of the main trans-shipment points of container transit between Europe and Asia.[40] Moreover, an accord has been reached on the international financing, with Finnish, Russian and EU funding, of the reconstruction of the 55 km road from Vyborg to the customs checkpoint at Serdyukov on the border of Finland.[41] Such projects will be vital for effective and efficient Russia–EU trade flows.

Putin pointed out in 2000 that northwestern Russia accounts for 20 per cent of total foreign investment in Russia and that 50 per cent of all products manufactured there are competitive on the international market. He stressed that freight handled by the Baltic states costs the country $1.5 billion a year in transit fees, arguing that Russia must concentrate on transport, communication and seaport development, particularly the Baltic pipeline system, in the future.[42] Although Russian transit routes compete with those of the Baltic states, when Putin met Semen Vaynshtok, the president of the Transneft joint-stock company, to discuss the commissioning of Primorsk port in Leningrad Region (the final point in the Baltic Pipeline System), he noted that 'Russia is gaining its own routes for the shipment of oil from Western Siberia, the Urals and even certain CIS countries, above all Kazakhstan'.[43] Putin stressed the need for the 'complete depoliticization of this project' and the necessity of making it 'economically attractive both to the participants of

40 ITAR-TASS News Agency, Moscow, 13 September 2000.
41 Ibid., 14 September 2000.
42 Russian Public TV, Moscow, 3 August 2000.
43 Ibid., 11 January 2002.

the market within our country and to our partners abroad. This means that our port must operate efficiently. Ships must be handled to high standards. Prices and tariffs which we charge the participants in the market must be no higher and, preferably, lower than what is being offered by our competitors in other countries.'[44]

However, as of early 2003 it remained to be seen whether it would be feasible for Russia to bypass the Baltic state ports, whether such a move could be depoliticized and whether EU support for the Transport Corridor Europe–Caucasus–Asia would compete with alternative Russian-dominated East–West transit corridors. If roads built to international standards were to link China to the South Caucasus and the EU states, then 'the shortest, cheapest, most suitable and safest transport corridor' would probably bypass the trans-Siberian corridor, undercutting all but the energy corridors from the Russian Federation.[45] Clearly, by 2003 the economic security agenda remained far from settled. A range of issues still had to be managed, and more were likely to emerge over the following decade with the potential to become politicized by the EU, Russia and the Baltic and CIS states.

MILITARY SECURITY: VALUES, CAPABILITY, CREDIBILITY AND TRANSITION TRAPS?

The growing defence and security sector is a relatively new issue in Russia–EU relations; it has developed rapidly and moved up the agenda during the Putin presidency.[46] The European Security and Defence Policy (ESDP) strengthened the EU's Common Foreign and Security Policy by giving it a military dimension (e.g. the EU's Rapid Reaction Force, civilian crisis management capability and increased defence-industrial cooperation). It responds to real and growing transnational threats that destabilize EU values by enabling diplomacy to be backed by the credible prospect of military action. Evolving ESDP was one of the main topics of the EU–Russia summit of October 2000. Russia's desire to have security issues in Europe resolved by European structures rather than within the framework of NATO is in large part the basis of its interest in ESDP.[47] Russia's justice minister Yuriy Chayka stated in April 2002 that his EU colleagues 'expressed their full understanding and support for Russia, as well as [sharing] common concerns

44 Idem.
45 Uzbek Radio second programme, Tashkent, 24 April 2002.
46 Dieter Mahncke, 'Russia's Attitude to the European Security and Defence Policy', *European Foreign Affairs Review*, Vol. 6, Issue 4, Winter 2001, pp. 427–36.
47 Clelia Rontoyanni, 'So Far, So Good? Russia and the ESDP', *International Affairs*, Vol. 78, No. 4, 2002, pp. 813–30.

about the anti-terrorist fight, migration and organized crime'.[48] Russia's strategic realignment post-11 September and its integration into the US-sponsored 'coalition of the willing' reinforced its security cooperation with neighbouring states.

Indeed, a cursory glance at Russia–EU cooperation in the security sphere indicates that it embraces sources of potential insecurity within both the 'hard' and the 'soft' security agendas. Putin has called for international cooperation and 'constructive interaction' against the main threats and risks to European security. These are 'non-military in nature' and include 'the proliferation of weapons of mass destruction, international terrorism, aggressive separatism, organized crime, drug trafficking and ecological disasters, which might upset the strategic stability as a whole'.[49] Russia has ratified the 1990 convention on money laundering, and there is also bilateral cooperation in the field of Justice and Home Affairs, particularly in fighting organized crime, trafficking in narcotic drugs and human beings, and illegal migration. Environmental security cooperation occurs in the form of TACIS (technical aid) projects and also within the Northern Dimension (including cross-border cooperation with Finland and the Baltic states), which includes water purification schemes in St Petersburg.

Cooperation in the non-proliferation and disarmament sector includes Russia's chemical weapons destruction programme and the conversion of arms grade plutonium programme, which receive funding from the EU budget. A meeting between the EU and Russia on 12 September 2001 broadened existing anti-terrorist cooperative efforts and reinforced joint action concerning the Middle East peace process. Russia is a co-sponsor of the peace process in the Middle East, and its foreign minister noted, 'The very nearness in approaches to this issue on the part of Moscow and Brussels allows us to act more in unison and, if required, collectively on this track.'[50]

When examining the viability of ESDP it is clear that positive Russian attitudes towards its development will be critical to its effectiveness.[51] The EU is formulating targets for civilian and military crisis management capabilities. The principal military target pertains to the European Rapid Reaction Force (ERRF), which was planned to become operational in 2003. Although it was deployed to Macedonia in March 2003, it is still too early to gain a sense of its effectiveness and ability and the extent to which it can

<hr>

48 Interfax News Agency, Moscow, 30 April 2002.
49 Ibid., 7 February 2001.
50 Ibid., 25 November 2000.
51 Tuomas Forsberg, 'Russia's Role in the ESDP', in Esther Brimmer (ed.), *The EU's Search for a Strategic Role: ESDP and its Implications for Transatlantic Relations* (Washington, DC: Center for Transatlantic Relations, 2002), pp. 85–100.

weather the internal tensions that disrupt the formulation of a coherent EU foreign and security policy.[52]

Two critical issues remain to be resolved: will the ERRF be deployed outside the Balkans region into former Soviet space and what will its rules of engagement be? The answer to these questions will determine Russian attitudes to the ERRF and thus define the nature of Russia's military security cooperation with the EU. The extension of the EU's holistic approach to military and non-military aspects of security into the Commonwealth of Independent States (CIS) – with military and economic sticks and carrots – will to a great extent stand or fall on the degree of Russian support. At present, the prospects of greater Russian cooperation appear weak; Russia exhibits a 'wait and see' attitude towards the ERRF. The experience of the Balkans and the EU's emphasis on peacekeeping might lead Russian policy-makers and analysts to conclude that the EU will use economic and financial means to 'buy peace' and that the role of the ERRF will be confined to ensuring that the conflicting sides respect the conditions of the 'purchase'.[53]

A difficulty in Russian participation in cooperative peacekeeping efforts within Europe was most apparent during the Kosovo campaign, when the 'Pristina Brigade' seemed to have slipped from Russian civilian control and it appeared that factions within Russia's Ministry of Defence had initiated an independent foreign policy. This incident highlighted the absence of the necessary preconditions to develop and sustain cooperative military security efforts between Russia and the EU.

First, it has been argued that they do not share the same fundamental strategic culture and value system that have underpinned the Euro-Atlantic security community over the past half-century. Indeed, the extent to which Russia will adopt EU norms, rules and values is in direct proportion to the expectations of EU membership, as the EU's normative power over Russia is weak. Moreover, although the EU is defined as Russia's main strategic partner in the National Security Concept of 2000, most analysts argue that relations with the United States remain of primary strategic importance to Russia and that Russia's preferred European security system would be based on an enhanced role for the Organization for Security and Cooperation in Europe (OSCE).

---

52 'National egoism, distinctly divergent foreign policy interests of the individual members and an inefficient decision-making system in CFSP, along with far reaching retention of sovereignty by individual states, all led to a lack of coherence in collective action and was thus a great handicap to the conduct of European foreign affairs.' Gisela Müller-Braneck-Bocquet, 'The New CFSP and ESDP Decision-Making System of the European Union', *European Foreign Affairs Review*, Vol. 7, 2002, pp. 259–60.

53 Stanislav Tkachenko, 'The EU's Crisis Management from the Russian Perspective', in Graeme P. Herd and Jouko Huru (eds), *EU Civilian Crisis Management*, Conflict Studies Research Centre, RMA Sandhurst, M22, May 2002, p. 56.

Is Russia–EU military security cooperation to be caught forever between the Scylla and Charybdis of a divergent strategic context and clashing norms and value systems? If Robert Kagan's thesis holds true, and Americans inhabit a strategic environment within which Hobbesian Realpolitik dominates while Europeans luxuriate in the illusory comforts of a Kantian liberal peace, then manifestly Russia might be thought to share the strategic outlook of the United States rather than of Europe. In the words of Kagan, 'Americans are from Mars, Europeans are from Venus.'[54] Indeed, US–Russian support for authoritarian but anti-fundamentalist Islamic regimes in Central Asia strengthens this observation – Russians too can inhabit Mars.

However, to suggest that Russia and the United States inhabit the same strategic universe is to overlook the complexity of both Putin's strategic reorientation and the ambiguity and ambivalence at the heart of ESDP. First, Putin's ability to undertake strategic realignment has been facilitated by fundamental disparities within the value system that underpins the Euro-Atlantic security community. Compare, for example, Gerhard Schröder's 'pre-emptive', 'unilateral' and instrumental anti-Americanism in the run-up to the German elections in 2002 with Putin's standing 'shoulder to shoulder' with the United States in support of the global war against terror in Central Asia. A paradox emerges, as the very weakness of the concept of a 'global war on terror' becomes its greatest strength as far as Russia is concerned: the inherent dilemmas and contradictions embodied by this 'war' provide Russia with an ideological pretext for strategic realignment, while the disparities and fractures within the Euro-Atlantic security community offer President Putin the opportunity to choose which of the core values and interests of a divided transatlantic community Russia shares.[55]

Secondly, there is a basic incompatibility between Russia and EU states in the military-technology sector, a capability gap which makes effective cooperation in that sphere difficult. The EU's determination to retain links with the United States in a strategic partnership further underscores the lack of a basis for meaningful cooperation between the EU and Russia. But it is the differences in technology, defence spending and collective security capability between the United States and its European allies within NATO – rather than between EU states and Russia – that have been highlighted

54 Robert Kagan, 'Power and Weakness', *Policy Review*, June–July 2002, Issue 113, pp. 3–28, available at *http://www.policyreview.org/Jun02/kagan/html.*

55 For a fuller elaboration of this argument, see Graeme P. Herd and Ella Akerman, 'Russian Strategic Realignment and the Post-Post Cold War Era', *Security Dialogue*, Vol. 33, No. 3, 2002, pp. 357–72. See also Igor Zevelov, 'Russian and American National Identity, Foreign Policy, and Bilateral Relations', *International Politics*, 39, December 2002, pp. 447–56.

since 11 September.[56] NATO's command and decision-making structures have been undermined by America's decision to create a 'coalition of the willing' for the purposes of the war in Afghanistan in 2001–2 rather than to harness NATO's collective security role in accordance with the Alliance's own strategic concept (as revised in Washington in April 1999). NATO's reaction has highlighted an apparently unbridgeable chasm. Europe's failure to modernize has left it marginalized: in danger of losing the ability to deploy effective EU fighting forces out of area to enforce the higher-end Petersberg tasks. The more marginalized Europe is, the more hegemonic the United States will tend to be. NATO is split between European member states, which are consigned to uphold the practically defunct collective defence role and to carry out limited peacekeeping and policing functions (primarily in the Balkans), and the United States, which concentrates on directing à la carte multilateral formations to wage war against 'global terror'. Such a perception is likely to fuel a drive by some EU member states (led by France) to use ESDP to counterbalance US 'hyper-power' (US primacy perceived as hegemony). Efforts in this direction, its protagonists assert, would aim to insure against the prospect of US and EU priorities differing or of US inability/unwillingness to cooperate with EU forces in future crisis management.[57] The coherence and sustainability of ESDP were brought into question over the splits in Europe over the best way to proceed on ensuring full and immediate Iraqi disarmament (UN Resolution 1441) with Russia siding with France and Germany ('Old Europe') and the US with the UK, Italy, Spain, Portugal and Denmark, and 'New Europe' – the 'Vilnius 10' of Albania, Bulgaria, Croatia, Estonia, Latvia, Lithuania, the former Yugoslav Republic of Macedonia, Romania, Slovakia and Slovenia.

Although the invasion of Iraq by a US-led 'coalition of the willing' has apparently exposed pre-existing fractures and cleavages in the Euro-Atlantic security community by posing choices that many governments would have preferred to evade and avoid, Russia's response at least was clear and nuanced. On 20 March 2003, at a Security Council meeting in Moscow, Putin argued in a keynote statement that the war was unjustified, that Iraq did not pose a threat to its neighbours and that military action represented a serious political mistake as it undermined the principle of state sovereignty and raised

56 Julian Lindley-French, 'Terms of Engagement: The Paradox of American Power and the Transatlantic Dilemma Post 11-September', *Chaillot Papers*, No. 52, May 2002, available at *http//www.iss-eu.org/chaillot/chai52e.pdf.*

57 Anthony Lake has argued that the danger of the ERRF is not that it will be too effective, thereby causing a decoupling with the US-initiated Rapid Response Force, 'but that it could create structures and institutions which in some senses could be competitive with NATO without developing the capabilities to make them real.' Anthony Lake, 'Interview', *Defensor Pacis*, Issue 12, September 2002, p. 14.

the spectre of an international order based on the principle of 'might is right' ('fist might', in Putin's words). Russia therefore joined France and Germany among the major European powers in opposing the war – a 'coalition of the unwilling', which Paris at least marked as a counterweight to US primacy.

Russia's response to the invasion raises interesting questions about its foreign policy priorities in the 21st century and how this might impact on relations with the EU. Russia's advocacy of a negotiated second resolution demonstrates its determination to maintain its status as a world power through the exercise of its seat on the UN Security Council. The Putin government's desire to reflect public opinion might be understood as a backlash against having conceded ground on the ABM Treaty, NATO enlargement, and the positioning of US troops in Central Asia and Georgia, and is particularly potent in the run-up to the 2004 Russian presidential elections. But the 'battle of Iraq' also demonstrates Putin's interest in maintaining a meaningful partnership with the US, and in the context of the Global War on Terrorism this partnership is likely to remain strong during both the Bush and Putin first- and second-term presidencies (until 2008). Although Russia has argued that 'invasion' of Iraq was 'illegal', it has done so with far more flexibility and tactical élan than either Berlin or Paris. The major foreign policy achievement of Putin's first-term presidency has been to dramatically improve and consolidate relations with the US; and Putin is unlikely to allow a fundamental deterioration of Russia's one key strategic partnership. Nevertheless, Moscow has successfully improved its relations with Berlin and Paris, moving its partnership to the strategic level. This trend is likely to have positive spillover effects on EU enlargement in the Baltic region in 2004 and 2005, and lead to an increased political willingness – at least in Paris, Berlin and Moscow – to explore more closely Russia–EU foreign and security policy alignment.

The capabilities gap, which has so weakened NATO's perceived utility, means Russia could make a greater potential contribution to the EU's development of instruments in the security sector. Russian Deputy Prime Minister Viktor Khristenko has noted that there is a real basis for cooperation in the military sphere, particularly between Russia's Global Orbiting Navigation Satellite System and the EU's Galileo global satellite navigation system. Cooperation could extend to other aspects of the defence and space complex, as well as to the settling of crises and emergencies.[58] Russian Foreign Minister Igor Ivanov has noted that the EU and Russia should develop

---

58 ITAR-TASS News Agency, Moscow, 28 September 2000. 'Russia may also provide technology for the EU's satellite centre in Torrejon (Spain), and a cooperation agreement is pending between the European Space Agency and Russia's Rosaviakosmos.' Rontoyanni, 'So Far, So Good? Russia and the ESDP', p. 824.

jointly operated mechanisms to resolve common concerns and coordinate possible contributions to the EU's crisis management operations.

Although obvious areas of military security cooperation that plug existing gaps in the ERRF capability profile are satellite reconnaissance and navigation programmes and heavy airlift (the US currently has 253 heavy airframes for transport, the EU only seven), the Russian satellites have poor reliability records. In addition, the further development of national satellite programmes by EU member states should not be overlooked, nor should the ability of the EU to purchase Boeing C-17s or Lockheed Martin S-130-JSs until the joint procurement of the French-constructed A-400M airbus comes on line in 2008.[59]

Thirdly, even if we accept that Russia has military assets that it might usefully contribute to enhance the ESDP and that the EU demonstrates a growing political willingness to accept that contribution, would Russia commit troops to projected ERRF peacekeeping missions? It can be argued that the implicit *raison d'être* of an active and operational ERRF brings it into direct competition, and possibly confrontation, with Russia in its 'zone of vital interest', undercutting the basis for cooperation. Were the ERRF to be deployed to Transniestria, Abkhazia, Nagorno-Karabakh, South Ossetia, to say nothing of Russian territory (Chechnya), Russia's reaction is likely to be negative, with accusations that the EU is actively undermining its traditional sphere of influence and attempting to encircle it in conjunction with NATO.[60]

Rontoyanni cites Trenin and Kobrinskaya respectively in arguing that for Russian elites, the EU is a politically less sensitive partner than NATO and that the Russian leadership 'might be more willing to accept an EU contribution to the onerous peacekeeping operation in Abkhazia'.[61] Despite the willingness of these analysts to accentuate the positive, the negative cannot be entirely eliminated. Yet Russia's policy on this issue is split, reflecting the fragmentation of policy-making structures and the penetration of the decision-making process by lobby groups, both domestic and transnational, within the Federation. It is likely that Russian business and criminal interests engaged in smuggling and other illicit economic activities in the separatist areas can mobilize political opposition to the resolution of conflicts in these

59 Mark Webber, 'Third-Party Inclusion in the European Security and Defence Policy: A Case Study of Russia', *European Foreign Affairs Review*, Vol. 6, 2001, pp. 418–20.
60 It is not entirely certain that Russia would object to an EU presence in the first two conflict regions, provided it had a say in planning the mission. In any case, the EU appears far from willing to venture into the CIS region, let alone against Russian opposition. See also Lynch, 'Russia Faces Europe', pp. 87–90.
61 Rontoyanni, 'So Far, So Good? Russia and ESDP', p. 822.

economic 'black holes', while the Russian military will not want the extent of their involvement in sustaining such conflicts to be highlighted. The conjunction of criminal groups, with access to military force, a monopoly of power within a contested territory and the desire to instigate ethno-nationalist state-building projects presents complex challenges and 'credibility traps' for the ERRF and the EU's crisis management capability. In particular, combatant and non-combatant roles are difficult to distinguish, and the status of the army, and of paramilitary and armed groups, cannot easily be separated. Moreover, it is in the interest of local power elites – criminal warlords – to maintain the instability, and so sustain the pathological nature of these *de facto* states.

For these reasons it might be argued that ERRF operations will not venture into such sensitive CIS space. However, despite these current obstacles to meaningful Russia–EU military security cooperation three further salient factors must also be considered. First, Russia's current military doctrine and national security concept assume that the greatest external threats to Russian stability will come from the south and the east, although the 2000 Military Doctrine lists the deployment of NATO troops close to Russia's borders as a threat. The 2000 National Security Concept (also currently in force) refers to Russia's tactical nuclear weapons as a deterrent in view of NATO's conventional supremacy. The deployment of the ERRF to the Caucasus or Central Asia might not pose such an insoluble dilemma for Russia, particularly as these regions remain destabilized and Russia's conventional military forces continue to decline. Indeed, it is clear that, at the very least, Russia's political support would be a necessary precondition for an ERRF deployment in these areas. Paradoxically, Russia's experience of these states and regions, and its very support for troublesome regions that are sources of insecurity with the potential to trigger an operational ERRF deployment in the future, means that its active support, perhaps as lead coalition partner, would greatly increase the chances of success of an EU peace-support mission.

Secondly, the EU and individual EU states, most notably Germany, have already begun to step up cooperation between their security services and those within the Russian Federation in an effort to combat terrorism. The 'global war against terror' has provided a stimulus to Russia–EU security services and intelligence exchanges and cooperation, an activity integral to the ESDP.[62]

---

62 M. E. Herman, '11 September: Legitimizing Intelligence?', *International Relations*, August 2002, Vol. 16, No. 2., pp. 227–41. See also Joint Statement on International Terrorism, EU–Russia Summit (Press: B42Nr 12423/01: Brussels, 3 October 2001).

Thirdly, Russian demographic trends will force the pace of military reform, albeit by a process of default rather than by design. Russia will move from a conscript-based to a hybrid professional-contract army, smaller and more mobile and with a force structure that is closer to the ERRF than the present Russian military. Moreover, Russia's geographical proximity to a post-Saddam Iraq, still attempting to implement post-conflict rehabilitation measures, and Iran, still a part of the so-called 'axis of evil', as well as Afghanistan, which remains far from stable, makes it highly likely that Russia's near neighbours to the south and east will constitute territory over which 'soft security' threats (trafficking of drugs, arms, sex trade and illegal migrants) and terrorism will undermine security and stability in the Russian Federation itself. If such a trend is emergent, then it could provide a stronger incentive for Russia to seek closer security cooperation with the EU.

If the first three of these counter-arguments to the proposition that Russia–EU military security cooperation cannot be meaningful are sustainable, then bureaucratic inertia and paralysis within both the Russian Federation and the European Union will be swept aside. Indeed, Russia's cooperation with the broad sweep of ESDP will unite a fractious Europe, having removed one important reason for inaction: 'but Moscow will object'. By October 2001 Russia had become the first non-member state 'to gain monthly consultations with the EU's Political and Security Committee, the main decision-making body of the ESDP'.[63] It is possible that the EU and Russia may find it politically expedient to coordinate positions and cooperate in the military security sphere outside Europe, in the Middle East, sub-Saharan Africa or Southeast Asia, and that such cooperation will allow the institutionalization of a partnership that is strong enough to survive the stress and sensitivities of cooperation in Russia's 'vital zone of interest'. This zone will become the EU's equivalent strategic 'zone of interest' as first- and second-echelon enlargement continues eastwards over the next decade.[64]

<hr>

63 Rontoyanni, 'So Far, So Good? Russia and the ESDP', p. 821. The EU Police Mission (EUPM) in Bosnia-Herzegovina launched in January 2003 has five Russian participants. As Dov Lynch, 'Russia Faces Europe', pp. 68–9, notes: 'The EUPM signals Russia's willingness to work under the EU in the Balkans'.

64 In April 2002, Russian Foreign Minister Igor Ivanov noted that talks between Russia and the EU helped 'to continue the long-term work on creating common space in respect of economy, energy, law and security. Russia and the EU have mutual interest in the search for shared answers to new global threats and challenges, in the settlement of crises in the Middle East, in Afghanistan and in the Balkans.' ITAR-TASS News Agency, Moscow, 2 April 2002. Gorm Rye Olsen, 'The EU and Conflict Management in African Emergencies', *International Peacekeeping*, Vol. 9, No. 3, Autumn 2002, pp. 87–102. See also Russia and EU Joint Statement of Concern in the Conflict between India and Pakistan: Annex 4, EU-Russia Summit, Moscow, 29 May 2002.

SOCIETAL SECURITY: HUMAN CAPITAL AND CONFLICT

The key dynamic currently shaping Russia's societal security agenda is the ongoing demographic crisis, which is unprecedented in peacetime: the population has been declining at a rate comparable only to that of the world wars and to the time of repression and the famine in the 1920s and 1930s in the Soviet Union.[65] The dynamics of Russian demography, their causes and the consequences of changing settlement and migration patterns will have both domestic policy-making and international security implications for the Federation well into the foreseeable future. Since the collapse of the Soviet Union the population of the Russian Federation has declined from 148.3m in 1992 to approximately 144m in 2001. On the basis of the trajectory established between 1992 and 2001, demographers generally agree that over the next decades Russia's population will fall to 142m in 2005, 138m in 2010 and between 132m and 134m in 2015–16. According to a UN forecast, in 2050 it will be little more than 121m, moving Russia from seventh to fourteenth among the world's most populated countries. Some assessments are even more pessimistic than this. Murray Feshbach, a leading US demographer, has calculated that if socio-economic conditions in Russia continue to decline, the Russian population could stand at 100m by 2050.

The effect of this decline is multifaceted, but it will be registered only gradually, in the form of trends that will begin to shape Russian policies and perhaps impact on Russian–EU relations. It can be argued that the instrumental use of the diaspora may no longer prove to be such an effective option if Russian citizens and ethnic-Russian or Russian-speaking residents return to Russia in increasing numbers.[66] Russia has complained that the human and civil rights of its Baltic diaspora could be undermined by the withdrawal of the OSCE missions from Estonia and Latvia and by the EU's insistence that their language laws and citizenship policies conform to European norms. Increasingly, however, given Russia's competition for population, the function of the Russian diaspora in Russian foreign policy may change, moving from being a means to an end (that is, a Russian lever of influence over national foreign and security orientations) to being an end in itself (a source of immigration for the Russian Federation). Although this may appear somewhat speculative, current policies being developed by the Ministry of Labour and the Nationalities Ministry, as well as discussions concerning Russia's developing security blueprint, all suggest that as its

---

65 *Moskovskiy Komsomolets*, Moscow, 29 November 2000.
66 Graeme P. Herd, 'Russia's Baltic Policy after the Meltdown', *Security Dialogue*, Vol. 30, No. 2, June 1999, pp. 197–212.

population declines, Russia may begin to compete within the former Soviet space for skilled workers and so-called 'technical intelligensia'.

The post-Schengen barriers to the free movement of people, that is the visa question, have also been raised as a societal security concern between Russia and the EU. Some analysts, most notably Dmitry Trenin, have argued that Russia's 'Euro-Balts' will prove to be a highly dynamic and entrepreneurial bridge rather than a barrier between EU and Russian markets.[67] But others within the Russian elite argue that even after the integration into the EU of the Baltic states and Poland, Russia will still have a legitimate state interest in the protection of diaspora rights, even as their instrumental value decreases. At the Council for Baltic Sea States meeting in Svetlogorsk in 2002, for example, Foreign Minister Ivanov stated that 'it would be unacceptable if the normal process of European Union enlargement would become a good thing for one group of states and a source of troubles for another.'[68] In early 2002, President Putin declared that Poland's admission to the EU should not 'create obstacles for a direct dialogue between our citizens'. He noted that in 2001 four million Russian citizens had visited Poland and three million Poles had travelled to Russia, and that trade turnover between the two countries might have reached $6 billion US dollars in that year.[69]

While the issue of immigration from former Soviet states to the Russian Federation impacts on Russia's relationship to the 'near abroad', the emigration of Russian citizens from the Federation will have a greater influence over Russia's 'far abroad' policy than ever before. Both the central and east European states and the EU states are becoming more interested in attracting skilled migrants – particularly the best and brightest within the high-technology-potential human capital-intensive industries. Such recruitment, along with the prospect of higher living standards and better employment opportunities, constitutes a pull factor for Russia's skilled population, particularly that in the European core. As Vladimir Kontorovich has noted, 'Migration aspirations of Russians now and in the foreseeable future will be mainly orientated westwards, towards developed countries.'[70]

---

67 The Schengen convention regarding residency status will apply to those ethnic Russians or Russian-speakers who are without citizenship. The travel rights of Russian citizens in Estonia and Latvia will conform to the bilateral agreements that exist between Russia and individual EU states in compliance with Schengen rules.
68 Interfax News Agency, Moscow, 6 March 2002.
69 ITAR-TASS News Agency, Moscow, 16 January 2002.
70 Vladimir Kontorovich, 'Can Russia Resettle the Far East?', *Post-Communist Economies*, Vol. 12, No. 3, 2000, p. 375.

CONCLUSIONS: DYNAMIC CONVERGENCE?

That Russia has ceased to be a global power and struggles to maintain the status of a regional power can hardly be disputed.[71] But it is precisely because of Russia's institutional, structural and systemic weaknesses that its cooperation and integration or its conflict and isolation from the European security order have become such a critical question. Russia still has nuclear, biological and chemical weapons, and since 11 September the danger that transnational terrorist networks might gain access to weapons of mass destruction of Russian origin has been highlighted. Russia's cooperation is necessary as transborder security threats, such as illegal migration, drugs, weapons and people-trafficking (including human body-part smuggling), the operations of organized criminal groups and terrorist networks and ecological disasters, all potentially threaten the stability of Europe and the integrity of common European institutions, values and interests.

Relations between the EU and Russia are at present finely balanced between the sides' respective interests in an age of terror in which these interests are being redefined. According to all official Russia–EU documents, strategies and press releases, by 2003 the Russia–EU relationship was based on closer cooperation and a long-term partnership, on the 'harmonizing of relations' – togetherness, or *sobornost*, in the words of Russia's Prime Minister Kasyanov – and on a mutually beneficial balance of interests. Russia has essentially entered into a 'partnership of the willing' with the EU. However, if the potential points of conflict as outlined in this chapter fail to be resolved or managed, then the Russia–EU relationship will become an enforced partnership. This potential outcome would entail an asymmetric trade relationship centred on Russian hydrocarbon exports and imports of manufactured goods from the EU, little foreign policy coordination, the establishment of hard and impermeable Schengen borders, and Russia's contradictory combination of economic dependency on, and societal isolation from, the EU as a source of friction and instability *within* the Russian Federation.

Although Russian–EU relations are stable and much progress in cooperation has been made in the past five years, it could be argued that Russia's cooperative capacity over the longer term will be hampered by its inability to integrate at a deep functional level with the EU. In particular, the political recentralization of power in Russia undermines economic cooperation among regions within the Federation, while the penetration of criminal activity into

71 Frank Umbach, 'Russia as a "Virtual Great Power": Implications for its Declining Role in European and Eurasian Security', *European Security*, Vol. 9, No. 3, Autumn 2000, pp. 87–122; Paula J. Dobriansky, 'Russian Foreign Policy: Promise or Peril?', *The Washington Quarterly*, Vol. 23, No. 1, Winter 2000, pp. 135–44.

all levels of the Russian economy also discourages foreign direct investment and economic collaboration with the EU.

At present, however, it seems that Russia and the EU face systemic pressures which propel them into long-term collaboration. Russia's integration into the global economy and its ability to develop its technological base and overcome demographic pressures, to name but a few of the key dynamics set to shape its development in the new century, suggest that its future lies with the West and that it can be anchored in security cooperation with the EU. In order to ensure a mutually supported partnership the EU needs to develop a long-term strategy that takes into account the current realities and dynamics of the Russia–EU relationship and moves beyond declarations to provide sustainable mechanisms for resolving outstanding issues. Russia and the EU must bridge the conceptual gaps that divide them and recognize the impact of systemic pressures which will create long-term sympathy, if not parity, between the two. Russia and the EU are able to promote increased network connectivity, two-way financial transactions, shared liberal media flows, norms and values and collective security systems. Russia will Europeanize under the pressure of internal dynamics, not least as its citizens internally migrate in greater numbers from the Russian Far East and Far North to urban centres west of the Urals. This process will reinforce the integration of Russia into the functional core of the transatlantic security community and it is clear that the strengthening of the Russia–EU axis will be pivotal in securing such a goal.

Many obstacles lie ahead, not least the danger that the current Global War on Terrorism-led discourse on transatlantic disunity may become a dominant trend, and that the apparent breakdown in transatlantic relations (some analysts talk of the possibility of 'strategic divorce' and 'strategic dissonance') will lead to the rise of ESDP as a counterweight to US primacy, perceived as hegemony. If such perceptions become widespread and consolidated, then Russia's relations with the EU will be shaped less by the former's unwillingness to cooperate across the board on a range of issues, and more by the EU's inability to identify, coordinate and implement common policies and projects which further peace, stability and prosperity with Europe's largest state. At its worst Russia's EU relationship will become an instrumental object of US–EU tensions and cleavages; at best, stronger Russia–EU ties will render Russia a more attractive US partner. Most probably, however, Russia will be forced to chose between the US and EU on issues critical to its own integrity and role as an international actor. As a consequence, neo-Soviet foreign policy (divide and rule) towards the EU may, paradoxically, become the most rational and effective Russian approach over the next decade.

8

Russia in the EU or the EU in Russia? Approaches to Kaliningrad

CHRISTOPHER PRESTON

The prospect of the European Union's enlargement to the borders of Russia has brought Kaliningrad to the forefront of the political debate concerning the future shape of Europe. The Kaliningrad *oblast* (region), situated on the Baltic Sea coast, is the most westerly of Russia's 89 regions. Following the accession of Poland and Lithuania to the EU it will be entirely surrounded by EU member states, territorially cut off from 'mainland' Russia. Previously known as East Prussia, Kaliningrad was created in the aftermath of the Second World War. Its status as an enclave was determined by the Potsdam conference of 1945, and it was split between Poland and the USSR. In the Soviet era, Kaliningrad was the main base for the Soviet Baltic fleet and was therefore a closed area, both to non-resident Soviet citizens and to foreigners.

Following the collapse of the Soviet Union and the independence of the Baltic states in 1991, Kaliningrad became a Russian exclave, its only land borders with Poland and Lithuania. In the immediate post-Soviet period, concerns focused on the destabilizing effect of the continuing presence of deteriorating nuclear weapons and the estimated 200,000 troops remaining in Kaliningrad. However, from the mid-1990s the withdrawal of all but about 16,000 of these troops, coupled with the general decline in the Russian military, significantly reduced this 'hard' security threat.

But as this perceived threat receded, a range of new issues emerged to confront policy-makers. The economic importance to it of the Russian military was part of Kaliningrad's economic dependence on 'mainland' Russia particularly for energy imports and as a market for its traditional manu-facturing outputs. By 2002 its economy had deteriorated to the point where average incomes were approximately 35 per cent of the already low Russian average. Environmental degradation was severe. Organized crime, especially drug-trafficking, was endemic, and the region's drugs problem had led to the highest level of HIV infection in Russia, and therefore the whole of Europe.

The future of Kaliningrad poses major challenges to its own citizens, to its neighbours and to policy-makers in Moscow and Brussels. On their own the economic, social and environmental issues are daunting enough. Now, the evolving political context created by EU enlargement poses additional challenges. As Polish and Lithuanian accession to the EU draws closer, the reality of a Russian region entirely surrounded by EU territory, and therefore subject to its external border policy, confronts all the key stakeholders. The most visible and sensitive issue concerns transit. After EU enlargement, Kaliningraders will need a Schengen visa to travel overland to 'mainland' Russia. To date neither Poland nor Lithuania has imposed such a requirement. The political symbolism of this, given traditional Russian sensitivity concerning national sovereignty, territorial integrity and the historical fear of encirclement, cannot be underestimated. Nor, from the EU side, can the symbolism of strengthening external EU borders as a prerequisite for creating an internal borderless Europe be ignored. This issue alone threatens both EU and Russian sensitivities.

This highly charged issue needs to be seen in its wider context. The present round of EU accession is raising larger questions about the future of the enlargement process and the future relations between 'insiders' and 'outsiders'. Assuming that in any likely scenario Russia will not be an EU candidate in the foreseeable future, Kaliningrad is a litmus test of EU–Russian cooperation. Thus it provides an opportunity to explore the inclusiveness or exclusiveness of the integration process. Can this process find solutions to deep-seated problems that originate from outside EU territory or will new barriers inevitably be created?

This chapter explores the issue of Kaliningrad within the context of EU enlargement. It examines:

- the perspectives of the key stakeholders, the EU, Russia, Kaliningrad itself, Lithuania and Poland, in the light of the several overlapping policy frameworks that shape their attitude to Kaliningrad;
- the key policy issues, in particular trade, visa and transit policies;
- current efforts by the EU to find solutions to these issues;
- the likely future development of the Kaliningrad issue.

The chapter argues that the sensitivity of the Kaliningrad issue, for the reasons noted above, imposes constraints on the key actors. However, practical solutions to the essential issues can be found if both the EU and Russia can be flexible. Developing this flexibility over Kaliningrad is critical for the future of the EU's broader relations with Russia.

Enlargement

The policy frameworks for enlargement, EU–Russia relations and the Northern Dimension shape EU policy towards Kaliningrad. Of these, EU enlargement is the dominant strategic framework, and is critical for the two candidate countries, Poland and Lithuania, which 'encircle' Kaliningrad. Both candidates have to work within the constraints of the EU's classical method of enlargement. This requires that upon accession candidates should take on the *acquis* in full, and that any adjustments necessary to achieve convergence must be limited in scope and duration. Despite the political and economic adjustment costs of this regulatory alignment, the *de facto* principle, established in the EU's first enlargement, has been sustained in subsequent rounds of enlargement. Despite the manifest pressures to adopt more differentiated solutions to problems presented by increasingly heterogeneous candidates, the principle has been strengthened, in order to avoid diluting integration as the EU widens.[1] Consistent with this principle Poland and Lithuania have been negotiating EU accession since 1998 and 2000 respectively. Both are set to join the EU in 2004, in time to participate in the next European Parliament elections, due in June of that year.

The key elements of the *acquis* that affect the Kaliningrad issue concern trade, visa and transit policies. Following the EU's enlargement, Kaliningrad, as part of Russia, will face the Union's common external tariff in trading with Poland and Lithuania. More significantly it will face the EU's visa regime, which will require Kaliningraders to obtain a full EU visa if they wish to cross Lithuanian or Polish territory to visit mainland Russia. Such a situation is unprecedented in the EU's experience of enlargement. Yet the EU's policy of strengthening its external borders in order to deal with 'soft' security issues as internal borders are liberalized is now a core element of the *acquis*. No derogation in principle is therefore permissible. Indeed, Kaliningrad's position as a transit route for illegal immigration, drugs and car smuggling poses precisely the threats for which the EU's external border regime was developed. Whatever the future status of Kaliningrad and the policy regime imposed upon it, the EU will continue to regard it as a source of 'soft' security threats.

---

1 See Christopher Preston, *Enlargement and Integration in the European Union* (London: Routledge, 1997).

EU–Russia relations

The enlargement process has brought into sharper focus the need for the EU to develop a new geopolitical relationship with Russia. Notwithstanding the debate about whether Russia itself could ever be a credible EU candidate, enlargement necessitates an enhanced bilateral policy framework covering political and economic issues. The EU's share of Russia's external trade is 33–35 per cent (compared to 20–21 per cent for the CIS, 11–12 per cent for the central and east European countries, 7–8 per cent for the United States and 4–5 per cent for China).[2]

EU–Russia relations are currently governed by the EU–Russia Partnership and Cooperation Agreement (PCA). Proposed in 1994 and signed in 1997 for an initial period of ten years, the PCA provides the institutional framework for enhanced cooperation in trade, energy, environment, transport, for enhanced political dialogue concerning observance of democracy and human rights, and for intensified cooperation in justice and home affairs. This framework was further strengthened by the adoption in June 1999 of a common EU strategy on Russia. This identified a series of ambitious goals for EU action, principally the consolidation of democracy, the rule of law and public institutions, the integration of Russia into a common European economic and social space, including WTO membership, and enhanced cooperation to strengthen stability and security in Europe and beyond.

At the core of the common strategy was the recognition of the critical importance of Russian stability to the EU and the proactive role that the EU needs to take if this is to be ensured. The strategy reaches beyond conventional models of bilateral cooperation with Russia and establishes the EU as the main catalyst for its internal reform and its regulatory convergence with EU norms. Such intensive engagement is critical to the Kaliningrad issue. Should the common strategy achieve incremental improvements to the economic and social fabric in Russia's regions, then the 'soft' security threats, on which the EU's tough external borders policy is based, are likely to diminish, leaving more space for a pragmatic resolution of the difficult *acquis* issues.

The Northern Dimension

The third element of the EU's perspective is the development of its Northern Dimension. Agreed at the Helsinki European Council in December 1999, the Northern Dimension represents an initiative to 'provide added value through reinforced coordination and complementarity in EU and member

---

2 See J. Baxendale, S. Dewar, and D. Gowan (eds), *The EU and Kaliningrad* (London: Federal Trust for Education and Research, 2000), p. 271.

states programmes, and enhanced collaboration between the countries in Northern Europe'. The major challenges driving the initiative were identified as the need to tackle environmental degradation, in particular risks from nuclear power plants, and the management of the Baltic Sea, energy and organized crime. Kaliningrad was identified explicitly as a 'pilot region' for the development of regional cooperation between the EU, Russia and the candidate countries. In June 2000 the Council endorsed an action plan drawn up by the Commission to improve policy coordination and to target EU financial assistance through its existing budgetary instruments on northern issues.[3]

Though not yet an EU member, Lithuania was active in promoting and supporting the development of the Northern Dimension, particularly in relation to Kaliningrad. The action plan acknowledged this, noting that

> the special geographical status of the Kaliningrad *oblast* means that cooperation on infrastructure projects, such as energy and transport, may have a multiplier effect. This being another aim of the Northern Dimension initiative, the Lithuanian-Russian agreement to cooperate within the Northern Dimension may prove helpful in this regard.[4]

The Northern Dimension did not propose any radical new policy initiatives or any financial aid. However, it did enhance awareness of the context in which Kaliningrad exists, and it has supported a more inclusive approach to how these issues, especially the role of the candidate countries in advance of accession, might be tackled.

These three interlocking policy frameworks provide the context for the EU's approach to Kaliningrad, which is pragmatic and incremental and motivated by a strong desire not to internalize additional problems after enlargement. But there are clearly limits to this pragmatism. They arise from internal constraints imposed by the classical method of enlargement and from external constraints imposed by the Russian response to EU initiatives.

THE RUSSIAN PERSPECTIVE

From Russia's perspective too, Kaliningrad needs to be considered within a number of overlapping frameworks: its policies towards the EU, Lithuania and Poland and its policy for the Kaliningrad region itself.

---

3 *Action Plan for the Northern Dimension with External and Cross Border Policies of the European Union 2000–2003*, Council of the European Union, Brussels, 14 June 2000, p. 5.
4 Ibid., p. 13.

Policy towards the EU

As with the EU's approach to Russia, Russia's approach to the EU has been cautious and incremental and also within well-defined limits. Under the Putin presidency Russia has pursued a policy of active cooperation with the EU as part of its broader geopolitical strategy of engagement with the West. The key political priority has been to liberalize trade, within the context of the Partnership and Cooperation Agreement, and specifically to gain EU support for full Russian membership of the World Trade Organization (WTO). The Putin government has recognized that internal reform is critical to achieving these objectives and has committed itself to a domestic reform programme.

The Russia–EU summit of October 1999 was where the key elements of Russia's strategy towards the EU first emerged. The strategy was a response to the common EU strategy towards Russia, presented in June 1999. The Russian policy has much in common with that of the EU, including the need for Russia to be closely involved in the development of the pan-European security architecture, the development of common economic and legal frameworks for trade and investment, and, wherever possible, the coordination of positions within international organizations. However, this commonality also conceals some important differences of emphasis, notably concerning how much active EU involvement Russia will accept in its internal reform process. As one commentator has noted, 'According to the Russian strategy paper, the systemic transformation within the country is defined not as a goal of partnership *with* the EU, but as the goal of the Russian strategy *towards* the EU.'[5] Thus Russian resentment, even when not stated explicitly, at being seen as the target or object of EU policy constrains the extent to which the EU can engage in Russia's internal transformation. This clearly impacts on the Kaliningrad issue, given the scale of the internal reform which will be necessary to transform it into an economically viable region geographically surrounded by the enlarged EU.

Policy towards Lithuania and Poland

Russia's policy towards the two EU applicant states that will enclose the Kaliningrad region has evolved incrementally over the past ten years in response both to changes in its foreign policy towards the Baltic region and to the growing EU aspirations of the two countries in question. The priority for Russia has been to keep its western borders as open as possible in order to

---

5 See Y. Borko, 'EU/Russia Cooperation: The Moscow Perspective', in Baxendale, Dewar and Gowan (eds), *The EU and Kaliningrad*, p. 63.

ensure easy transit and, wherever possible, to develop cross-border economic links. Given Lithuania's position as the main rail transit corridor to Kaliningrad, Russia's relations with Lithuania concerning the enclave have been more important than those with Poland.[6]

In the early years following independence Kaliningrad was used as the main staging post for the withdrawal of Russian troops and munitions from eastern Europe. This caused worries for Russia's neighbours. In 1991, Russia concluded a favourable bilateral agreement with Lithuania covering border issues as a matter of priority.

Since the conclusion of Lithuania's Europe Agreement with the EU in 1995 and the opening of its negotiations for full EU membership in 2000, Russia has had to come to terms with its neighbours aligning all their legislation with EU norms. Thus Russian policy has increasingly had to take account of the multilateral dimension of Lithuanian policy, in contrast to its traditional bilateral approach.

Policy towards the Kaliningrad region

Kaliningrad also needs to be considered within the framework of evolving regional-federal relations within Russia. Following the collapse of the USSR and the decline in Kaliningrad's military significance, there was recognition in Moscow that special measures might be necessary in order to overcome the region's economic and geographical disadvantages. In 1991 Kaliningrad was granted the status of a Free Economic Zone (FEZ), allowing the duty-free import of materials from all third countries in an attempt to create a Baltic Hong Kong.[7] Despite the efforts made between 1991 and 1995, few positive benefits accrued to the region, in part owing to Russian ambivalence during that period about free market activity.

In 1995 President Yeltsin cancelled the FEZ, only to restore many of its privileges the following year in the form of a Special Economic Zone (SEZ). Nevertheless, Kaliningrad failed to attract foreign direct investment in the 1990s, reflecting both the seriousness of its underlying economic problems and the unpredictable policy regime for investors.[8] In addition, there was the historical tension in centre–periphery relations in Russia. During the Yeltsin era, policy tended, albeit erratically, towards granting a measure of regional

6 In 1992 Poland concluded a bilateral agreement with Russia covering the Kaliningrad issue.

7 For an evaluation of Kaliningrad's economic potential see S. Dewar, 'Myths in the Baltic', in Baxendale, Dewar and Gowan (eds), *The EU and Kaliningrad*, Chapter 10.

8 In December 2000 the main customs office of the Russian Federation suddenly issued a new regulation abolishing the SEZ's tax advantages. Within one month manufacturing by foreign investors shut down, and started again only following repeal of the regulation in February 2001.

autonomy. However, the Putin government has pursued a policy of centralization, reducing the degree to which regions can pursue autonomous economic policies. The present government's policy, which sees Russian territory as 'indivisible' within the context of its external relations, creates tensions with its desire to see Kaliningrad as a 'pilot region' in developing Russia's relations with the EU.

THE KALININGRAD PERSPECTIVE

It is necessary to consider the future of Kaliningrad from the perspective of Kaliningrad itself, lest the region be regarded solely as the object rather than the subject of policy. The historical experience of the region, having been settled by 'mainland' Russians after the war and then acting as a Russian military base, has meant that Kaliningrad has not developed a distinct regional or separatist identity, in contrast to other Russian regions. Thus the main concerns of the regional administration have been to ensure that transit and economic links are maintained with Russia and that local initiatives can be taken to tackle the region's serious economic problems. From the early 1990s, the regional administration lobbied in both Moscow and Brussels to have Kaliningrad recognized as a priority region for the EU's TACIS programme.[9] Although this was achieved in 1994, the limited budget and the complex and opaque procedures for selecting projects for support during this period led to little tangible benefit. More recently, the regional administration has opened trade missions in Gdansk and Vilnius, supported by the region's own budget. Yet the degree of local initiative that the regional administration can exercise is severely circumscribed, and it depends on the state of broader federal–regional political relations outlined above. The inconsistencies in the implementation of the SEZ noted earlier are symptomatic of Kaliningrad's vulnerability. Moreover, it has been argued that 'Kaliningrad itself has displayed limited abilities to manoeuvre towards the more process-oriented challenges. The skills needed to utilise the opportunities have turned out to be modest.'[10]

THE POLISH AND LITHUANIAN PERSPECTIVES

The perspectives of Poland and Lithuania on the Kaliningrad issue have also changed in order to take account of these countries' evolving orientation

---

9 Technical Assistance to the CIS. Regions eligible for aid and project priorities are drawn up by the European Commission's delegation in Moscow in collaboration with the federal ministries responsible for foreign aid.

10 P. Joenniemi and J. Prawitz, 'Kaliningrad: A Double Periphery', in *Kaliningrad: The European Amber Region* (Aldershot, Hants: Ashgate, 1998), pp. 226–61.

towards western Europe, and specifically their impending EU membership. A key objective for both countries in the early post-Soviet period was to maintain good bilateral relations with their powerful eastern neighbour. This led to the early conclusion of bilateral agreements with Russia, as mentioned above. Given its position as the main transit corridor, Lithuania has been particularly active in seeking to bring Kaliningrad to the forefront of its developing relations with the EU. In 1999 Lithuania proposed the 'Nida' initiative for enhanced cooperation and joint development projects between Russia and Lithuania, chiefly concerning energy and environment, within the framework of the Northern Dimension initiative. The 'Nida' initiative was designed both to deal with the specific problems of Kaliningrad and to demonstrate Lithuania's willingness to act in advance of accession as if it were already an active EU member with responsibility for external EU borders.

Although less concerned with transit issues, Poland has sought closer engagement with Russia, particularly through cross-border cooperation. Poland established a cooperation council between its northeastern *voivods* (municipalities) and Kaliningrad. Cross-border trade between Poland and Kaliningrad started in 1994, and increased in value from $64m initially to $292m in 1998. Over 400 Polish businesses, the majority involved in intermediary trade, are registered in Kaliningrad. They make up about 32 per cent of all foreign capital investment.[11]

KALININGRAD WITHIN AN ENLARGED EU: THE KEY POLICY ISSUES

The perspectives set out above provide the context in which the key policy issues affecting Kaliningrad are being played out within an EU that is soon to be further enlarged. Three major policy areas – trade, visas, and transit – are at stake.

Trade policy

Polish and Lithuanian accession to the EU will confront the Kaliningrad region with the need to adapt to the EU's common commercial policy, including its common external tariff and other trade policy instruments. Thus Kaliningrad will be confronted with the classic issues facing all third countries trading with an enlarging EU. It will need to evaluate the extent to which the post-enlargement trade regime is likely to create or divert trade, what the appropriate policy responses should be and how far the EU and Russia are willing to adapt their own trade policies in order to take account of their specific impact on Kaliningrad.

11 Data provided by the Polish Foreign Ministry.

These challenges can be explored by examining trade between Kaliningrad and Lithuania. The trade patterns have been analysed in an impact study commissioned by the Lithuanian government.[12] The study noted that exports from Lithuania to Kaliningrad are unlikely to be affected by Lithuania's accession to the EU, as Russia applies Most Favoured Nation (MFN) treatment to goods originating in Lithuania as well as to those originating in the EU. Owing to the Kaliningrad region's status as a Special Economic Zone, Russia applies special treatment to some goods imported from the region, but no major changes to Russia's import regulations are likely to arise from EU enlargement.

However, exports from Kaliningrad to Lithuania will be directly affected by the replacement of Lithuania's foreign trade regime by that of the EU. Trade between Kaliningrad and Lithuania is highly asymmetric. In 1997 Lithuania was the second-largest market for Kaliningrad's exports, with a share of 9.4 per cent (though this had declined to 5 per cent in 1999). By contrast, Lithuanian imports from Kaliningrad amounted only to 0.78 per cent of its total imports.[13] And while Russia as a whole is more important as a source of imports (particularly minerals and fuels) for Lithuania than as a destination of exports, the opposite is true for Lithuania's trade with Kaliningrad.

Because exports from Lithuania to Kaliningrad considerably exceed its imports, trade turnover is unlikely to be much affected from the Lithuanian perspective. Also, Lithuanian imports from Kaliningrad are more diversified (covering a range of manufacturing and agricultural products) than those from Russia. Given that some of these product categories are subject to EU tariffs (and other non-tariff barriers in the case of food and agricultural products), the general level of protection against Kaliningrad exports is likely to rise. However, the study concluded that owing to the small volume of total trade, the overall negative effects are likely to be small, and will depend on the performance of specific product groups. It is important to note that this is essentially a static analysis of trade. It ignores the dynamic potential that may arise from the creation of a Russia–EU free trade area, identified as an EU priority in its common strategy on Russia; thus the situation may alter more than the report suggests.[14]

12 P. Joenniemi, R. Lopata, V. Sirutavicius and R. Vilpisauskas, *Impact Assessment of Lithuania's Integration into the EU on Relations between Lithuania and Kaliningrad Oblast of the Russian Federation* (Vilnius University, October 2000).

13 Data provided by the Lithuanian Customs Department. Quoted in ibid., p. 17.

14 'Common Strategy of the European Union of 4 June 1999 on Russia' (1999/414/CFSP), *Official Journal of the European Communities*, L157/1, 24 June 1999.

Visa policy

Whereas adapting to the EU's trade policy may have some limited consequences for specific groups, adapting to the EU's visa policy will have more wide-ranging consequences and be problematic. Here Kaliningrad confronts one of the fundamental principles of the EU: that internal liberalization can be sustainable only if it is balanced by strong external borders in order to minimize the 'soft' security threats that arise from crime, illegal immigration and smuggling. During the 1990s the trend within the EU was to reduce the importance of internal borders in order to facilitate trade within the single market after 1992. However, following the 1997 Treaty of Amsterdam and with the prospect of EU borders extending eastwards, the emphasis has shifted towards creating an 'area of freedom, security and justice' with common policies dealing with asylum, immigration and all aspects of cross-border movement.

Striking the balance between freedom, security and justice has been challenging for the EU. Member states are proving reluctant to transfer national competences to the European level, and the whole area of justice and home affairs remains opaque and legally complex, despite efforts made in the Nice Treaty to rationalize the EU's multi-pillar structure and despite some progress on counter-terrorism in the wake of 11 September 2001. The need to strengthen the EU's external borders poses real difficulties for those candidate countries that to date have maintained liberal border policies with eastern neighbours, designed, for instance, to facilitate cross-border trade and retain existing patterns of social interaction.

These policy issues are vital to Kaliningrad. Both Poland and Lithuania have maintained liberal visa regimes for Kaliningrad. Lithuanians and Russians can cross their mutual border on internal passports and identity cards, and may remain in the other's territory for up to 30 days. Kaliningrad-resident Russian citizens can transit through Lithuania by train without any visas as long as they do not get off in Lithuanian territory. Movement between Poland and the Russian Federation is regulated by two agreements, one between the USSR and Poland on mutual visa-free travel dating from 1979 and a 1986 one on simplified procedures for residents living near the border.[15]

These liberal border policies have important symbolic as well as practical importance for the residents of Kaliningrad. They help to reduce the sense of isolation felt by Kaliningraders and allow them to engage in mutually

---

15 *Polish Official Journal of Laws* No. 13, item 41 of 1980 and *Polish Official Journal of Laws* No. 24, item 114 of 1986. Russian and Polish citizens residing in specified border areas are entitled to make visa-free tourist trips (for up to seven days) to visit friends and relatives solely on the basis of travel documents.

beneficial cross-border trade, which is critical given the dire economic conditions within the Kaliningrad region.[16]

As is consistent with the classical method of EU enlargement, Poland and Lithuania have no alternative but to take on the *acquis* in full. Thus the liberal border regimes noted above will in due course be replaced by an arrangement whereby these border states must issue full Schengen visas to Kaliningraders wishing to enter Poland and Lithuania or to transit to 'mainland' Russia. But although signing up to the Schengen Agreement is one of the accession requirements, the process of admission to Schengen varies from that of the main body of the *acquis*: states are not automatically full members of Schengen from the date of accession to the EU; it depends on the EU's evaluation of the preparedness of the accession state to operate its external border policy. This in effect allows some flexibility in the phasing in of the relevant visa regimes in Poland and Lithuania. Lithuania's policy is to adopt the Schengen *acquis* in 2004 on entry into the EU, even though it may not become a full member of the Convention upon accession. Kaliningraders will therefore face a differentiated visa regime in the near future. As a consequence it is also likely that Russia will introduce a reciprocal visa regime for Poles and Lithuanians. There is thus a real risk that attitudes may harden, creating a new division between 'insiders' and 'outsiders' in eastern Europe.

Transit policy

The transit issue concerns not only the movement of Kaliningraders across EU territory but also the free movement of goods. Here the overall economic dependency of Kaliningrad on transit and external factors of production is critical to an evaluation of its general future when enclosed within the territory of an enlarged EU. Power generation in Kaliningrad is totally dependent on coal and oil imported from 'mainland' Russia (making up 80 per cent of the total) and on natural gas (making up a further 15 per cent). By far the greatest amount of coal and oil is sent by rail.[17]

Since its independence Lithuania has operated a liberal, non-discriminatory regime for Russian goods crossing its territory. Bilateral agreements on trade, based on WTO principles of non-discrimination, guarantee transit trade free from customs duties.[18] However, despite the liberal legal regime its

16 In 2000, approximately 1 million Polish citizens and 1.2 million 'foreigners' (all but a few of whom were Russians) crossed the Poland–Kaliningrad border. In 2000, 3.6 million persons crossed the Lithuanian–Kaliningrad border. Data provided by the Polish Foreign Ministry.

17 In 1999, 5.7 million tonnes of goods crossed Lithuania by rail; 379,000 tonnes were sent by road. Figures provided by the Lithuanian Customs Department. Quoted in Joenniemi et al., *Impact Assessment*, p. 9.

18 Agreements signed in 1991, 1993, 1995 and 1999 set out the details of this regime.

effectiveness is compromised by inadequate border infrastructure and crossing delays.

On accession Lithuania will adopt the Community's customs code, its convention on common transit procedure and other, related areas of the *acquis*, in particular its developing common transport policy. But the changes brought about by the adoption of these elements of the *acquis* are unlikely to be very great. The Lithuanian customs code, which came into effect in 1998, was drafted with EU assistance and is consistent with the EU customs code. The transit regime applied to Kaliningrad after enlargement will, in any case, depend on the EU's review of its own transit system in order to make it both more flexible and secure.

SOLUTIONS TO THE KALININGRAD ISSUE: THE EU'S APPROACH

Taken together, these *acquis* policy issues, and the wider problems raised by the economic, social and environmental conditions of Kaliningrad, constitute a set of major challenges to the enlarging EU and its developing relations with the Russian Federation. The EU has experienced difficulties with border regions in the past; since Finland's accession, it has had almost a decade's experience of managing a border with Russia. However, Kaliningrad's future enclave status is unprecedented. The need to find flexible solutions is now higher on the EU's policy agenda, as a result of both the imminence of enlargement and the need to deepen EU–Russia relations.

The EU's policy on Kaliningrad was set out by the Commission in a communication to the Council in January 2001.[19] As the Commission itself acknowledged, the paper did not set out formal proposals; it outlined a range of options that could form the basis of specific proposals in the future. The Commission addressed the critical *acquis* issues outlined above. Concerning the movement of goods, it noted that since the EU's MFN tariffs for trade with Russia under the PCA were already lower than those of Poland (15.8 per cent) and Lithuania (5.3 per cent), the general effect of enlargement should create trade for Kaliningrad. However, the paper acknowledged that the new trade regime would need to be analysed in order to assess its effect on different product categories before an overall judgment could be made. The Commission recognized that the 23 border crossings between Poland, Lithuania and Kaliningrad required attention in order to facilitate cross-border trade.

Concerning the movement of people, the Commission stated that the visa-free transit currently available would no longer be possible after enlargement and that Kaliningrad citizens would be obliged to travel in possession

19 'The EU and Kaliningrad', Communication from the Commission to the Council, COM (2001) 26 Final, Brussels, 17 January 2001.

of a full passport.[20] The Commission thereby restated the orthodox position that the principles of the *acquis* are not negotiable. However, it argued that the new rules need not necessarily impede the movement of people given that the *acquis* provides for a range of options, including transit and short-term, long-term and multiple-entry visas. The Commission also stated its willingness to consider further developing the rules on small border traffic – simplified procedures for individuals making regular border crossings, for instance to work close to the border – to facilitate cross-border economic links and to look further at a range of supporting measures, including the cost of visas, the presence of EU consular offices in Kaliningrad and a range of measures to upgrade the efficient operation of border crossings.[21]

Beyond these specific *acquis* issues, the paper identified the wider issues of EU engagement in Kaliningrad, notably the need to contribute to the region's economic development through TACIS-funded training and small and medium-sized enterprise (SME) development and also support for governance, health and environment initiatives. The key elements of the Commission's strategy for Kaliningrad were set out in its summary of recommendations. The main suggestions were that:

- the EU and Russia should jointly examine the trade impact of enlargement within the framework of the EU–Russia PCA;
- the EU, Russia, Poland and Lithuania should examine the functional management of border crossings and the region's linkages into the main pan-European transport corridors;
- assistance should be provided to contribute to the creation of a functioning border control system, including fake-proof travel documents;
- the EU and Russia should quickly conclude a readmission agreement;
- the EU should provide more information to the administration and the people of Kaliningrad on the implications of enlargement and especially on how the future external borders will function.[22]

Consistent with its enlargement strategy, the Commission argued that these proposals should be widely discussed by the EU, Russia, Poland and Lithuania. Certainly the paper has stimulated a debate among these interests as to how the questions should be addressed in the future, and Poland has produced a detailed response from Poland, setting out its policy for Kaliningrad.[23]

20 See 'EU–Russia relations special meeting in Kaliningrad', 15 May 2002, available at *http:// europa.eu.int/extenal_relations/north_dim/news*.
21 Ibid., p. 2.
22 The paper also indicated the need to discuss a wide range of other issues, including fishing, the environment and energy.
23 Ministry of Foreign Affairs, Republic of Poland, *Position vis-à-vis Communication from the European Commission: The EU and Kaliningrad* (2001).

This policy is illustrative both of the detailed response to the specific proposals in the Commission's paper and of the wider approach that Poland takes in dealing with relations with the EU and Russia. The essential principle for Poland is to regard Kaliningrad as an integral part of its bilateral relations with Russia, '… based on respect of the rule of territorial integrity of the Russian Federation'.[24] The paper thus acknowledges that priority must be given to negotiating with Moscow over the future of Kaliningrad, but it also identifies a range of local initiatives that complement the high-level bilateral and multilateral negotiations over the region's future.[25]

The key elements of the Polish strategy towards Kaliningrad are based on working within the framework of the *acquis* while trying, wherever possible, to make it more flexible and responsive to the specific needs of the region. Procedures and costs for multiple-entry visas are critical in this respect,[26] and the Polish government has expressed concern that once visa-free travel is abolished, significant delays can be expected in Russia's issuing of visas to Poles.[27] Poland regards the Commission's proposals for the speedy conclusion of an EU–Russia readmission agreement as a signal for Russia to speed up its conclusion of a readmission agreement with Poland.

The Polish position paper argues strongly in favour of a more active approach to cross-border cooperation (beyond the proposals for small border traffic), utilizing the experience already gained on the Polish–German border of combining the EU's aid programme for all EU candidate countries (PHARE) and INTERREG, the EU's Inter-regional Assistance funds, an initiative concerning border development, cross-border cooperation and selected energy networks. This cooperation would also extend to concluding an agreement on joint border controls, leading to the progressive harmonization of crossing formalities and certification.[28]

The Commission's communication on the EU and Kaliningrad formed the basis of discussions between the key stakeholders from early 2001 in an effort to prevent the Kaliningrad issue from compromising EU enlargement or the future of EU–Russia relations. Kaliningrad was discussed by senior Russian and Commission officials meeting as the Russia–EU Cooperation

---

24 Ibid., p. 1.
25 Poland places considerable emphasis on the Council for Cooperation between its north-eastern *voivods* and Kaliningrad and on local economic development along the border region.
26 Polish visa charges for Russians are set at $5 (single entry) and $14 (multiple entry), lower than those applied by EU member states (30 euros and 50 euros respectively).
27 Poland's position paper argued in favour of similar charge levels, given that in 2001 charges for Russian visas were 10 times higher than Polish visas for Russians. Polish Foreign Ministry, *Position vis-à-vis Communication from the European Commission: The EU and Kaliningrad*, p. 12.
28 Ibid., p. 14.

Committee in Kaliningrad on 15 May 2002. The meeting discussed all the key critical issues: visas, border control, organized crime, environmental pollution, energy supplies and transport links. The conclusions of the meeting reconfirmed that after enlargement, EU visas, based on internationally acceptable passports, would be required. Russian proposals for special visa-free transit corridors were not acceptable; the EU side stressed that practical border cooperation would therefore be even more necessary in the future and promised substantial funding for infrastructure improvement with regard to border control.[29] The EU side also pressed Russia to permit the opening of EU consulates in Kaliningrad, to issue passports to its citizens, to ratify its border agreement with Lithuania and to conclude a readmission agreement with the EU.[30]

KALININGRAD'S FUTURE WITHIN THE ENLARGED EU

Four scenarios

The future of the Kaliningrad region depends on the flexibility of all the crucial stakeholders and on how far 'top-down' initiatives can be integrated with 'bottom-up' initiatives. The study of Kaliningrad's future commissioned by the Lithuanian government posited four scenarios, all dependent on the willingness of Russia and the EU to be innovative in finding solutions.[31]

Using the existing PCA framework, the first scenario foresees a commitment by both Russia and the EU to utilize the instruments of the PCA to reduce the regulatory gap between Russia and the EU so that over time trade and transit issues become less politically charged. Here the commitment to create a free-trade zone between the EU and Russia, involving the gradual harmonization of product standards, would remove trade barriers; it would gradually open up the region economically, making the borders less important. Although these ultimate objectives are clearly stated and are shared by both the EU and Russia, at least at the level of official agreements, they are closely linked to progress on accession to the WTO and internal reform, and are therefore likely to remain problematic.

The second scenario, creating new initiatives between the EU and Russia, envisages an even closer EU–Russia engagement, leading to the possibility of an association agreement between the two parties. However, this is a longer-term scenario, as the intermediate steps of Russian membership of the WTO, Free Trade Area implementation and confidence-building would

---

29 The meeting reported that the current border-crossing time is five hours.
30 EU–Russia relations special meeting in Kaliningrad, IP/02/721, Brussels, 15 May 2002.
31 Joenniemi et al., *Impact Assessment*, pp. 15–20.

need to take place.[32] The present policy agenda is demanding enough with-out the addition of new, more ambitious initiatives.

The third, Northern Dimension, scenario involves using the existing frameworks and instruments available to the EU (particularly through sectoral and TACIS funding initiatives) to improve regional and cross-border cooperation. Clearly this framework can be used to build confidence, but it will not radically change the overall policy framework within which the Kaliningrad issue is managed.

The fourth scenario involves developing Kaliningrad as a 'pilot region'[33] in EU–Russia relations and searching for innovative solutions unique to the region, for instance by liberalizing trade between Kaliningrad and the EU and allowing the liberal transit and visa regimes currently operated by Poland and Lithuania to continue beyond enlargement. This implies greater trade policy differentiation in the EU's treatment of Kaliningrad compared to the rest of Russia. Apart from the technical problems of differentiation[34] (for instance over rules of origin and certification) it is debatable how far the EU and Russia would be willing to allow differentiation to be taken in view of the precedents it might set. At the time of writing, this scenario did not seem likely to occur given the agreement reached prior to the EU's Copenhagen summit in December 2002.[35] The future of Kaliningrad within the enlarged EU therefore depends on the developing policy positions of the key stakeholders and the relative importance that they ascribe to Kaliningrad.

Policy developments

From the EU's perspective, all the evidence suggests that the strategic imperative of enlargement is the dominant concern. Although this has already

32 The EU's Common Strategy for Russia envisages the incremental integration of Russia into a 'common European economic and social space'. To achieve this the EU has pledged to provide support for institutional and administrative reforms, particularly those that promote the transparent regulation of the market economy. This will include legislative approximation in the fields of customs, standards and certification, and competition policy. However, no specific timetable is proposed for this work. See 'Common Strategy of the European Union of 4 June 1999 on Russia', pp. 4–6.

33 The reference to Kaliningrad as a 'pilot region' appeared in the General Affairs Council's Action Plan for the Northern Dimension presented to the European Council in Feira on 19–20 June 2000. However, the designation has no formal status (at least at present). It reflects the political importance that both the EU and Russia give to the enclave.

34 Differentiation means that the rules applied to EU–Kaliningrad trade may differ from those applied to EU–Russian trade in general. The EU would need to know whether imported goods came from Kaliningrad or 'mainland' Russia, hence concerns about rules of origin and certification.

35 The agreement treats Kaliningrad as part of Russia and does not differentiate between Kaliningraders and mainlanders.

caused difficulties in its dealings with Russia, the EU is not willing to compromise its basic principle that the *acquis* is not negotiable. Thus, despite vociferous protests by Mosow Russians will face the EU's external border policy when it enlarges and will need visas to transit EU territory. Any solutions will therefore be drawn from those already outlined in the Commission's paper as compatible with the *acquis*, such as cheaper and more easily available visas.

Despite its unwillingness to compromise on the basic principle, the EU has demonstrated some flexibility over the way in which a visa regime might operate. The idea of a jointly funded and staffed EU consulate in Kaliningrad, in addition to the Polish and Lithuanian missions already present, has been discussed. This could serve to increase Kaliningraders' access to visas and prevent the issue becoming even more politically contentious.

The Russian side has shown a slightly more pragmatic approach to the visa issue. On 2 September 2002, the Russian government presented the EU's External Relations Commissioner Chris Patten with a draft 'memorandum of intentions' setting out its latest thinking on Kaliningrad in the light of the EU's determination to maintain the *acquis*.[36] On 18 September 2002, the Commission proposed a package of special measures to resolve the Kaliningrad issue. The most important of these was the proposal to introduce a special facilitated transit document (FTD) for Russian citizens who need to travel frequently to and from Kaliningrad.[37] The Commission also proposed that the feasibility of a non-stop high-speed train service linking Kaliningrad with the rest of Russia through Lithuania and Belarus should be studied and that better use of international conventions for road and rail transit should be explored. The long-term goal of visa-free travel between Russia and the EU was restated, conditional on Russia strengthening border and internal security in an effort to combat organized crime.[38] The proposals

36 The memorandum conceded that Kaliningrad residents would need special transit documents to cross Lithuanian and Polish territory and that full visas could be issued to car-drivers. However, it opposed the imposition of full EU visas for residents transiting by bus or train and proposed instead that the precise status of the travel documents should be determined by a joint EU–Russia working group, to include Lithuania. Reported in *European Voice*, 5 September 2002.

37 The Commission proposed that this securitized document could be issued at low cost by the consulates of candidate countries after examining approved lists provided by the Russian authorities. The FTD would allow individuals short periods to transit through EU territory by road or rail. Where Russian citizens do not yet possess internationally valid passports (the usual prerequisite for issuing visas but not commonly held by Russian citizens), the FTD could be considered valid for a short transition period, up to the end of 2004, when accompanied by an internal Russian travel document.

38 European Commission, 'Kaliningrad: Commission Proposes Set of Measures to Ease Transit after Enlargement', IP/02/1331, Brussels, 18 September 2002.

were discussed by the European Council in Brussels on 24–25 October 2002 in order to adopt a common position before the EU–Russia summit in Copenhagen on 11 November. This summit was seen as the last opportunity to resolve the transit issue prior to the Copenhagen European Council in December 2002, at which the details of the general enlargement package were to be finalized.

In the event, the EU–Russia summit concluded an agreement closely based on the Commission's September proposals. Russia accepted the introduction of a low-cost FTD for Russians transiting only between Kaliningrad and the 'mainland', to be operational by 1 July 2003.[39] It was also agreed to launch a feasibility study on the visa-free non-stop train proposal in 2003, for possible implementation following Lithuania's accession to the EU. Both sides agreed to extend the number and capacity of Lithuanian and EU consulates in Kaliningrad as a way to support the new transit regime, and Russia confirmed its intention to conclude a readmission agreement with Lithuania, to be implemented by June 2003.[40]

The agreement represents a pragmatic resolution of the issues and removes the risk of the Kaliningrad issue further blocking either the wider goals of EU enlargement or closer links with Russia. The agreement can be presented as '*acquis*-compatible', in that the EU and Lithuania will issue specific documents to control Russian transit across their territory. Moreover, at least for the moment, it saves Russia's face by not requiring fully compatible international visas for Russian transit.

The explicit inclusion of Lithuania in the development of EU policy towards Kaliningrad, and its critical role in implementing the transit agreement, is further evidence that the enlargement imperative dominates the EU's approach. The evidence shows that by 2002 Poland and Lithuania were already taking a critical role in border management and cross-border economic development, suggesting that the enlargement dynamic in this region is largely positive.

Polish and Lithuanian perspectives also evolved during the 1990s. Both candidate countries were eager to establish their EU credentials in advance of full membership. They therefore fully accepted the 'orthodox' EU position that the principle of Schengen is not negotiable and focused their efforts on the practical implications of introducing the new policy regime in as flexible

---

39 The agreement provided for two types of document: a multiple-entry visa obtainable from a Lithuanian consulate and, for those Russian citizens making only one return journey, a facilitated rail travel document available on the basis of personal data supplied at the time of purchase. The Lithuanian authorities will be able to refuse entry to Russian citizens if they consider them unacceptable to cross their territory.

40 EU–Russia Summit, *Joint Statement on transit between the Kaliningrad region and the rest of the Russian Federation*, 11 November 2002.

a way as possible. Given their historical experience of bilateral relations with Russia and their 'front-line' position on the EU's new eastern external border, giving precedence to EU relations is very important to them.

From the Russian perspective, resolving the Kaliningrad question involves complex issues of both principle and practice. Overall, the Putin government is the most pro-Western post-Soviet Russian government to date and its orientation has been reinforced since 11 September 2001. Despite tensions over Iraq, Russia is strongly committed to closer integration with global institutions, in particular the WTO, and sees its national self-interest as lying in the pursuit of good relations with the EU. But Russia also has deeply rooted historical anxieties about the possible risks of fragmentation, and territorial integrity is critically important to Russian national identity. This accounts for the sensitivity about the post-enlargement need for Russians to possess EU documentation to travel from one part of Russia to another. Nevertheless, the terms of the November 2002 agreement confirm the Russian government's positive general orientation towards the EU and its desire to focus on wider EU–Russia bilateral issues.

Although a flexible and affordable transit regime is clearly in the interests of Kaliningraders themselves, local issues, in particular the state of the enclave's economy, predominate. In this respect it is recognized that cooperation with the EU is likely to bring more benefits. There is evidence that the local perspective is changing, especially among the younger generation. A recent survey found that around 80 per cent of Kaliningraders under the age of 25 had been to western Europe (including Poland), whereas only 15 per cent had visited other parts of Russia.[41] This suggests that in the longer term, local links are likely to assume greater importance than the connection with the 'mainland'. However, it is far too soon to argue that Kaliningrad is in the process of detaching itself from the Federation. The region lacks the administrative capacity and a sufficiently clear sense of its own identity to consider a more ambitious strategy. Even if the federal government took a benign view of such a development (for which there is currently no evidence), there is no sign that the EU would wish to assume greater responsibility for the region given the problems it would bring.

Although the Russian federal government has been willing to recognize the economic problems of Kaliningrad by granting it SEZ status, there are very strict limits as to how far differentiation can go. An entirely new status for Kaliningrad, explicitly recognizing its enclave position, was not under consideration at the time of writing. The transit agreement represents as much differentiation as is acceptable to the federal government. Nor has the

41 See 'Between Two Worlds', *The Economist*, 29 June 2002.

EU pressed for further differentiation. It has repeatedly stated that it is willing to provide financial and other support to the region but that Kaliningrad remains a Russian responsibility. Similarly, Poland and Lithuania have stated that they are not pursuing any form of differentiation.[42]

CONCLUSION

In the case of Kaliningrad, it is easier for the EU to be in Russia than for Russia to be in the EU. For the foreseeable future, Kaliningrad will be dealt with pragmatically and incrementally, within the policy framework agreed in November 2002. Given the wider range of issues at stake in EU–Russia relations it is unlikely that the government in Moscow will risk jeopardizing them over Kaliningrad. But Kaliningrad could remain an emotional issue, vulnerable to being exploited by nationalist politicians in Russia.

The future of Kaliningrad depends only partly on the policy regime imposed on it by Brussels and Moscow. Seeing Kaliningrad as a potential Baltic Hong Kong is overly optimistic, but visa and transit issues might decline in political importance should the government and people of Kaliningrad themselves begin to tackle the formidable economic problems of the region.[43] In the longer term, Kaliningrad's position depends on the effects of the wider dynamics of the integration process in Europe. Should eastern enlargement provide economic and political benefits to existing and new members and positive spillover effects for the enlarged EU's neighbours, then indeed some entirely new models for Kaliningrad's position could become possible. However, over the next five years or so, managing the effects of enlargement, implementing existing EU policies and starting to address Kaliningrad's internal problems will be more than enough to occupy policy-makers in Russia and the EU as well as the residents of Kaliningrad themselves.

42 'Poland's policy vis-à-vis Kaliningrad Oblast of the Russian Federation – one of 89 entities of the state of Russia – remains a part of bilateral relations with Russia. Such an approach to relations with Kaliningrad is based on respect for the rule of territorial integrity of the Russian Federation', Polish position paper (see above, note 27), p. 1.
43 See Dewar, 'Myths in the Baltic', in Baxendale et al., *The EU and Kaliningrad.*

9

Croatia, Bosnia-Herzegovina and Serbia

PETER FRANKOPAN

Croatia, Bosnia-Herzegovina and Serbia will not be among the first group of central and east European countries to join the European Union in 2004. The reasons for this are numerous and do not stem solely from the wars that have engulfed the Balkan region in the past decade or so. Delay in starting negotiations for accession to the EU may in any case be beneficial, both for the EU, which will have been able to identify 'teething problems' from the first enlargement to post-communist Europe, and for the former Yugoslav republics. In the latter case, the promise of eventual membership should encourage self-critical debate within these aspiring countries about their recent past, the failure of their judicial systems to build up an atmosphere of trust and the potential resurgence of extreme nationalist politics.

BACKGROUND

The bloody wars of secession in 1991–5 gave the former Yugoslav republics a reputation in the West for engaging in fratricidal conflict based on ancient ethnic hatreds. However, the reality was much more complex, as shown by variations within and between the republics and by the clever manipulation of antagonisms and local hardships by opportunistic politicians. Tensions had been present within Yugoslavia since its inception, revolving almost exclusively around questions of identity and the delicate balance between, and autonomy of, its constituent republics and provinces. The Serbs held the balance of power in the post-Treaty of Versailles Kingdom of Serbs, Croats and Slovenes. During the Second World War, the occupation of Yugoslavia by Nazi Germany provided the opportunity for systematic persecution in this region as a whole, with the Ustashe regime in Croatia particularly notorious for atrocities committed against Serbs from 1941 onwards. The 'Croatian Spring' of 1971 was an attempt to re-establish Croatian cultural autonomy in the light of the perceived hegemony of a 'Serbian' bureaucracy. The response of Josip Broz Tito, who had ruled the country since the end of

168

the Second World War, was to undertake a series of reforms, culminating in the 1974 Constitution, which devolved substantial autonomy to the six republics and to the autonomous provinces of Kosovo and Vojvodina. This system came to be cynically exploited by Milosevic 15 years later, immediately before and indeed during the break-up of Yugoslavia.

The friction between the various national and ethnic populations in this region was inflamed by the economic chaos that characterized the years following Tito's death in 1980. This period saw spiralling inflation, repeated devaluation of the dinar and increasingly desperate measures to appropriate foreign currency in order to service the burgeoning national debt. With regular shortages of goods and power throughout the country, the authority of central government was challenged more and more often, both by the media and by wide sections of the population, as exemplified in the late 1980s by increasingly regular large-scale demonstrations.[1] In the confusion, opportunistic leaders such as Serbia's Slobodan Milosevic and Croatia's Franjo Tudjman were able to gather substantial support by appealing to nationalist sentiments, thereby establishing effective personal control over the state apparatus. As nationalist rhetoric became increasingly vociferous the economies of the republics became ever more divergent, and with the federal structure straining under the weight of centrifugal forces, the disintegration of Yugoslavia became only a matter of time.

The first war after the collapse of communism, when the Yugoslav People's Army (JNA) invaded Slovenia following its secession from the Federation on 26 June 1991, lasted ten days. The JNA was defeated and the secession was both swift and successful, partly because of the high degree of ethnic homogeneity in that republic.

Croatia, on the other hand, was in no such position, although President Tudjman had planned to secede in tandem with President Kucan, his Slovenian counterpart. The Serb-Croat war resulted from Milosevic's determination not to let Croatia secede while it still contained Croatian Serbs; he was not against secession *per se*. In fact, in March 1991 Milosevic and Tudjman had met secretly to decide the fate of Bosnia-Herzegovina, which was to be carved up between a greater Croatia and a greater Serbia.[2] The failure of the international community to anticipate or manage the transition

---

1 See M. Tanner, *Croatia: A Nation Forged in War* (London: Yale University Press, 1997), pp. 208–16. For more extensive surveys of the build-up to and the collapse of Yugoslavia, see M. Glenny, *The Fall of Yugoslavia: The Third Balkan War* (London: Penguin, 1992), and B. Magas, *The Destruction of Yugoslavia: Tracking the Break-up, 1980–92* (London: Verso, 1993).

2 M. Glenny, *The Balkans: Nationalism, War and the Great Powers* (London: Granta, 1999), p. 633.

to independence of Slovenia and Croatia motivated concerted action to prevent bloodshed in Bosnia. The United Nations Security Council passed a resolution at the start of 1992 authorizing the deployment of a substantial force, but the force was not given a strong enough mandate to stop the advance of the (now) Serb army into Bosnia. However, by 1995 the military balance of power had shifted dramatically and, after a series of NATO airstrikes on Bosnian Serb positions, all parties signed the Dayton accords marking an end to the war.

Tensions within the Serbian province of Kosovo had been kept under control during the conflicts in Croatia and Bosnia-Herzegovina.[3] By 1998, however, forces from the rump state of the Federal Republic of Yugoslavia had entered the province with the aim of disarming local insurgents and reimposing federal authority. Following the collapse of mediated talks at Rambouillet between the Yugoslavs and the Kosovo Liberation Army, further NATO bombings, this time in Serbia itself, resulted in UN Security Council Resolution 1244 and the Military Technical Agreement. This recognized Yugoslav sovereignty in Kosovo, allowed for the deployment of a stabilization force (KFOR) and installed a UN mission to oversee the transition to peace and, ultimately, democracy.

DEALING WITH THE PRESENT, FACING THE PAST

The final major obstacles to reconstruction and reconciliation were removed in 2000, by which time moderates were in power in Croatia, Bosnia-Herzegovina and Serbia proper. Relations within and between these young states could now be re-examined and rebuilt. Potential accession to the EU acted as a strong motivation for elites across the Balkans to reconsider the merits of their political systems and economic policies. It was now more vital than ever to provoke debate within the countries in question over the potential costs and benefits of membership of the EU, partly in order to move away from the idea that the EU would provide an arena as well as the means to solve internal socio-economic and political problems. These problems had to be dealt with *before* membership could be considered.

The tendency to mythologize the past and to fail to confront truths which can be uncomfortably close to home goes some way towards explaining the reluctance of all three states in question to cooperate with the International Criminal Tribunal for the former Yugoslavia (ICTY) except when under extreme pressure from the international community, and

---

3 See, however, Helsinki Watch, *Human Rights Abuses in Kosovo, 1990–1992* (New York: Human Rights Watch, 1992).

particularly in the past few years from the United States. Put simply, in much the same way that unpleasant facts were looked at in Germany following the collapse of the Third Reich in 1945, those facts need to be addressed so that they can then be considered closed; and they need to be addressed as well in order to allow the local populations some insight into what happened during the break-up of the former Yugoslavia and why it happened. Without such a process taking place, it is hard to see how relations between the successor states will be normalized except over the very long term, and only when those who were too young to have been involved in or witnessed the atrocities have come through to dominate the high positions of state. Even then, there is no guarantee that animosities and prejudices will not be handed down and continue to restrict growth and stability in the region as a whole.

There has been a considerable effort to invest in education in all the countries of southeastern Europe, as this provides at least one way of breaking the cycle of emotional rather than rational reactions both to the 'other' and to the 'self'. Whether this is an effective way to confront the past remains to be seen, for it is, of course, a prerequisite that nationalist tendencies and mythologies are not simply stored up for future generations. Crucial to this education, therefore, is cooperation with the ICTY and the process of bringing those indicted for war crimes to trial in a court of law. However, it is indicative of just how much reform beyond the purely administrative and institutional is required that as late as the summer of 2002 the Americans felt it necessary not to approve a $10 million grant for educational projects in Serbia, in order to apply yet more pressure for indictees to be handed over to the ICTY. It seemed to be necessary to take extreme measures to compel the various governments to confront the actions of their populations.

It is not without irony, then, that there is considerable local support in this region for the concept of bringing to justice those guilty of instigating and taking part in atrocities. The objection, as articulated at governmental level, especially in Croatia and Serbia, is that the ICTY is not the correct arena in which to try those who are charged. It is, of course, a challenge for the various governments to have the political courage to surrender to the ICTY, or even to submit to trial at home, those who are perceived to have played a prominent and heroic role in the defence of their respective countries. The indictment of General Norac and General Gotovina provoked considerable opposition in Croatia, to the point where it seemed that the government might not survive the pressure applied by the media and a hostile public. The indictment of another figure, General Bobetko, proved to be only marginally less divisive, although in this case at least ill health (confidentially verified by

ICTY doctors) has made extradition unlikely, thereby minimizing domestic fallout.[4] Although a number of high-profile individuals were brought to The Hague, most notably Slobodan Milosevic, former Yugoslav president Milan Milutinovic and the Serbian nationalist politician Voijslav Seselj, at the time of writing many others who have been indicted remain at large. The reluctance to surrender these people to the ICTY is a major stumbling block. Nor is it clear yet whether trials which are conducted in the respective country with the Tribunal's agreement, as in the case of Norac, will have an outcome that allows for the necessary degree of closure for these matters to be dealt with in a truly satisfactory manner.

This discussion paints a gloomy picture in which there appears to be little sense of confronting the immediate past, an inability to move forward in a constructive manner and a reluctance to seek to learn from the break-up of Yugoslavia. But it is important to set this into the wider context of the post-communist world, where these problems and symptoms strike a familiar chord. The point to emphasize is that the key difference between the states of the former Yugoslavia and the other countries of central and eastern Europe is that for the latter, emergence from the Soviet bloc did not involve sustained, consistent or even substantial use of force.

It is of some significance that although the use of force was certainly not endemic in Yugoslavia before its break-up, it had played a prominent and regular role from the time of the country's creation. This is revealing, not only in providing an understanding of how the conflicts of the 1990s came to be militarized so quickly, but also in allowing us to pinpoint the key weakness that lay at the heart of the Yugoslav ideal – namely that of maintaining a federal identity in the face of competing and often contradictory ethnic, religious, cultural and even linguistic claims and counter-claims. Because Yugoslavia's creation, even from an internal perspective, had essentially been a means to an end rather than a goal in itself, it was always unclear how local differences should best be managed. Thus the birth of Yugoslavia was marked, almost from the very beginning, by the efforts and struggles of those

4 Croatian generals Mirko Norac, Ante Gotovina and Janko Bobetko were the three most senior and high-profile military figures indicted by the ICTY for war crimes allegedly committed in Croatia during the early 1990s. Norac's arrest in 2001 prompted widespread outcry as well as several large public demonstrations in Croatia. Norac subsequently went on trial in Rijeka in a Croatian court as part of a deal struck between the chief prosecutor, Carla Del Ponte, and the Croatian authorities. He was found guilty in March 2003 and sentenced to fifteen years in (Croatian) prison. At the time of writing, Gotovina had yet to face trial, having apparently fled the country in 2001. News that Bobetko was unlikely to be extradited in view of his poor health prompted a rise in the popularity of the government in Zagreb, even though there was no obvious reason why any credit should have gone in that direction. General Ademi, yet another senior military figure indicted by the ICTY, surrendered himself to The Hague in summer 2001.

172

within the state both to express themselves in terms of a more devolved identity and to seek greater autonomy at a local level. Likewise, it is significant that such efforts were consistently rejected and dealt with by force throughout the twentieth century.

However clear the tensions within Yugoslavia were from the start, they were not uniform or consistent, and it would be easy to overstate the case that the country was made up of constantly warring factions. There were long periods, especially after the Second World War, of cooperation and tolerance during which coercion from the centre was limited. But this was the fatal weakness of Yugoslavia, as such periods of calm were the product, in the first instance, of political liberalization, of the devolution of power into local hands. The inevitable by-product of this was the shift of focus, at least passively, onto the constituent republics and onto other regions, such as Vojvodina and Kosovo, which either enjoyed or aspired to an increasing degree of autonomy, and away from the higher ideal of Yugoslavism. As local desires found an opportunity for expression and articulation, it was not long before they came to demand concessions, such as recognition of languages, social freedoms and the use of national and regional symbols, which did not sit comfortably with the centre.

These pressures were by no means unique to Yugoslavia or even, for that matter, to the various socialist and communist states of central and eastern Europe. What made Yugoslavia distinctive, however, was an inability to deal with liberalization in a coherent way; it resorted instead to knee-jerk reactions which fostered not only increasing resentment but also the climate of force that was to prove so telling at the start of the 1990s. And there had already been the response of the federal government to demonstrations in Kosovo in 1981, soon after the death of Tito, which saw the use of force, large-scale purging and a clumsy re-enforcement of the pan-Yugoslav ideal, on the one hand, and the blanket condemnation of opponents of this as nationalists, on the other. This convinced many inside and outside the country that it was only a matter of time before the government would be unable to control tensions or to impose its will.

That the government was ill-equipped to deal with the issue of managing liberalism within a wider Yugoslav context was not helped by the fact that the Communist Party proved to be highly ineffectual in bringing new blood into the federal apparatus. Thus by the time of the collapse of the Berlin Wall in 1989, the machinery of state was still largely dominated by the partisan generation. The importance of this cannot be overemphasized, for two reasons. First, there was little readiness to deal with, or comprehension of what lay behind, the sudden and rapid transition of the world around Yugoslavia and particularly the collapse of communism as a genuine alternative political, social and economic system – at least in its extant form. Second, the failure to grasp the implications of transition in a region where this was bound to give rise to some efforts to decentralize had important consequences. Opportunities arose for individual strong men, most notably Slobodan Milosevic in Yugoslavia and Serbia, Radovan Karadzic in Bosnia-Herzegovina and Croatia's Franjo Tudjman, to impose themselves and their wishes essentially unopposed by a bewildered and impotent hierarchy and to capture if not fuel the desires of the relevant populations in order to pursue their own agendas.

This goes some way towards explaining Yugoslavia's descent into anarchy. However, it is important to bear in mind that for all the optimism that followed the removal of Milosevic and Tudjman from the political scene (albeit in different circumstances) and the marginalization of other nationalist figures across the region, many of the issues raised during the break-up itself, particularly minority rights, remain to be dealt with satisfactorily in the three countries under consideration. In Croatia, for example, the government has struggled to convince the minority Serb population that it will be adequately protected and represented in public life. In the rump of Yugoslavia, now renamed Serbia and Montenegro, the status of the ethnic Albanian and Hungarian populations also remains unclear and they are in practice accorded only limited rights; moreover, the uncertain political future of Kosovo means that the relationship between the different ethnic, religious and political groups within that province is managed by the United Nations Interim Administrative Mission in Kosovo (UNMIK) instead of finding its natural local balance. This dependence on the UN mission brings the danger of unpredictability when the mandate finally ends.

CURRENT PROBLEMS: OBSTACLES TO REFORM

Even the most cursory look at the region reveals that the major structural problems have been put on ice rather than tackled head on. At the time of writing, there seems little immediate prospect of a final resolution of the dispute between Croatia and Slovenia concerning the extent and division of territorial waters in the Bay of Piran in the northern Adriatic or over the question of ownership of the Krsko nuclear plant, which was jointly owned by both countries. More progress has been made on the issue of the Prevlaka peninsula and Croatia's southeastern border, with a joint declaration by the Croatian and Yugoslav foreign ministers in April 2002 that sought to reach a final settlement by the end of the year. Agreement was finally reached in December 2002, just before the expiry of the UN mandate: joint patrols by Croatian and Serbian and Montenegrin forces replaced those of the United

Nations Mission in Montenegro, which had previously been responsible for monitoring and maintaining peace in the area.[5]

Less of a concern in Croatia, at least at present, is the relatively high level of popular support for political parties in Istria advocating, in the most extreme cases, greater levels of self-rule and closer ties with Italy. Such calls may increase if economic and political reforms stall, as they appeared to be doing at the start of 2003.[6] Moreover, while the prognosis in terms of sovereignty was essentially a positive one, there was still a great deal to be done in order to clear the major obstacle of the return of refugees, a topic which inflamed local passions and which, in spite of recent promises, has not yet been dealt with decisively by the government in Zagreb.

In Bosnia-Herzegovina, there are outstanding problems as well, although the agreements reached in Geneva and New York in 1995, and enshrined finally at Dayton, Ohio remain intact. Bosnia-Herzegovina, which saw the worst of the fighting and bloodshed in the early 1990s, has remained essentially peaceful in recent years. However, the state of affairs at the time of writing, at least in terms of a political and administrative establishment, clearly does not suffice to stand the test of time, and it appears inevitable that there will be changes in due course, although it is difficult to anticipate what such changes will be or involve. Bosnia-Herzegovina is made up of two entities. The Republika Srpska controls 49 per cent of the territory and the Federation of Bosnia-Herzegovina controls the remainder. Each has its own parliament, devised and intended to cooperate at a federal national level in two houses of representatives. This arrangement is over-complicated if not actually unworkable, but it does preserve a status quo based on the post-

5 The Bay of Piran saw a series of increasingly acrimonious confrontations between Croatian and Slovenian fishing boats and coast guards during the summer of 2002. The dispute centred on access to the Adriatic and to international waters and on whether and to what extent Croatia was prepared (and obliged) to provide such access. Although settlement of this issue is not specifically linked to the Krsko nuclear plant, this latter topic was also a subject of increasingly bitter debate in both countries, with the Croatian parliament failing to agree to a settlement. The Prevlaka question revolves around the precise sea border off the Prevlaka peninsula. Yugoslavia (now Serbia and Montenegro) has been keen to win the right for its commercial and naval shipping to pass unimpeded through Croatian waters, thereby preserving the value of its own deep-water port in Montenegro.

6 The main party in Istria, the Istrian Democratic Assembly (IDS) is strongly represented in all parts of the peninsula and has performed consistently well at the local level, suggesting that there is a desire to express an Istrian identity. The party has overtly liberal tendencies, however, and there has as yet been little attempt to bring an irredentist programme to public discussion. Nevertheless, the weakness of the coalition government, which the IDS supports, may mask debate and focus on this subject. Increasing frustration with the privatization process and with the political process in general (as seen in a series of strikes in late 2002 and early 2003) have begun to impact on the IDS's own future orientation, as it has on other political parties with and without a regional focus.

break-up settlement. All the same, there is considerable mutual suspicion between the two entities, which not only has the effect of sustaining latent hostilities based on ethnic, religious and cultural grounds but also condemns the country as a whole to a stalemate and an uneasy truce.

In Serbia, animosities and tensions are arguably even more of a barrier to development, although important steps were made in this respect in 2001–2. In particular, the question of Serbia's association with Montenegro within the former Republic of Yugoslavia, which dominated public discussion in both countries from early 2001, retreated somewhat. This was in no small part due to the efforts of the EU to postpone debate in the short term, the formal replacement of the state of Yugoslavia with that of Serbia-Montenegro and the promise of formal referenda in (a maximum of) three years from 2003. Kosovo continued to present a rather more difficult series of problems, not least because of the large-scale exodus of Serbs during and immediately after the NATO bombings of 1999. The Kosovo question was put on ice, at least for the time being, owing to the arrival of UNMIK. Nevertheless, it was unclear how and when Serbian sovereignty would be reconciled with the aims and ambitions of the local population or what effect this might have on Kosovo and on the politics and political development of Serbia itself. Although Kosovo is the most obvious and most dramatic future flashpoint in Serbia, there are other regions too – notably Vojvodina, which in January 2002 was granted a greater degree of autonomy by Belgrade, but also the Sandzak and the Presevo valley – where minority rights and sensitivities must be addressed carefully.[7]

The grounds for optimism in Croatia, Bosnia-Herzegovina and Serbia stem largely from the relief that the militarized and highly aggressive atmosphere which prevailed in the 1990s appears to have settled down. The arrival of a new generation of politicians to replace the old partisan generation and the appointment of leaders who do not carry the intellectual and psychological baggage of communism or of the past decade, and who do not have

7 The Sandzak is a predominantly Muslim enclave on the border between Serbia and Montenegro, based on the town of Novi Pazar. Although the Sandzak was never a province in the former Yugoslavia (as Vojvodina and Kosovo were), there has been a growing desire for this area to be designated as a separate political and territorial unit within current Yugoslavia. Although its leader, Sulejman Ugljanin, openly opposed the further disintegration of Yugoslavia, in March 2001 he proposed that the country be divided into five components, of which the Sandzak would be one, the others being Serbia, Montenegro, Kosovo and Vojvodina. The Presevo valley is an ethnically Albanian area in southern Serbia. It saw a significant dispersal of its population during the Yugoslav military initiatives in Kosovo in the late 1990s. This period also saw increasing militarization in the region. Since 2001, the situation has stabilized significantly, with the return of refugees during the summer of 2001 and the disbanding of insurgents, overseen directly and successfully by the Serbian deputy prime minister, Nebojsa Covic.

the debts and bonds of patronage that tied the ruling class so closely to Tudjman and to Milosevic, mean that there is at last a platform on which to build for stability in the region.

This platform remains shaky, however. In all three countries, the government was formed by a coalition of parties, often with widely differing agendas and outlooks on economic, political, social and constitutional development. In each case, this has made for an uneasy balance between the major party and its junior partners, who have often been able to extract an inordinately high price in return for their support. The problems go well beyond the issue of securing positions (often in non-governmental roles) for prominent supporters. In the case of Croatia, for example, the decision by the leader of the Liberal Party, Drazen Budisa, to withdraw members of his party from cabinet positions (causing considerable damage to his standing within the party as well as among the electorate) succeeded in bringing down the government of Ivica Racan in July 2002. Although Racan's party, the Social Democrats, held enough seats in parliament to form a solid minority government, the confusion caused by the resignation and by the reappointment of a new government served to divert attention from more pressing matters of reform, particularly regarding the economy and the judiciary. Perhaps more importantly, it undermined the government and further disenfranchised a public that was already having to contend with an unemployment rate of over 20 per cent.

The situation continued to deteriorate during 2002, partly because of continued in-fighting within the new coalition but above all because of increasing disenchantment about the speed and effect of reform. This culminated in a series of strikes by various public-sector workers and also in the suspension of the board of the Croatian Privatization Fund after a series of embarrassing and damaging sales of state-owned companies, above all the Sisak steelworks and Suncani Hvar hotels (the sale of the latter was revoked in February 2003). As a result, there was a loss of confidence in the government itself. These difficulties came as unwelcome distractions, actively hindering the process of democratization and inflicting further damage upon the political establishment.

The obvious weaknesses of a coalition government and domestic political uncertainty during a time of reform were also clear in Belgrade, even before the assassination of the prime minister, Zoran Djindjic, in March 2003. These stemmed from more than the cosmetic changes to the status of Yugoslavia, with its renaming as Serbia and Montenegro and the ratification of the Constitutional Charter on Serbian and Montenegrin Union, and the failure of the electorate to elect a new Serbian president following elections in December 2002 and February 2003, which were both judged void because of low turn-out. The problems arose principally from the tensions between the coalition umbrella Democratic Opposition of Serbia, particularly between Prime Minister Djindjic and the President of Yugoslavia, Vojislav Kostunica, which characterized and dominated the period following Milosevic's fall from power. The tensions had the effect of personalizing the debate and destabilizing an already limited and difficult programme of reform. The antagonism between Kostunica's party, the Democratic Party of Serbia (DSS) and Djindjic's Democratic Party remained at a fever pitch for much of 2001–2, with petty, tit-for-tat politics fought for the sake of limited political capital as politicians jockeyed for position in the public eye.

As in Croatia, the effect of disruption was containable because the principal opposition parties in each case – the Socialist Party of Serbia and the Croatian Democratic Union, the vehicles that had propelled Milosevic and Tudjman respectively to power – enjoyed only limited support. Nevertheless, the disruption and, above all, the energy and time required to anticipate, counter and deal with these parties were unwelcome diversions from more pressing matters. Worse, the fluid domestic situation in both countries did little to attract or reassure investors who might otherwise have provided much-needed funds for the economy as well as employment in a highly depressed labour market.

It remains to be seen what effect Djindic's murder will have both on Serbia's internal politics and on the perception of the country from outside. At the time of writing, however, the crack-down on organized crime, the purging of corrupt state officials, and the appointment of one of Djindic's allies, Zoran Zivkovic, as prime minister suggest that the assassination may ironically have a beneficial impact if it delivers a much-needed boost to the pace of and appetite for reform, while at the same time providing cohesion and support for the moderates' programme. Whether or not this will form the basis for consolidation in anything other than the short term, however, is uncertain.

The situation in Bosnia-Herzegovina at the start of the twenty-first century was little better than that of its neighbours in terms of political in-fighting. The governing coalition in the Federation, known as the Alliance for Change, only belatedly began to act in a way deserving that name, setting aside personal as well as the expected ethnic and religious differences to reach an agreement on the key issue of constitutional reform. Likewise, in the Serb-dominated Republika Srpska, spoiling tactics designed to score personal rather than substantive points receded from late 2001, and it seemed the outlook was improving. As in Croatia and Serbia, the limited alternatives to the existing coalitions suggested that, for the time being, moderates in all three states would retain the opportunity to pursue reform without having to deal with nationalist rhetoric, and that there was little likelihood of extremists being returned to power.

The fact that the political scene was still being affected by squabbles within the ruling coalitions was all the more frustrating because 2001–2 offered an unparalleled opportunity for reform: the opposition was weak, and there was enormous goodwill from the international community towards the incoming governments in Croatia and Serbia in 2000, and a continued logistical, military and financial commitment to Bosnia-Herzegovina and Kosovo. It will be disappointing indeed if this turns out to have been an opportunity missed.

Encouraging signs could be identified, and it seemed that there was a genuine desire to implement the key, and sometimes painful, reforms necessary for each of these states should they, like Croatia, seek eventual membership of the EU. There are certainly discrepancies in the attitudes of the ruling parties, and indeed of the oppositions, in Croatia, Bosnia-Herzegovina and Serbia to the role played by the West, including the EU, from the break-up of Yugoslavia to the NATO bombings of 1999. But there is a clear consensus, albeit by default in the absence of any debate on this matter, that accession to the EU is an essential and fundamental goal. This at least partly reflects the thirst prevalent throughout the post-communist European states for acceptance in the wider international community, stoked in turn by a fear of exclusion from the political, socio-economic and cultural mainstream. Thus membership of the EU is not just an undisputed goal. It is one that is pursued with seemingly relentless optimism, as much for the psychological security it offers as for any other, concrete, benefits it may bring.

PROSPECTS FOR MEMBERSHIP

Discussion and analysis of the expansion of the EU to include countries in southeastern Europe is somewhat premature, however. With the exception of Slovenia, there is little realistic prospect of membership, at least in the short term, for Croatia, Bosnia-Herzegovina and Serbia (whether as a single entity or as Serbia and Montenegro). It was never likely that any of those three states would have formed part of the first wave of candidates due to join the EU in 2004 given the conflict in the former Yugoslavia and that it was only with the removal of Milosevic and the installation of UNMIK that the region as a whole finally found stability. It is difficult to assess how quickly reform may occur. But leaving aside the question of whether the EU will be able or willing to take in new members, it does not seem likely that Croatia, Bosnia-Herzegovina and Serbia will either be ready or be offered the chance to accede before 2007 at the very earliest, although Croatia has expressed a desire to join in 2007 along with Bulgaria and Romania.

In some ways, Croatia, Bosnia-Herzegovina and Serbia might benefit from being late candidates for EU membership, as they should be able to draw lessons from the difficulties encountered by those states that join in 2004 and by Romania and Bulgaria, whose applications are not quite so far advanced. The first eastward enlargement will be important in highlighting the ease or difficulty with which former communist states can make the transition to EU membership. Moreover, by the time these states begin to negotiate accession, assuming that they choose to apply, the EU should have completed the protracted institutional reforms that have to some extent overshadowed the first wave of negotiations.

Although their status as latecomers might be beneficial to Croatia, Bosnia-Herzegovina and Serbia, however, their palpable optimism about the process brings considerable drawbacks, not least because it indicates a fundamental misunderstanding of what is involved in becoming a member of the EU. In the case of Croatia, for example, the enthusiasm with which accession is pursued at the national and the local level brings with it the risk of identifying and focusing only on the advantages, real or imaginary, of membership and failing to identify the disadvantages and costs (particularly in social and economic terms) which membership also entails. More serious is the danger of failing to understand just how far away the goalposts are, of promising too much too soon at a political level, which might in turn lead the electorate to develop very negative perceptions of the credibility of the EU as an institution. There is a clear example of this danger in the announcement by the government in Croatia immediately after the signing of a Stabilization and Association Agreement (SAA) with the EU in December 2001 – and without any consideration of when or if this agreement would be ratified by the other member states. In this statement, which was widely reported and commented on in the national media at the time, the minister responsible for relations with the EU, Neven Mimica, declared that although EU negotiators had advised Croatia to wait for the six-year duration of the SAA before applying for full EU membership, the government would seek to apply for this status within 12 months – with an application formally lodged in Athens in February 2003.[8]

Such unbridled optimism should not be ignored or presumed to be benign because, quite apart from the problem of raising expectations only to have them disappointed, it also arouses more substantive concerns. First, except at the highest political and administrative levels, there is a very limited if not negligible ability or desire to consider, understand or address what the EU wants and expects. Secondly, there is a profound misunderstanding of

8 For Mimica's statement, see, for example, EIU Country Report Croatia, January 2002, p. 2.

where Croatia (for example) truly stands in terms of future and potential membership. In reality, the programme of reforms still required in all three countries before accession can be contemplated seriously is so extensive, and progress in all three so sluggish, that there is a danger that such unrealistic attitudes may in due course turn to frustration and then hostility.

The need to avoid this predicament will be of crucial importance in the short to medium term. All three countries are currently going through a process of profound change, a process which is, and will continue to be, painful as unemployment remains high and austerity measures hit large numbers of the population. Eventual membership of the EU can, and perhaps even should, be used prudently to justify the price that will continue to be paid. However, this must be done in a manner that does not compromise either the EU itself or the respective governments in the successor states to the former Yugoslavia, where the primary concern must be stability. Under no circumstance should this be jeopardized by over-enthusiastic promises which prove to be undeliverable. There is a fine balance to maintain in all three cases, and it is by no means difficult to envisage a case where frustrations about the course, pace and rewards of reform lead to the replacement of moderates by those with more extreme views, with the problems this would bring not only to the programme of reform but also to the stability of the wider region.

It is vital, then, for the EU in its formal and informal discussions with the governments in Zagreb, Sarajevo and Belgrade not only to avoid raising expectations too high but also actively to seek to manage and even dampen local aspirations. Although this will almost certainly be seen as an attempt to diminish the strategic and economic importance of the individual country, or even of the region as a whole, upsetting these sensitivities at an early stage will be a small price to pay in the long run. The great danger in the coming years will be that an increasingly powerful extremist voice begins to be heard in response to the slow pace of reform or, to be more precise, the low rate of return of the rewards of reform. With unemployment above 20 per cent in all three countries, indeed as high as 40 per cent in Bosnia-Herzegovina, and with still very limited amounts of foreign direct investment (FDI) in the region generally, there are clearly ingredients in place for the relative stability enjoyed since 2000 to be eroded rapidly – and for the programme of reform to be stopped or even reversed.[9] This would appear to be the principal threat to the stability and security of the countries of the former Yugoslavia, at least

9 For unemployment figures and levels of foreign direct investment in each country, see Economist Intelligence Unit, *Country Profile Yugoslavia* (2002); *Country Profile Croatia* (2002); *Country Profile Bosnia-Herzegovina* (2002).

for the foreseeable future. With that in mind, the EU can and should play its hand sensibly and carefully.

There is a further issue for leaders in these countries to address: it remains unclear how the EU will cope with the accession of ten new members in 2004. If that process is very difficult there may be little appetite for further expansion. In the particular cases of Croatia, Bosnia-Herzegovina and Serbia, specific concerns might emerge about potential migration. In fact, the level of immigration from the first wave of candidate countries is surprisingly small at present. Even the large number of asylum-seekers and illegal immigrants in the late 1990s who were, or purported to be, from Kosovo during the end of the 1990s dropped sharply after the end of the NATO bombing of Yugoslavia in 1999. Nevertheless, immigration is a live topic in political debate across the EU, not only in countries, such as Germany, Austria, Italy and Greece, which have exterior borders with candidate states but also in those that do not, including Belgium, the United Kingdom and the Netherlands. Thus it is possible that expansion will occur in a climate of suspicion both with regard to the increased costs that it will bring to existing member states and over the availability of a cheap and highly educated labour force. It stands to reason that these pressures will be magnified if the current depressed economic conditions do not improve.

On a more positive note, in the 1990s the EU did come to understand the need to take a proactive role in the region and also how to do so. It was heavily involved in brokering the moratorium between Serbia and Montenegro. This appears finally to have put on hold the question of the future relationship between the two remaining constituent republics of the former Yugoslavia, which Brussels feared could have opened up issues of devolution and secession elsewhere in the former Yugoslavia or in southeastern Europe more widely. That the EU was highly visible and also decisive in its prescription of renaming Yugoslavia and backing future referenda in both Serbia and Montenegro says a great deal about how the Union has adapted to play a role beyond its borders.

There are other examples of this foresight, and of the Union taking the lead in the region, even if it did not offer any signals about membership. One instance was the scale of the EU's involvement in the Stability Pact Donor Conference in Brussels in 2000. Another was its quick and pre-emptive move to help prop up the Albanian and Macedonian economies immediately after the NATO bombings in 1999, which hit trade badly.[10] The effect of the EU involvement, coupled with the *de facto* independence of Kosovo under

10 World of Information, *Business Intelligence Report: Federal Republic of Yugoslavia* (2000), pp. 19–20.

UNMIK, suggests that the territorial and ethnic issues that dominated the region may now finally be subsiding – although it would also be fair to say that the Union's desire (and ability) to continue committing resources to all three countries has diminished sharply.

After months of debate about the future of the rump of Yugoslavia and before renaming the state and announcing an agreement to postpone referenda on independence, a senior Serbian cabinet minister, Bozidar Djelic, suggested in 2000 that the Serbians should hold their own referendum about the divorce from Macedonia and the dissolution of Yugoslavia. This rather bullish proposal was interesting for two reasons. It represented a keen desire to bring this matter to a conclusion – as finance minister, Djelic was acutely aware that the level of investment was directly proportional in the first instance to political stability. Above all, it provided a clear sign that Belgrade was now prepared to loosen its grip when it so chose, a major departure from the Milosevic years. The return of autonomy for Vojvodina to the level it had enjoyed before Milosevic was another important and useful example of an increasing liberalization and consolidation within Serbia, although it should be stressed that the concessions to Vojvodina were not approved by all members of the ruling coalition, notably the DSS, the party of President Kostunica.

This aside – and it is worth noting that the DSS did not vote against the coalition, it abstained from the vote – the eagernesss to enforce Yugoslavism as a geographical and political concept appears to have dissipated significantly since the fall of Milosevic. In the case of Kosovo, the presence of UNMIK, and of the forthright and eminently sensible Special Representative of the Secretary General of the UN, Michael Steiner, meant that there was little prospect of dramatic change in the province, at least in the short term. It remains to be seen what will happen in Kosovo over the longer run, for the exodus of perhaps as many as 200,000 Serbs during and immediately after the NATO bombings of 1999 altered the ethnic and political balance significantly. At the time of writing, it seems unlikely that there will be a substantial return of the Serbian minority; this would have serious implications for the status of Kosovo within Serbia because the progression of the province to full independence would be likely to become inexorable. The EU is aware of this and will sanction a change of Kosovo's current status only if it can be handled smoothly and, equally importantly, if the effects and precedents can be contained. The deferral of key questions is due in large measure to conditions on the ground and to the aspirations and interests of local politicians and businesses.

The pace of change in Croatia, Bosnia-Herzegovnia and Serbia in terms of the replacement of key individuals who had dominated the political scene in the 1990s, market reform, attraction of investment and moving away from reliance on Western aid was nowhere near as dramatic and fast as those within and those outside them wished it to be. In particular, the privatization processes in the three countries were desperately slow and well behind schedule, mainly because foreign investors were reluctant to make long-term financial commitments in the light of reports and rumours of organized crime and cartels working even at the government level in all three countries. Clearly, the assassination of Zoran Djindic in March 2003 and the subsequent investigations – which not only revealed the extent of the influence and power which criminal gangs were able to extert in Serbia but also the links enjoyed by high-ranking members of the government – only served to confirm what was widely thought to be the case already. Many public officials, including 35 judges, seven of whom sat in the high court, as well as the deputy public prosecutor, Milan Saraljic, were either charged with criminal offences or forced to resign in the weeks which followed Djindic's murder. This gives a good indication of how deep the problems of open government run in this country. Likewise, the dismissal of the Chief State Prosecutor in Croatia, Radovan Ortynski, in the middle of 2002, following rumours and speculation about a report being prepared on corruption in Croatia (although it had yet to present any concrete findings), did little to reassure the international and local business communities that this issue was being looked at as earnestly and diligently as it should and evidently needs to be.[11]

Even if crime and corruption have not deterred the investor, the slow pace of judicial reform in particular has proved hard to overcome. Apart from the fact that the judiciary is politicized, there are substantial problems owing to the lengthy judicial process and the overly bureaucratic administration that deals with it. Worse still, concrete steps have yet to be taken to deal with the question of land and asset ownership – in terms of compensation where nationalization occurred after 1945 but also in terms of being able to offer investors clean title to that land. The effect is that there are obvious barriers to inward and local investment, which in turn hinders social and economic development in the region.

Of course, foreign investment is not an end in itself. It is a means to stimulate the economy and to allay social concerns brought on by

---

11 Ortynski was removed following his failure to produce any evidence to support his allegations of corruption and links to organized crime in the political establishment and the judiciary. This followed a public challenge by Prime Minister Racan to provide details to support his comments about corruption. Having voted to remove him, the Croatian parliament nominated Mladen Bajic as his successor. Although the evidence Ortynski had gathered was passed to Bajic, the parliament decided not to set up an enquiry into Ortynski's allegations.

unemployment or by the cancellation or reduction of pensions coupled with the rising cost of living. But foreign investment can also bring its own problems and difficulties – the Croatian government, for example, is well aware of this with respect to the banking sector, which is now dominated entirely by Italian and Austrian (i.e. non-Croatian) concerns. However, foreign investment, carefully handled, can be highly beneficial, as it has been in Slovenia, Hungary and the Czech Republic, in prompting and forcing more open government, and in offsetting the social costs of economic reform.

Certainly, there are positive signs about progress in and prospects for this region, not least in the increasing normalization of relations between the ex-Yugoslav republics, notably between Croatia and Serbia, and in the fact that there is a path open towards acceptance and recognition by the major international institutions. For example, Croatia's membership of the World Trade Organization as of 2000, its signing of a Stability and Association Agreeement with the EU in 2001, its admittance to the Central European Free Trade Agreement in 2002 and its invitation in the same year to join NATO's Membership for Action Plan were widely welcomed boosts for it. They were used to show that the country was finally playing a part in the European and international mainstreams and thus that the sacrifices and costs of the past decade had been worthwhile.

There is still a long way to go in Croatia, Bosnia-Herzegovina and Serbia before admission to the European Union becomes a real possibility. Of particular concern at present is the position of Bosnia-Herzegovina, where progress towards normalization and reform is much harder to envisage than for its two neighbours, not least because of its complex and often contradictory political and social organization. It will be interesting to see the effect of Belgrade's softening in its relations with and attitudes towards its neighbours, particularly those areas and regions considered to be key, such as Kosovo, Montenegro and Vojvodina.

Certainly, Belgrade is starting to stand much farther away from the Republika Srpska in Bosnia than it did under Milosevic – and farther than many in the Republika Srpska would want it to do – in part, no doubt, because propping up the Serbian part of Bosnia comes at a financial as well as a political price. In Bosnia as a whole, therefore, much depends on whether the Republika Srpska can sell, and deliver, a political solution to its inhabitants which looks for solutions from Sarajevo rather than from farther away and which does not deal with them in the same way as in the past. Milosevic's removal has also led to a revision of the concept of 'Greater Serbia' which had dominated the political debate in Serbia proper as well as in the Serb part of Bosnia. Once talk of an international community of Serbs as a distinct entity was used to whip up support for Milosevic, but now the concept of Serbia taking direct responsibility for Serbs outside its territorial boundaries has moved quietly into the background.

Part of the reason for this is the moderate stance of the current leadership in Belgrade and its understanding that there are priorities closer to home that require its attention. Furthermore, the pressure of economic and social reform in Serbia is sufficiently severe for there to be obvious limitations as to how far Republika Srpska could be propped up, even if there were a genuine desire to do so. As a result, it is not just rhetoric which has been softened; the ties which bound the fate of federal Yugoslavia to the Bosnian Serbs so strongly during the 1990s have also been loosened.

This is not for lack of effort from the Republika Srpska, which sees Belgrade as its natural focal point and which has consistently sought to rely on Serbia as a source not only of spiritual guidance but also of investment. Thus, Serbia's own preoccupations act as a very welcome restraint on the ambitions that the Republika Srpska can realistically entertain in terms of assessing its own medium- and long-term future. However, as economic recovery and social reform gather pace in Croatia and Serbia, Bosnia should naturally emerge as a beneficiary, profiting from increased trade with its neighbours. It is likely that the Federation of Bosnia-Herzegovina (the predominantly Croatian and Muslim entity) will gain disproportionately should the Republika Srpska not re-evaluate its direction and play a full and cooperative role in Bosnia; for, as is already clear, there is an economic and social price to be paid for the intransigent policies pursued even since the settlements at Dayton.

CONCLUSION

At the time of writing, the region as a whole is at a crossroads, with many positive signs amid the inevitable problems. In the short term, the most important priority is for moderate parties to stay in power. If austerity measures are too severe, if inflation rises too rapidly or if unemployment is not countered by the creation of new jobs, there is a real danger that extremists could again attract the levels of popular support that made these republics of former Yugoslavia an economic basket case for much of the 1990s.

In this respect, reform of the judiciary is the most essential and pressing concern, as it is a critical part of the democratization of the region. Indeed, the importance of judicial reform has been pinpointed regularly and repeatedly by EU and OSCE missions to all three countries. The necessity of an efficient and transparent legal system underpins future social stability because it is a key indicator of the governments' openness and thus a benchmark of their authority. Moreover, the imposition and clarity of mechanisms for governing disputes is a central plank in attracting future foreign (and local) investment. Although the low level of FDI in Croatia, Bosnia-Herzegovina and Serbia is partly a reflection of continued fears about the stability of the former Yugoslavia, it also suggests that the lack of protection through a functioning, efficient legal system has been a major deterrent. In short, the construction and maintenance of a transparent legal system is a significant factor in the pace of regional development, the springboard for long-term progress in these countries.

For all the problems still to be addressed in the former Yugoslavia, there are signs that the corner has been turned and that the region will now settle down and put the terrible events of the 1990s behind it. Although the pace of reform has often been painfully slow, the fact that the violence of those years appears to have been decisively curtailed is an important development in itself, even allowing for the assassination of Zoran Djindic. Another sign is that moderates are in power in all three states, with agendas that seek to push forward into the future rather than rake up the immediate and the mythological past. It is worth noting that many of the factors that caused the break-up and accompanying violence in the former Yugoslavia still simmer under the surface. In this respect, therefore, the transition to socio-economic stability needs to be carefully handled within the countries themselves, as well as by those international institutions, such as the EU, that have a vested interest in preserving the peace and continuing democratization beyond their current territorial boundaries.

10

An ever larger Europe: destined to remain divided?

CHARLES JENKINS AND JULIE SMITH

For half a century 'Europe' has been used as shorthand for Western Europe, or, more precisely, for the European Community, even when that body comprised only six states. As the Community and later Union grew from six to nine to its current 15 members, the shorthand term became more apposite; with the prospect of expansion to an EU of 25 it might seem entirely appropriate to equate the Union with 'Europe'.

Yet even the 25 do not constitute the whole of Europe; important parts of the continent remain outside. Russia, for instance, was a significant player in both the major European wars of the nineteenth century (Napoleonic and Crimean) and those of the twentieth century. However, even though many consider Russia to be European in culture and history (despite remaining on the other side of the Iron Curtain for forty years), there is little prospect of its acceding to the European Union in the foreseeable future: its size, its poor economic prospects and, for some, even the values it espouses all militate against this. The United States – like France and Germany – may recently have come to see Russia as an ally, but that does not mean it would be welcome as a member of the enlarging EU.

Nor, with the exception of Slovenia, are the successor states to the Former Republic of Yugoslavia likely to join the European Union or NATO in the near future, although Croatia hopes to accede to the EU in 2007. The position of the former Yugoslav republics is somewhat different from that of Russia: few would question their European credentials but they have not yet fully come to terms with recent ethnic conflicts. Nor have they entirely succeeded in making the transition to free market economics and fully democratic systems, including effective and independent judiciaries. Thus for the time being they will have to work with the European Union within the framework of the EU's stabilization and association process for the region, which encourages Balkan states seeking to join the Union to engage in regional cooperation first and at the same time offers them the prospect of eventual EU membership. By making the accession process conditional on the fulfilment of human and minority rights and a conciliatory approach to any disputes with neighbours, the process should help the establishment of stable democracies in that part of the continent, as has already occurred in central Europe. In addition, it should facilitate the eventual accession process for would-be members from southeastern Europe.

Relations with some of the other Eastern outsiders, notably Moldova, Ukraine and Belarus, are likely to remain somewhat distant in the medium to long term. Although Poland has sought to bring Ukraine towards the EU and Western values, its efforts have so far met with little success either in Ukraine or among current EU members, which appear reluctant to accept Ukraine as a potential member. Thus, as with Russia, it will be important for the Union to develop relations with Ukraine that facilitate economic and political cooperation falling short of prospective EU membership. Some barriers will inevitably remain – the concept of a Schengen border is, after all, intended to ensure internal security *within* the enlarged Union and by its very nature necessitates strict controls. Yet, as the chapters by Wolczuk and Wolczuk and by Partos demonstrate, such borders need not inevitably exclude those who wish to visit the Europe Union legitimately, whether for personal or business purposes; the aim is only to keep illegal migrants and would-be criminals out of the Union, something which is in the interests not just of current EU members but of Europe more generally.

Security issues have changed considerably since the end of the Cold War. There is less likelihood than at any time in history of invasions by or of any of the countries considered in this volume, but there are increased terrorist threats and therefore a mutual interest in cooperating to prevent terrorists acquiring weapons of mass destruction. These are matters which concern both the EU and NATO, making parallel enlargement processes highly desirable. There are also environmental issues such as the dangers of ageing nuclear power stations and the transport and disposal of nuclear waste and hazardous chemicals. Nor should concerns over human rights stop at the EU's eastern frontiers; pressure should be put on Russia, Ukraine, Belarus and Moldova to meet their commitments as members of the Council of Europe in cases (e.g. with Russia over Chechnya) where they clearly fall short of them. The willingness to abide by the Council of Europe's rules would enhance the prospects for EU membership of applicant states and render more politically acceptable cooperation with those that do not seek or would not be eligible for full EU membership.

At the economic level, there is still a large gap in prosperity between the EU-15 and most of the accession states; the gap between the latter and their eastern neighbours is even larger. Such economic disparities, rather than formal membership or non-membership of Western institutions, may continue to represent the greatest division in Europe. While the central European countries that were already richer than their ex-Soviet neighbours have continued to make strong economic progress since 1989, the countries further east (at least until the last two or three years) experienced a decline in living standards following the collapse of communism, reflected most dramatically in a fall in life expectancy. Countries with such levels of poverty are never likely to be stable neighbours, so the greatest priority must be to foster closer economic relations with the aim of promoting sustainable development. If suitable projects and means of monitoring them can be found, it might therefore be appropriate for the European Union to increase significantly the very small amount of aid provided to the former Soviet states via the TACIS programme. It is desirable to bring about a 'common economic space' as outlined by Graeme Herd in Chapter 7, with the expectation that countries would meet the requirements for and thereby gain membership of the World Trade Organization. While imports of energy and other natural-resource-based goods will continue to be crucially important in economic relations between Russia and the EU, the other western ex-Soviet countries have far fewer natural resources of interest to the Union. Exports of manufactured goods from these countries to the EU are very low; a substantial increase could produce economic benefits for the exporting countries without causing any noticeable economic disruption in the EU. Such exports should be encouraged as a way of enhancing relations between Europe's new member states and their neighbours.

Enlarging the EU and NATO will inevitably lead to the creation of new 'insiders' and 'outsiders' in Europe. Whether it will also lead to tension or a greater sense of 'us' and 'them' across the continent is rather less clear. To the extent that the two organizations are (or are perceived to be) exclusive clubs, with high costs attached both to joining and to remaining outside, there will be challenges for new and existing member states as well as for the new outsiders. In the short term it is likely that enlargement will create some difficulties for those in border regions both inside and outside the Union who have become used to informal cross-border trade. In the medium to long term, however, such difficulties could be significantly reduced if the Union were to adopt the Commission's proposals on 'Wider Europe', which would enable non-member states in eastern Europe and the southern Mediterranean to strengthen their economic links with the Union, gaining some of the benefits of the internal market while remaining formally outside the Union.[1]

1 Commission of the European Communities, 'Wider Europe – Neighbourhood: A New Framework for Relations with our Eastern and Southern Neighbours', Communication from the Commission to the Council and the European Parliament, COM (2003) 104 Final, Brussels, 11 March 2003.

This could reduce the impact of Europe's new boundaries, creating, as James Gow advocates in Chapter 4, *inclusive* new frontiers rather than *exclusive* new borders. Frontiers should not only permit but encourage the flow of people who are not long-term migrants, and of trade in goods and services. As the current EU member states prepare to adapt to the prospect of free flows of labour for the ten new members after 2004 (in some cases with a seven-year transition period), they are unlikely to be enthusiastic about opening up to long-term migration from further afield, from the south or southeast. Nevertheless, opportunities for both studying and working in western Europe should be provided. There needs to be more cooperation between local and regional authorities on economic development, environmental issues, tackling crime and encouraging cultural exchanges, which would all enhance the quality of life in the enlarged EU and among its new neighbours.

The current enlargement of the European Union will not be the last. Apart from Romania and Bulgaria, which are already negotiating accession, Croatia and Turkey, which have applied and are waiting to start negotiations, and the Former Yugoslav Republic of Macedonia, which is expected to apply in the course of 2003, a whole raft of states in eastern and southeastern Europe may apply in the coming years. How fast their applications progress will depend in part on the speed at which these states reach the standards set out in the Copenhagen criteria, in part on more subjective issues such as perceived historical, religious and cultural identity; it may also depend on the Union's ability to deal with the 2004 enlargement. The last factor will in turn hinge on the EU's ability to reform its own decision-making structures, a question that was fudged in the latter part of the 1990s but which was hotly debated during 2002/3 and will form the core of the 2003/4 Intergovernmental Conference.

However slow the enlargement and reform processes may be, they are unlikely to deter would-be members from applying, thereby creating yet more new 'insiders/outsiders' issues in Europe, this time reaching to North Africa and Central Asia. If current questions of insider/outsider relations can be neatly circumvented by enhanced cooperation with third countries falling short of membership, the question will become simpler: the extent of the EU's formal borders, as opposed to its much broader diplomatic and economic relations. For those who fear that enlargement means a dilution of the integration process as well as those with slim prospects of ever joining the Union, closer and more imaginative forms of cooperation between the Union and its neighbours might in the long term be the way to reduce the possibility of Europe being divided by a new paper curtain.

Bibliography

Agh, A., *The Politics of Central Europe* (London: Sage, 1998).

Akkoyunlu, S., *European Labour Markets: Can Migration Provide Efficiency? The Polish-German Case*, ESRC 'One Europe or Several?' Programme, Working Paper 31/01, University of Sussex, 2001.

Akkoyunlu, S. and R. Vickerman, 'Migration and the Efficiency of European Labour Markets', in J. Brocker and H. Herrmann (eds), *Spatial Change and Interregional Flows in the Integrating Europe – Essays in Honour of Karin Peschel* (Heidelberg: Physica-Verlag, 2000), pp. 157–70.

Alexander, Michael and Tim Garden, 'The Arithmetic of Defence Policy', *International Affairs*, Vol. 77, No. 3, July 2001, pp. 509–29.

Alexander, S., *Church and State in Yugoslavia since 1945* (Cambridge: Cambridge University Press, 1984).

Allen, D., 'EPC/CFSP, the Soviet Union, and the Former Soviet Republics: Do the Twelve Have a Coherent Policy?', in E. Regelsberger et al. (eds), *Foreign Policy of the European Union: From EPC to CFSP and Beyond* (Boulder, CO and London: Lynne Rienner, 1997).

Baleanu, V. G., *In the Shadow of Russia: Romania's Relations with Moldova and Ukraine*, CSRC Research Paper G85, Royal Military Academy Sandhurst, Camberley, 2000.

Baleanu, V. G., *Romanian-Hungarian Relations: From Mutual Misunderstanding to Irrational Rationality*, CSRC Research Paper G71, Royal Military Academy Sandhurst, Camberley, 1999.

Banac, I., *The National Question in Yugoslavia: Origins, History, Politics* (Ithaca, NY: Cornell University Press, 1984).

Baranovsky, Vladimir, 'Russia: A Part of Europe or Apart from Europe?', in *Europe: Where Does it Begin and End?*, Special Issue of *International Affairs*, Vol. 76, No. 3, July 2000, pp. 443–58.

Bauer, T., P. T. Pereira, M. Vogler and K. F. Zimmermann, 'Portuguese Migrants in the German Labor Market: Performance and Self-Selection', *International Migration Review*, Vol. 36, No. 138, 2002, pp. 467–91.

Bauer, T. and K. Zimmermann, *Assessment of Possible Migration Pressure and its Labour Market Impact Following EU Enlargement to Central and Eastern Europe: Part 2*, DfEE Research Report RR 139 (London: Department for Education and Employment, 1999).

Baxendale, James, Stephen Dewar and David Gowan (eds), *The EU and Kaliningrad: Kaliningrad and the Impact of EU Enlargement* (Federal Trust for Education and Research, 2000).

Bennet, C., *Yugoslavia's Bloody Collapse* (London: Hurst, 1995).

Bilandzic, D., *Jugoslavija poslije Tita* (Zagreb: Globus, 1986).

Bíró, Gáspár, 'Bilateral Treaties between Hungary and its Neighbours after 1989', in Ignác Romsics and Béla Király (eds), *Geopolitics in the Danube Region – Hungarian Reconciliation Efforts, 1848–1998* (Budapest: Central European University Press, 1999).

Boeri, T., H. Brücker et al., *The Impact of Eastern Enlargement on Employment and Labour Markets in the EU Member States*, Report to European Commission, DG Employment and Social Affairs, DIW, CEPR, FIEF, IAS, IGIER, Berlin and Milan, 2000.

Borjas, G. J., 'Self-Selection and the Earnings of Immigrants', *American Economic Review*, Vol. 77, 1987, pp. 531–53.

Borjas, G. J., 'The Economics of Immigration', *Journal of Economic Literature*, Vol. 32, No. 4, 1994, pp. 1667–1717.

Borko, Yuri, 'EU/Russia Co-operation: The Moscow Perspective', in Baxendale et al., *The EU and Kaliningrad*.

Borko, Yuri, 'The European Union's Common Strategy on Russia: a Russian View', in Hiski Haukka and Sergei Medvedev (eds), *The EU Common Strategy on Russia: Learning from the Grammar of CFSP* (Helsinki: The Finnish Institute for International Affairs, 2001).

Boswell, Christina, *EU Enlargement: What are the Prospects for East–West Migration?*, European Programme Working Paper (London: Royal Institute of International Affairs, 2000).

Botic, I. and S. Djurekovic, *Yugoslavia in Crisis* (New York and London: Croatian National Council, 1983).

Centre for International Relations, Warsaw, 'Polish Policy vis-à-vis Ukraine and How it is Perceived in EU Member States' (transcript of a debate), *Reports & Analyses*, No. 2/00.

Chiswick, C. V., 'The Impact of Immigration on the Human Capital of Natives', *Journal of Labour Economics*, Vol. 7, 1988, pp. 464–86.

Cibotaru, Viorel, 'The Foreign and National Aspects of Moldova's Strategic Foreign Policy', in Igor Munteanu and Trevor Waters (eds), *Highway or Barrier? The Republic of Moldova's Integration into Euro-Atlantic Structures*, CSRC Research Paper G96, Royal Military Academy Sandhurst, Camberley, 2001.

Cigar, N. and Stjepan G. Mestrovic, *Genocide in Bosnia: The Policy of 'Ethnic Cleansing'*, Eastern European Series No. 1 (College Station, TX: Texas A & M University Press, 1995).

Collinson, Sarah, Hugh Miall and Anna Michalski, *A Wider European Union? Integration and Cooperation in the New Europe*, RIIA Discussion Paper No. 48 (London: RIIA, 1993).

'Common Strategy of the European Union of 4 June 1999 on Russia' (1999/414/CFSP), *Official Journal of the European Communities*, LI57/1, 24 June 1999.

Council of the European Union, *Action Plan for the Northern Dimension with external and cross border policies of the European Union 2000–2003*, Brussels, 14 June 2000.

Crampton, R. J., *Eastern Europe in the Twentieth Century – and After* (London: Routledge, 2nd edn, 1997).

CSIS Global Organized Crime Project, 'Russian Organized Crime', CSIS Panel Report (Center for Strategic and International Studies, Washington, DC, 1997).

Danspeckgruber, Wolfgang, 'Self-Determination and Regionalization in Contemporary Europe', in Wolfgang Danspeckgruber (ed.), *The Self-Determination of Peoples: Community, Nation and State in an Interdependent World* (Boulder, CO: Lynne Rienner, 2002).

De-Coulon, A. and M. Piracha, 'Self-Selection and the Performance of Return Migrants: The Case of Albania', mimeo, Centre for Economic Performance, London, 2002.

Dewar, S., 'Myths in the Baltic', in Baxendale et al., *The EU and Kaliningrad*.

Dyker, David, Agnes Nagy, Hedvika Spilek, Peter Stanovnik, Jeffrey Turk and Peter Vince, 'East-"West" Networks and their Alignment: Industrial Networks in Hungary and Slovenia', mimeo, ESRC 'One Europe or Several?' Programme Working Paper No. 10, January 2002.

EBRD, *Transition Report* (London: European Bank for Reconstruction and Development, various years).

European Commission, *Action Plan for Skills and Mobility*, Communication from the Commission to the Council, the European Parliament, the Economic and Social Committee and the Committee of the Regions, COM (2002) 72, 13 February 2002.

European Commission, Comext database, published in CD format (Luxembourg: Office for Official Publications of the European Communities).

European Commission, *External and Intra-European Union Trade: Statistical Yearbook* (Luxembourg: Office for Official Publications of the European Communities, 2000).

European Commission, *The EU and Kaliningrad*, Communication from the Commission to the Council, COM (2001) 26 Final, Brussels, 17 January 2001.

European Commission, *Kaliningrad: Commission Proposes Set of Measures to Ease Transit after Enlargement*, IP/02/1331, Brussels, 18 September 2002.

European Commission, *New European Labour Markets, Open to All with Access to All*, Communication from the Commission to the Council and the European Parliament, COM (2001) 116 Final, Brussels, 28 February 2001.

European Commission, *A Northern Dimension for the Policies of the Union*, COM (1998) 589 Final, 25 November 1998.

European Commission, *On a Community Immigration Policy*, Communication from the Commission to the Council and the European Parliament, COM (2000) 757 Final, Brussels, 22 November 2000.

European Commission, *Wider Europe – Neighbourhood: A New Framework for Relations with Our Eastern and Southern Neighbours*, Communication from the Commission to the Council and the European Parliament, COM (2003) 104 Final, Brussels, 11 March 2003.

EU–Russia Summit, *Joint statement on transit between the Kaliningrad region and the rest of the Russian Federation*, 11 November 2002.

Faini, R., 'Increasing Returns, Migrations and Convergence', *Journal of Development Economics*, Vol. 49, 1996.

Fischer-Galati, Stephen, *Twentieth Century Romania* (New York: Columbia University Press, 2nd edn, 1991).

Fowler, Brigid, *Fuzzing citizenship, nationalising political space: a framework for interpreting the Hungarian 'status law' as a new form of kin-state policy in Central and Eastern Europe*, ESRC 'One Europe or Several?' Programme Working Paper 40/02, University of Sussex, Falmer, Brighton, 2002.

Friedberg, R. M. and J. Hunt, 'The Impact of Immigrants on Host Country Wages, Employment and Growth', *Journal of Economic Perspectives*, Vol. 9, 1995, pp. 23–44.

Galen Carpenter, T., *Nato's Empty Victory* (Washington, DC: Cato Institute, 2000).

Galeotti, Mark, 'Crime, Corruption and the Law', in Mike Bowker and Cameron Ross (eds), *Russia after the Cold War* (London and New York: Longman, 2000).

Galor, O. and O. Stark, 'Migration, Human Capital Formation and Long-run Output', in H. Siebert (ed.), *Migration: A Challenge for Europe* (Tübingen: Institut für Weltwirtschaft an der Universität Kiel, 1994), pp. 59–70.

Gang, I. and F. L. Rivera-Batiz, 'Labour Market Effect of Immigration in the United States and Europe: Substitution vs. Complementarity', *Journal of Population Economics*, Vol. 7, 1994, pp. 157–75.

Gaston, N. and D. Nelson, 'The Employment and Wage Effects of Immigration: Trade and Labour Economics Perspectives', in D. Greenaway, R. Upward and K. Wakelin (eds), *Trade, Investment and Labour: Proceeding of IEA Conference* (Palgrave: Basingstoke, 2002).

Glenny, M., *The Balkans: Nationalism, War and the Great Powers* (London: Granta, 1999).

Glenny, M., *The Fall of Yugoslavia: the Third Balkan War* (London: Penguin, 1992).

Glover, S., C. Golt, A. Loizillon, J. Portes, R. Price, S. Spencer, V. Sirinivasan, and C. Willis, *Migration: An Economic and Social Analysis*, Research, Development and Statistics Directorate Occasional Paper No. 67, The Home Office, London, 2001.

Gowan, David, *How the EU Can Help Russia* (London: Centre for European Reform, 2000).

Grabbe, Heather, 'The Sharp Edges of Europe: Extending Schengen Eastwards', *International Affairs*, Vol. 76, No. 3, July 2000.

Grabbe, Heather, *Profiting from EU Enlargement* (London: Centre for European Reform, 2001).

Grabbe, H. and K. Hughes, *Enlarging the EU Eastwards* (London: Royal Institute of International Affairs/Pinter, 1998).

GUS, *Rocznik Statystyzny Handlu Zagranickneg* [Central Statistical Office, *Statistical Yearbook of International Trade*], Warsaw, 1999.

Haisken De New, J. P. and K. F. Zimmermann, 'Wage and mobility effects of trade and migration', in M. Dewatripont, A. Sapir and K. Sekkat (eds), *Trade and Jobs in Europe: Much Ado about Nothing?* (Oxford: Oxford University Press, 1999).

Hanson, G. H. and A. Spilimbergo, 'Illegal immigration, border enforcement and relative wages: evidence from apprehensions at the US-Mexico border', paper to CEPR Workshop on Location and Regional Convergence/Divergence, Louvain-la-Neuve, 1996.

Haukkala, Hiski, 'The Making of the European Union's Common Strategy on Russia', Working Paper No. 28, The Finnish Institute of International Affairs, Helsinki, 2000.

Helsinki Watch, *Human Rights Abuses in Kosovo, 1990–1992* (New York: Human Rights Watch, 1992).

Henderson, K., *Back to Europe: Central and Eastern Europe and the European Union* (London: UCL Press, 1999).

Herd, Graeme P., 'Russia's Baltic Policy and the August Meltdown', *Security Dialogue*, Vol. 30, No. 2, June 1999, pp. 197–212.

Herd, Graeme P. and Ella Akerman, 'Russian Strategic Realignment in the Post-Post Cold War Era', *Security Dialogue*, Vol. 33, No. 3, 2002, pp. 357–72.

Hopkinson, William, *Enlargement: a New NATO*, Chaillot Papers No. 49, Institute for Security Studies, Paris, 2001.

Hungary Country Report (London: The Economist Intelligence Unit, 1996–2001).

IMF, *Directory of Trade Statistics Yearbook* (Washington, DC: International Monetary Fund, 2000).

Joenniemi, Pertti and Jan Prawitz, 'Kaliningrad: A Double Periphery', in *Kaliningrad: The European Amber Region* (Ashgate: Aldershot, Hants, 1998), pp. 226–61.

Joenniemi, P., R. Lopata, V. Sirutavicius and R. Vilpisauskas, 'Impact Assessment of Lithuania's Integration into the EU on Relations between Lithuania and Kaliningrad Oblast of the Russian Federation', Vilnius University, October 2001.

Kadare, I. et al., *The Southern Balkans: Perspectives from the Region*, Chaillot Papers, No. 46, Institute for Security Studies, Paris, 2001.

Kadijevic, V., *Moje Vidjenje Raspada* (Belgrade: Politika, 1993).

Kagan, Robert, 'Power and Weakness', *Policy Review*, June–July 2002, pp. 3–28; available at *http://www.policyreview.org/Jun02/kagan/html*.

Kaminski, Antoni Z. and Jerzy Kozakiewicz, *Polish-Ukrainian Relations 1992–1996: Report* (Warsaw: Centre for International Relations at the Institute of Public Affairs, 1997).

Kempe, Iris (ed.), *Beyond EU Enlargement, Vol. I: The Agenda of Direct Neighbourhood for Eastern Europe* (Gütersloh: Bertelsmann Foundation Publishers, 2003).

King, Charles, *The Moldovans: Romanians, Russia and the Politics of Culture* (Stanford: Hoover Institution Press, 2000).

Kingston, Klara, 'The Hungarian Status Law', in *RFE/RL East European Perspectives*, Vol. 3, No. 17, 3 October 2001.

Komornicki, T., *Potowe Towarowe Polskiego Handlu Zagranicznego a Międzynarodowe Powiązania Transportowe* [Commercial Commodities Flows of Polish Foreign Trade and International Transportation Connections], Prace Geograficzne Nr 177, Instytut Geografii i Przestrzennego Zagospodarowania, Polska Akademia Nauk, Warsaw, 2000.

Kontorovich, Vladimir, 'Can Russia Resettle the Far East?', *Post-Communist Economies*, Vol. 12, No. 3, 2000.

Kovrig, Bennett, 'European Integration', in Aurel Braun and Zoltan Barany (eds), *Dilemmas of Transition: The Hungarian Experience* (Lanham: Rowman & Littlefield Publishers, 1999).

Krenzler, Horst and Kataryna Wolczuk, *EU Justice and Home Affairs in the Context of*

Enlargement, Policy Paper, No. 4, The Robert Schuman Centre for Advanced Studies, European University Institute, 2001.

Kule, D., A. Mancellari, H. Papapanagos, S. Qirici and P. Sanfey, *The Causes and Consequences of Albanian Emigration during Transition: Evidence from Micro Data*, Studies in Economics 00/04, Department of Economics, University of Kent at Canterbury, *International Migration Review*, Vol. 36, No. 137, 2002, pp. 229–39.

Leon-Ledesma, M. and M. Piracha, *International Migration and the Role of Remittances in Eastern Europe*, Studies in Economics 01/13 (revised version of paper to European Society of Population Economics Conference, Athens, June 2001), Department of Economics, University of Kent at Canterbury.

Light, Margot, John Löwenhardt and Stephen White, 'Russian Perspectives on European Security', *European Foreign Affairs Review*, Vol. 5, No. 4, 2000, pp. 489–505.

Likachev, V., 'Russia and the European Union: A Long Term View', *International Affairs* (Moscow), Vol. 46, No. 2, 2000, pp. 116–26.

Löwenhardt, John, Ronald J. Hill and Margot Light, 'A Wider Europe: the view from Minsk and Chisinau', *International Affairs*, Vol. 77, No. 3, July 2001, pp. 605–20.

Lydall, Yugoslavia in Crisis (Oxford: Clarendon Press, 1989).

Magas, B., *The Destruction of Yugoslavia: Tracking the Break-up 1980–1992* (London: Verso, 1993).

Mahncke, Dieter, 'Russia's Attitude to the European Security and Defence Policy', *European Foreign Affairs Review*, Vol. 6, Issue 4, Winter 2001, pp. 427–36.

Malcolm, N., *Bosnia: A Short History* (London: Macmillan, 1994).

Malcolm, N., *Kosovo: A Short History* (London: Macmillan, 1998).

Massey D., J. Arango, G. Hugo, A. Kouaouci, A. Pellegrino and J.E. Taylor, 'Theories of International Migration: A Review and Appraisal', *Population and Development Review*, Vol. 19, No. 3, 1993, pp. 431–66.

Milanovic, Branko, *Income, Inequality and Poverty during the Transition from Planned to Market Economy* (Washington, DC: The World Bank, 1998).

Mis, Jan Stanislaw (ed.), *Polska Droga do Schengen: Opinie Ekspertow* (Warsaw: Instytut Spraw Publicznych, 2001).

Mortensen, J. and S. Richter, *Measurement of Costs and Benefits of Accession to the European Union for Selected Countries in Central and Eastern Europe* (Vienna: Vienna Institute for Economic Studies, 2000).

Müller-Braneck-Bocquet, Gisela, 'The New CFSP and ESDP Decision-making System of the European Union', *European Foreign Affairs Review*, Vol. 7, 2002.

Nicoll, W. and R. Schoenberg, *Europe Beyond 2000* (London: Whurr, 1998).

Nyberg, René, 'Russia and Europe', *European Security*, Vol. 8, No. 2, Spring 1999, pp. 15–21.

OECD, *International Mobility of the Highly Skilled* (Paris: OECD, 2002).

OECD SOPEMI, *Trends in International Migration* (Paris: OECD, 2001).

Official Journal of the European Communities, 'A Common Strategy of the European Union of 4 June 1999', L 157I/1, 24 June 1999.

Olsen, Gorm Rye, 'The EU and Conflict Management in African Emergencies', *International Peacekeeping*, Vol. 9, No. 3, Autumn 2002, pp. 87–102.

Owen, D., *Balkan Odyssey* (London: Gollancz, 1995).

Papapanagos, H. and P. Sanfey, 'Intention to Emigrate and Actual Emigration: The Case of Albania', paper to European Society of Population Economics Conference, Athens, June 2001.

Papapaganos, H. and R. Vickerman, 'Borders, Migration, and Labour-market Dynamics in a Changing Europe', in M. van der Velde and H. van Houtum (eds), *Borders, Regions, and People* (London: Pion Ltd, 2000).

Parker, Noel and Bill Armstrong (eds), *Margins in European Integration* (Basingstoke: Macmillan, 2000).

Partos, Gabriel, 'Persistent Diplomacy', *War Report*, No. 58, February–March 1998, pp. 62–3.

Partos, Gabriel, 'Romania', in Alan Day (ed.), *The Annual Register: A Record of World Events, 1988; 1989* (London: Longman, 1989 and 1990).

Pavliuk, Oleksandr, *The European Union and Ukraine: The Need for a New Vision*, Policy Paper Based on the Study on the Current State and Prospects of Relations Between the European Union and Ukraine (Kiev: East-West Institute, 1999).

Phinnemore, David, 'Romania and Euro-Atlantic Integration since 1989: A Decade of Frustration?', in Duncan Light and David Phinnemore (eds), *Post-Communist Romania – Coming to Terms with Transition* (Basingstoke: Palgrave, 2001).

Piracha, M. and R. Vickerman, 'International Migration and European Integration', paper presented to the 40th Annual Meeting, Western Regional Science Association, Palm Springs, CA, Department of Economics, University of Kent, February 2001.

Pischke, J.-S. and J. Velling, 'Employment Effects of Immigration to Germany: An Analysis Based on Local Labor Markets', *Review of Economics and Statistics*, Vol. 79, No. 4, 1997, pp. 594–604 .

(Poland) Ministry of Foreign Affairs, *The Eastern Policy of the European Union in the run-up to the EU's enlargement to include the countries of Central and Eastern Europe – Poland's Viewpoint*, Warsaw, 2001.

(Poland) Ministry of Foreign Affairs, *Position vis-à-vis Communication from the European Commission: The EU and Kaliningrad* (2001).

Pozdniakov, V. and S. Ganzha, 'New Countries on the EU's doorstep', *International Affairs* (Moscow), Vol. 45, No. 3, 1999.

Preston, Christopher, *Enlargement and Integration in the European Union* (London: Routledge, 1997).

Ramet, Sabrina and Christine Ingebritsen (eds), *Coming in from the Cold War: Changes in US–European Interactions since 1980* (Oxford: Rowman and Littlefield, 2002).

Rawlinson, P., *Russian Organised Crime and the Baltic States: Assessing the Threat*, ESRC 'One Europe or Several?' Programme, Working Paper 38/01, University of Sussex, 2001.

Reichlin, P. and A. Rustichini, 'Diverging Patterns with Endogenous Labor Migration', *Journal of Economic Dynamics and Control*, Vol. 22, Issue 5, May 1998, pp. 703–28.

Report on Preferential Treatment of National Minorities by their Kin-State, adopted by the Venice Commission, Document CDL-INF, Council of Europe, Strasbourg, 22 October 2001.

Rontoyanni, Clelia, 'So far, so good? Russia and the ESDP', *International Affairs*, Vol. 78, No. 4, October 2002, pp. 813–30.

Rothschild, Joseph, *Return to Diversity: a Political History of East Central Europe since World War Two* (Oxford: Oxford University Press, 1989).

Russinow, D., 'Nationalities Policy and the National Question', in S. Ramet (ed.), *Yugoslavia in the 1980s* (Boulder, CO: Westview, 1985).

Samardzija, V. (ed.), *Economic Aspects of Croatia's Integration into the European Union* (Zagreb: Institute for International Relations, 1997).

Sherr, James, *Ukraine's New Time of Troubles*, CSRC Research Paper G67, Royal Military Academy, Sandhurst, Camberley, 1998.

Sherr, James, 'The Dismissal of Borys Tarasyuk', Conflict Studies Research Centre Occasional Brief No. 79, Royal Military Academy Sandhurst, Camberley, 6 October 2000.

Silber, L. and A. Little, *The Death of Yugoslavia* (London: Penguin, 1995).

Simms, B., *Unfinest Hour: How Britain Helped to Destroy Bosnia* (London: Allen Lane/Penguin, 2001).

Smith, Alan, *The Return to Europe: The Reintegration of Eastern Europe into the European Economy* (London and Basingstoke: Macmillan, 2000).

Smith, Julie, *An Ever Larger Europe?*, RIIA Briefing Paper New Series No. 14, May 2000.

Smith, J. and E. Teague (eds), *Democracy in the New Europe: The Politics of Post-Communism* (London: Greycoat Press, 1999).

Spence, David, *Enlargement Without Accession: The EC's Response to German Unification*, RIIA Discussion Paper No. 36 (London: RIIA, 1991).

Stent, A., 'American Views on Russian Security Policy and EU-Russian Relations', prepared for the IISS/CEPS European Security Forum, Brussels, 14 January 2002.

Straubhaar, T. and M. Wolburg, 'Brain Drain and Brain Gain in Europe – An Evaluation of the East-European Migration to Germany', paper presented at Winter 1998 Workshop on *Managing Migration in the 21st Century: CIIP and Institute of Global Conflict and Cooperation*, Centre for US-Mexican Studies, University of California, San Diego, 1998.

Straubhaar, T. and K.F. Zimmerman, 'Towards a European Migration Policy', *Population Research and Policy Review*, Vol. 12, 1993, pp. 95–128.

Surovell, Jeffrey, 'Western Europe and the Western Alliance: Soviet and Post-Soviet Perspectives', *Journal of Communist Studies and Transition Politics*, Vol. 11, No. 2, June 1995.

Tanner, M., *Croatia: A Nation Forged in War* (London: Yale University Press, 1997).

Terriff, Terry, Stuart Croft, Elke Krahmann, Mark Webber and Jolyon Howorth, '"One in, all in?" NATO's next enlargement', *International Affairs*, Vol. 78, No. 4, October 2002, pp. 713–29.

Tkachenko, Stanislav, 'The EU's Crisis Management from the Russian Perspective', in Graeme P. Herd and Jouko Huru (eds), *EU Civilian Crisis Management*, CSRC Research Paper M22, Royal Military Academy Sandhurst, Camberley, May 2002.

Trifunovska, S. (ed.), *Yugoslavia Through Documents: From its Creation to its Dissolution* (Dordrecht: Martinus Nijhoff Publishers/Kluwer, 1994).

Tsygankov, Andrei P., 'From International Institutionalism to Revolutionary Expansionism', *Mershon International Studies Review*, Vol. 41, No. 2, November 1997.

Umbach, Frank, 'Russia as a "Virtual Great Power": Implications for its Declining Role in European and Eurasian Security', *European Security*, Vol. 9, No. 3, Autumn 2000.

(United Kingdom) House of Lords, *Working in Europe: Access for All*, 15th Report of the Select Committee on the European Union, Session 2001–2002, The Stationery Office, London, 2002.

Victims of Trafficking in the Balkans (Vienna–Geneva: International Organization for Migration, 2001).

Wallace, Claire and Dariusz Stola (eds), *Patterns of Migration in Central Europe* (Basingstoke: Palgrave, 2001).

Wallace, William, *The Transformation of Western Europe* (London: Royal Institute of International Affairs/Pinter, 1990).

Webber, Mark, 'Third-Party Inclusion in the European Security and Defence Policy; A Case Study of Russia', *European Foreign Affairs Review*, Vol. 6, 2001, pp. 418–20.

Williams, Phil (ed.), *Russian Organised Crime: The New Threat?* (London: Frank Cass, 2000).

Wolczuk, Roman, 'Ukrainian-Polish Relations between 1991 and 1998: From the Declaratory to the Substantive', *European Security*, Vol. 9, No. 1, Spring 2000, pp. 127–56.

Wolczuk, Roman, *Ukraine's Foreign and Security Policy 1991–2002* (New York and London: RoutledgeCurzon, forthcoming 2003).

Wolczuk, Kataryna and Roman Wolczuk, *Poland and Ukraine: A Strategic Partnership in a Changing Europe?* (London: Royal Institute of International Affairs, 2002).

Wolfmayr-Schnitzer, Yvonne, 'Trade Performance of CEECs According to Technology Classes', in *The Competitiveness of Transition Economies*, prepared by WIFO (Paris: OECD, 1998).

Zimmerman, K. F., 'European Migration: Push and Pull', *International Regional Science Review*, Vol. 19, 1996, pp. 95–128.

Zorlu, A., *Ethnic Minorities in the UK: Burden or Benefit?*, Working Paper No. 2001 14, Institute for Social and Economic Research, University of Essex, 2001.

News sources

Agence France Presse (AFP)
Associated Press (AP)
BASA Moldovan news agency
BBC Summary of World Broadcasts
BNS news agency
The Day (Kiev)
Diplomatichesky Vestnik
Duna TV

The Economist
Ekho Moskvy News Agency (Moscow)
Elektroni Visti (Kiev)
Gazeta.ru website, Moscow
Gazeta Wyborcza (Warsaw, published by Agora)
Heti Világgazdaság
Interfax news agency (Moscow)
International Herald Tribune
ITAR-TASS News Agency (Moscow)
Izvestiya (Moscow)
Kaunas Diena (Kaunas)
Mediafax news agency (Moscow)
Moldpress news agency (Chişinău)
Moskovskiy Komsomolets (Moscow)
Le Monde Diplomatique
Népszabadság (Hungary)
Polityka (Warsaw)
Radio Free Europe/Radio Liberty
Reuters news agency
Rzeczpospolita (Warsaw)
Der Standard (Vienna)
Unia i Polska (Warsaw)
UNIAN news agency (Kiev)
Vjesnik (Zagreb)

Index

Page references in *italic* refer to tables

EUROPEAN MIGRATION POLICIES IN FLUX

NEW

Changing Patterns of Inclusion and Exclusion

Christina Boswell

Hamburg Institute of International Economics and

Royal Institute of International Affairs

"This outstanding book cuts in a lucid and accessible way to the core of the key migration policy dilemmas facing Europe. It will be an indispensable guide for anyone with an interest in these important questions."

ANDREW GEDDES, UNIVERSITY OF LIVERPOOL

Timely book examining the nature and impact of the changing migration policies in Germany, Italy and the UK.

Analyses the content of new legislation, as well as the policy debate and party political treatment of migration issues in each country.

September 2003   168 pages   229 x 152 mm / 6 x 9 in
1-4051-0295-0 hb / 1-4051-0296-9 pb

For more information on the other books in the Chatham House Papers series please visit the book series section of **www.blackwellpublishing.com**